Negotiating Nuclear Arms Control

Studies in International Relations
Charles W. Kegley, Jr., and Donald J. Puchala,
Series Editors

Marvin S. Soroos
Beyond Sovereignty: The Challenge of Global Policy

Manus I. Midlarsky
*The Disintegration of Political Systems:
War and Revolution in Comparative Perspective*

Lloyd Jensen
*Bargaining for National Security:
The Postwar Disarmament Negotiations*

Lloyd Jensen
Negotiating Nuclear Arms Control

NEGOTIATING NUCLEAR ARMS CONTROL

by LLOYD JENSEN

UNIVERSITY OF SOUTH CAROLINA PRESS

Published in Columbia, South Carolina, by the
University of South Carolina Press

Manufactured in the United States of America

Library of Congress Cataloging-in-Publication Data

Jensen, Lloyd.
    Negotiating nuclear arms control / by Lloyd Jensen.
       p. cm. — (Studies in international relations)
    Bibliography: p.
    Includes index.
    ISBN 0-87249-530-2 (pbk.)
       1. Nuclear arms control—United States. 2. Nuclear arms control
—Soviet Union. 3. United States—Foreign relations—Soviet Union.
4. Soviet Union—Foreign relations—United States. I. Title.
II. Series: Studies in international relations (Columbia, S.C.)
JX1974.7.J447 1988
327.1'74'0973—dc19   87-30142
                                                              CIP

Contents

Acknowledgments   vii

1. The Search for National Security   1
Security through Deterrence   3
Arms Control and Deterrence   7
Why Negotiate?   10

2. The Nuclear Test Ban Negotiations   14
Early Skirmishing   15
Negotiating the Limited Test Ban Treaty   19
  Verification   22
  The Moratorium on Testing   27
  The Third Party Role   29
  Evaluating the Limited Test Ban Treaty   31
The Threshold Test Ban Treaty   34
Peaceful Nuclear Explosives   36
Carter and the Test Ban Issue   39
Reagan and the Test Ban Issue   41
Conclusion   48

3. Nonproliferation of Nuclear Weapons   52
The Effect of Nuclear Spread on Security   53
Early Proposals for Preventing Nuclear Spread   54
The Nuclear Nonproliferation Treaty   58
The Safeguards System   61
Security Assurances   63
The Peaceful Atom   69
The Nonproliferation Policies of Carter and Reagan   71
Conclusion   75

4. The Strategic Arms Limitation Talks   78
Pre-SALT Negotiations   78
The Strategic Arms Talks   86
  Defensive Weapons Control   87
  Offensive Weapons Control   89
  Forward-Based Systems   90
  The Issue of Equivalence   91
  Qualitative vs. Quantitative Limits   94
  Verification   98

Was SALT Worth Its Salt?   **104**
Who Gave up What?   **109**
Conclusion   **114**

5. Arms Control in the Eighties   117
Intermediate-range Nuclear Force Limitations   **118**
    The INF Negotiations   **119**
    INF Deployment and Its Aftermath   **131**
Strategic Arms Reductions   **137**
    Complying with SALT   **137**
    A New Start with START?   **144**
    The Gorbachev Initiatives   **151**
The Strategic Defense Initiative   **156**
Anti-satellite Weapons   **165**
Conclusion   **169**

6. Toward a More Secure World   172
Negotiable Weapons Systems   **172**
Obstacles to Disarmament   **176**
Toward More Effective Bargaining on Arms Control   **178**

Notes   183
Glossary   193
Index   196

Tables

1.1   Propaganda Themes Used for Explaining Disarmament Goals
       (1945–60)   **11**
2.1   Known Nuclear Test Explosions   **33**
4.1   Results of SALT II Compared to the Two Sides' Preferred
       Positions   **110**

Acknowledgments

My debts in producing this study are many. I would like to thank Kenneth J. Scott and Warren Slesinger of the University of South Carolina Press for their interest in producing this abridged text edition of my *Bargaining for National Security: The Postwar Disarmament Negotiations* (Columbia: University of South Carolina Press, 1988). Parts of Chapter 3 have been drawn from my previously published book, *Return from the Nuclear Brink: National Interest and the Nuclear Nonproliferation Treaty* (Lexington, MA: D. C. Heath, 1974) and brief sections of chapters 4 and 6 were previously included in "SALT on the Shelf: Problems and Prospects," *Parameters: Journal of the U.S. Army War College,* Vol. 10 (December 1980), pp. 57–64.

Support for part of the research on the book was provided by Temple University in the form of a study leave during the academic year 1982–83. Stephen Saetz and Jongduck Park served as able research assistants. The project could not have been completed without the word-processing skills of Gloria Basmajian.

Several colleagues have read portions of the manuscript and have been generous in providing useful advice. These include James Bennett, Daniel Druckman, and Lynn H. Miller. I have also benefited from the advice and encouragement of the editors of this series, Donald J. Puchala and Charles W. Kegley, Jr. My wife Jane has again taken time away from her own professional activities to serve as both loving critic and editor. Needless to say, I am grateful to all, but none need share the blame for any of the limitations found herein.

Negotiating Nuclear Arms Control

1

The Search for National Security

The advent of the nuclear age brought with it increased concern about national security as well as human survival. Since the first atomic bomb was exploded over Hiroshima on August 6, 1945, advances in nuclear technology and delivery systems have only served to enhance the potential dangers. Whereas almost 100,000 people lost their lives on the fateful day in Hiroshima, nuclear weapons currently threaten the lives of hundreds of millions. The nuclear revolution has resulted in the development of bombs measured in megatons (millions of tons of TNT equivalent). The Hiroshima bomb, estimated at about 13 kilotons, is a mere toy compared to contemporary thermonuclear devices—one of which was detonated by the Soviet Union and measured more than 50 megatons. In terms of TNT equivalence, such a device is about four thousand times the size of the Hiroshima bomb. Nuclear weapons of this size, however, make little military sense, for they tend only to dig deeper holes. Several bombs in the low megatonnage range spread over an area are likely to be more efficient and can be delivered by intercontinental ballistic missiles.

Not only has there been a revolution in the destructiveness of nuclear warheads, but the means for delivering those warheads have improved substantially in terms of capacity, speed, and accuracy. Since nuclear weapons have been reduced in size over the years, more destructive payloads can be carried in each delivery system. The bombs dropped on Hiroshima and Nagasaki were of such a size and weight that only one atomic weapon could be carried in a bomber. Today that same destructive capability can be transported in an attaché case. The miniaturization of nuclear bombs became particularly significant as the world entered the missle age, for missles have a more limited carrying capacity than bombers.

Missiles have also substantially reduced the delivery time required in transporting nuclear warheads to their destination. A thirty-minute warning time is all that is available for an intercontinental ballistic missile (ICBM) traveling between the Soviet Union and the United States. This time is cut to fifteen minutes or less with the submarine-launched ballistic missile (SLBM) or intermediate-range ballistic missile (IRBM).

Also contributing to the nuclear weapons threat is the increased accuracy of missiles. Whereas early missiles might be accurate only within several miles, both sides now have ICBMs capable of hitting within about three hundred feet of target. This pinpoint accuracy not only guarantees maximum destructiveness but also makes ICBM silos highly vulnerable to attack even when these silos are hardened with reinforced concrete.

As the technology race proceeds unabated, there is increasing concern with the potential destructiveness of nuclear war. Reflective of this concern is the growth of an extensive nuclear freeze movement and the publication of a number of treatises pointing out the dangers involved. Among the most influential of these is Jonathan Schell's *The Fate of the Earth*, which calls attention not only to the immediate death and destruction that could result from nuclear war but also to the long-term harm resulting from the destruction of ozone layers, lingering radiation, genetic damage affecting future generations, and agricultural and ecological damage.[1] Carl Sagan and other eminent scientists have estimated that only 500 to 2,000 nuclear warheads would be required to induce a climatic catastrophe.[2] The explosions from these weapons would create what they called a nuclear winter by shutting off sunlight for a considerable period of time. Nuclear war could indeed produce a world in which the living would envy the dead.

At the same time that the United States and the Soviet Union seemed to be marching toward Armageddon in what appeared to be an almost unrestrained arms race, the two were energetically involved in negotiations designed to restrain that race. Dozens of proposals have been made during hundreds of meetings in what sometimes seems to have been an almost futile effort to constrain various weapons systems. There have, of course, been some achievements along the way such as the successful negotiation of the Limited Test Ban Treaty in 1963, the Nuclear Nonproliferation Treaty in 1968, the SALT I and SALT II Treaties during the 1970s, along with a host of other less noteworthy agreements which will be examined in this study. But, on the whole, it must be said that the United States and the Soviet Union have chosen to rely principally upon military deterrence in their attempts to provide for their national security.

Before turning our attention to the long and tortuous course of U.S.-Soviet bargaining in the postwar disarmament negotiations, which is the subject of this study, it might be well to examine the role that nuclear deterrence can and has played in providing whatever security the world has enjoyed since World War II. It will be argued, however, that arms control negotiations can be useful in enhancing the stability of nuclear deterrence and should therefore be given serious consideration in the search for national security even though the achievements to date have not been overwhelming.

SECURITY THROUGH DETERRENCE

While nuclear weapons threaten the survival of the earth, they may have also provided a certain level of international stability by virtue of their deterrent value. The nuclear age has witnessed one of the longest periods of peace in European history. Advocates of nuclear deterrence argue that this phenomenon can be attributed to the existence of a deterrent system that has made war between the two superpowers unthinkable. In the past, other destructive weapons systems have been viewed as playing a similar role. For example, the airplane, because of its perceived deterrent value and the initial lack of any defense against it, was believed by some political leaders to make war in the future unlikely.

Establishing a causal link between the existence of nuclear weapons and the deterrence of war is not a simple matter. In order to prove that deterrence has been effective, it is necessary to demonstrate that the opposing power had the intention of attacking but failed to do so only because of the existence of nuclear weapons. Though a state may retreat in a confrontation, the retreat may be attibuted to factors other than the nuclear deterrent, such as a recognition that the possible gain is not worth other negative repercussions like adverse world opinion, loss of support of allies, or perhaps even internal opposition.

In examining Soviet behavior in the postwar world, there is reason to doubt whether it has been U.S. nuclear superiority that has deterred the Soviet Union from being more aggressive than it might have been. The fact of the matter is that the Soviet Union engaged in greater risk-taking behavior vis-à-vis the West before the Soviets achieved nuclear parity with the United States.[3] The Soviet Union pursued an adventurous foreign policy during the Stalin period despite the fact that the United States enjoyed an atomic monoply until 1949 and considerable military superiority for many years thereafter. In many respects, Nikita Khrushchev was more erratic and willing to take risks than his successor, Leonid

Brezhnev, yet the balance of military forces was more favorable to the Soviet Union during Brezhnev's tenure. A Brookings Institution study revealed that the Soviet Union engaged more frequently in "coercive action" in the late 1960s than in the mid-1970s, although it was only in the latter period that Soviet strategic nuclear strength had begun to approach that of the United States.[4]

Despite a strategic balance that has become more favorable to Moscow, an analysis of 215 postwar incidents in which the United States used or threatened the use of force revealed that the outcomes have actually been more favorable to the United States when U.S. military superiority has been less extreme. Short-term outcomes were found to be positive for the United States in its confrontations with the USSR in only 43 percent of the cases when the strategic balance was 100 to 1 or greater in favor of the United States, but this figure increased to 92 percent when the ratio of superiority decreased to less than 10 to 1.[5]

Even the events during the 1962 Cuban missile crisis, which is often used to illustrate the efficacy of nuclear deterrence, fail to prove that Khrushchev backed down primarily because of U.S. nuclear superiority. His willingness to concede had perhaps more to do with the asymmetry of interests between the two superpowers. Cuba and the missiles were peripheral issues for the Soviet Union but central to American concerns. Had the national interests of the two parties been more equivalent, the results may well have been different.

While it might be argued that nuclear deterrence has been effective in reducing the frequency of war in Europe, there is still reason for being wary about relying upon the balance of nuclear terror for world peace since that balance is a delicate one at best. A number of factors threaten the stability of the nuclear deterrent system, particularly those factors that might lead to an accidental nuclear war. The number of false warnings about an imminent Soviet missile attack has been substantial. One study noted at least 147 false indications during an eighteen-month period.[6] In one instance during June 1980, American forces were on nuclear alert for six minutes because of a computer error created by the malfunction of a circuit chip worth 46 cents. Accidental war might also arise because of psychological or physical problems among those who have charge of the nuclear deterrent. A House subcommittee reported that in 1977, a typical year, 1,219 American military personnel with some form of access to or responsibility for nuclear weapons were removed from duty because of mental disturbances, 265 for alcoholism, and 1,365 for drug abuse.[7] Political leaders themselves have not been immune from psychological breakdown, and the intense pressures resulting from international crises and fear serve only to increase the dangers of nuclear hostilities.

In addition to the possibility of nuclear war erupting by accident, there is also the danger of such a war arising by miscalculation. If one side or the other believes a nuclear strike is imminent, there would be considerable pressure to deliver the first blow. Such pressures would be particularly acute whenever one's retaliatory capability is felt to be vulnerable.

The threat of miscalculation is enhanced by virtue of the rapid pace of technology. The fear that the other side may be close to a scientific breakthrough is likely to cause particularly anxious moments. Most threatening would be a system capable of intercepting the bulk of the incoming missiles, thus signaling the end of deterrence. Since the incentives would be high to assure that the adversary never attain such a position, a preemptive strike would have to be seriously considered by the state fearing that it was about to lose the technological race for an effective strategic defense shield.

Miscalculation may result from concern about the viability of command and control structures in the nuclear age. John Steinbrunner has estimated that 50 to 100 nuclear weapons could disrupt the central nervous system of the U.S. command structure and a similar number could probably disable the Soviet Union.[8] In October 1981 President Reagan announced a $20 billion effort to improve command and control structures—a task he viewed as having higher priority than building new weapons systems.

The danger of nuclear weapons spreading to other nations and perhaps even falling into the hands of terrorist groups adds yet another threat to the stability of the nuclear deterrent system. Not only does increasing the number of nuclear powers increase the statistical probability that one of them might unleash a nuclear war but the new nuclear weapons state is perhaps more likely to use its recently gained nuclear capability than are existing nuclear powers. Any new nuclear weapons state is likely to have a less protected nuclear weapons capability since the costs of protecting offensive weapons may be prohibitively expensive for a state that has had to spend so much of its limited resources to develop its nuclear capability. In making the sacrifice to build a nuclear weapons capability, the state has also undoubtedly neglected its conventional capability, giving that state little option but to use its nuclear weapons in the event of war. Finally, since many of the potential nuclear powers are confronted with problems of internal political instability, it would require a very strong leader to resist domestic pressures for using the ultimate weapon in a serious conflict situation if such a weapon were available.

Given the many factors affecting the stability of the nuclear deterrent, several suggestions have been made for reducing the threat of a possible breakdown. Chief among these are actions designed to reduce the dangers of war by accident or miscalculation. Efforts have been made to minimize the danger of unauthorized use of nuclear weapons by centralizing command and control functions. In the United States the president is the only person empowered to initiate a nuclear strike, although there are contingencies in case the president is incapacitated. At every step in the decision to use nuclear weapons at least two individuals are made reponsible for setting in motion a nuclear strike under the so-called two key system. This procedure has been designed to reduce the danger of someone in the chain of command going berserk and initiating a nuclear attack. It might be noted that the system does not actually involve "two keys," for this would create the possibility of one of those involved overpowering the other and initiating a nuclear strike. Instead, each participant has critical information that is usable only if coordinated with the information available to the other.

If a nuclear bomb is accidentally dropped or a missle unleashed by accident or unauthorized action, it would become critical that the decision makers be able to communicate promptly and effectively with each other in order to reduce the possibility of an all-out nuclear war. To aid such communication, the two superpowers agreed in 1963 to establish a "hot line" between Washington and Moscow. Initially a cable was constructed between the two countries, but, with the development of satellite communication systems, the old cable system was replaced with a direct satellite communication link in accordance with an agreement reached by the two parties in 1971. Although one might have visions of the hot line's enabling the leaders of each state to be in direct telephone communication with each other, the current hot line actually uses teletype capability. In July 1984 agreement was reached between the United States and the Soviet Union to replace the twenty-year-old teleprinter capable of producing only sixty words per minute with modern machinery able to send nearly instantaneous exchanges of block messages and maps. To date the hot-line system has been used sparingly, most notably at the time of the 1967 Arab-Israeli war and again during the Afghanistan crisis in 1979.

Because of the danger of war arising by accident, it is desirable to delay a retaliatory response as long as possible in order to be certain that a nuclear reponse is justified. This can be done most effectively by creating what defense planners call an invulnerable retaliatory capability. Such a capability can be achieved by utilizing mobile vehicles, as in the case of submarines; dispersing existing retaliatory capabilities to make it more difficult to eliminate those capabilities; or by hardening the weapons which, in the case of missiles, involves placing them in underground silos with a thick cover made of reinforced concrete in order to assure survivability from all but the most direct hit.

Not only will the development of an invulnerable retaliatory capability reduce incentives for launching on warning because of the fear that one's retaliatory force and command centers will not survive a first strike, but such a capability assures the stability of deterrence by guaranteeing to the would-be attacker that a first strike will not be effective because of the assured destructive capability of the potential victim.

Finally, arms control and disarmament measures themselves may contribute to deterrent stability. Violence and the threat of voilence can be reduced by cutting the number and quality of weapons available to each party, particularly if the affected weapons include those that threaten the stability of deterrence.

ARMS CONTROL AND DETERRENCE

The relationship between arms control and deterrence is a complex one involving more than opposite approaches to the search for national security. Indeed, each approach may bolster the other. Deterrence is vital to arms control, for whatever agreement is reached, the remaining weapons on each side, along with the potential of accelerating the arms race, can serve to minimize the threat of violation of an arms control agreement. Even if the arms agreement involves reducing arms to the level necessary for internal defense, as envisioned in the general and complete disarmament proposals, deterrent force would still be required, perhaps in the form of a United Nations police force.

It has also been suggested that a deterrent arms buildup is necessary to produce "bargaining chips" that can be used to induce the other side to accept an arms control or disarmament agreement. This argument became the primary selling-point used by the Reagan administration for the development and production of the MX missile and its deployment in existing Minuteman missile silos. Since the MX basing-system in stationary silos made little sense from the perspective of the administration's concern about ICBM vulnerability, the bargaining chip argument perhaps provided the only rationale for proceeding. It should be noted that this argument has been used to justify almost every new weapons system. To the extent that bargaining chips have been ineffective in facilitating the reaching of arms control agreements, they have only helped to fuel the arms race. As will be shown subsequently, the latter seems more often to have been the case.

Arms control can contribute to the stability of deterrence by regulating or reducing any weapon that threatens to destabilize the system. The two kinds of weapons systems of most interest in this regard are those weapons capable of a first strike and those weapons or devices that threaten to provide a highly reliable defense against the other side's deterrent capability. Some defense analysts have asserted that the large land-based missiles of the Soviet Union with their ability to carry huge and multiple warheads represent a serious threat to the American ICBM. In May 1983 the U.S. Air Force estimated that by 1989 the Soviet Union could have so many accurate nuclear warheads that as little as one percent of the U.S. land-based missile force might survive "a well-executed Soviet first strike."[9]

Similarly, the MX missile, due to its great accuracy and heavy payload, is regarded by some as having first-strike potential and therefore would be highly threatening and provocative to the Soviet Union. If the primary mission of a missile is one of retaliation, such capabilities are not required, and small, mobile missiles as proposed in April 1983 by President Reagan's Commission on Strategic Forces make more sense from the standpoint of deterrence, particularly since mobile missiles are less vulnerable to a Soviet first strike.

Arms control agreements may be used to slow down the modernization of weapons systems, thereby enhancing the stability of deterrence. The fear that the other side might develop the ultimate defensive or offensive weapon fuels the arms race and creates pressures for a preventive strike if the balance is seen as slipping too far in the other side's favor. Past arms agreements, although not terribly successful, have sought to reduce such fears by placing restrictions on the testing of new weapons systems and by imposing limits on the size and power of any replacement delivery systems.

Arms control can be an important adjunct to military planning itself since quantitative arms agreements can lend predictability to the arms competition. In the absence of such quantitative constraints "force planners would be more inclined to base their weapons development and deployment decisions on worst case projections of the adversary's force. Therefore, numerical constraints can obviate some pressures for arms races and decrease costs associated with force acquisition and deployment."[10]

Finally, it has been argued that arms control negotiations are useful for deterrent stability even if agreement is not reached, for the debates themselves serve as useful seminars enabling each side to communicate its concerns on strategic issues. Since both sides have a vested interest in the stability of nuclear deterrence, both are likely to listen, or ought to listen, carefully to the presentation of the other side. During times of crises it is particularly useful to have a forum available where each might be able to reassure the other. Recent proposals for the creation of U.S.-Soviet, jointly manned crises control centers reflect this concern.

While there is compatibility between arms control and deterrence as approaches to national security, there are some obvious conflicts. Chief among these is the arms control objective of verification and the deterrent objective of creating an invulnerable retaliatory capability. Mobile basing-systems assure the greatest invulnerability, but mobile weapons are difficult to count if one wants to verify that arms control celings are not being violated. This conflict explains in large measure the difficulties in determining how to base the MX missile as over thirty basing-plans have been proposed at one time or another. In order to meet the verification requirements of the SALT II Treaty, the Carter administration settled upon a ''racetrack'' system that would allow verification of 200 MX missiles as they moved in open trenches between 4,800 protective covers. This was not only a costly plan but also a plan that ran into considerable political trouble in Utah and Nevada because of the extensive land area required for such a basing-system. After toying with other possible basing-plans, the Reagan administration eventually chose to emplace a scaled-down number of MX missiles in fixed silos, only to reverse itself in 1987 by proposing that MX be positioned on train cars.

A second incompatibility between arms control and a stable deterrent system arises from the role played by satellite observation. The same satellites that are so vital for verifying compliance with arms control agreements are equally available for finding targets for a disarming counterforce attack, thus threatening the stability of deterrence.

Third, certain unilateral arms control efforts designed to reduce the danger of nuclear war, or at least to minimize the damage from such a war, may actually destabilize deterrence. This is especially the case with respect to the hardening of command and control centers to lessen the danger of decapitation and the building of shelters to protect civilians from nuclear fallout. Such actions may be viewed by the adversary as provocative indications of plans to initiate a first strike, which in turn create pressures for preemption.

Finally, some of the incompatibility between arms control and deterrence derives from the fact that individual policy makers tend to concentrate upon one approach to national security while neglecting the other.

This is particularly true in the United States where the arms-controllers are found primarily in the State Department or the Arms Control and Disarmament Agency while the Defense Department focuses more upon deterrent strategies. In the Soviet Union the role of the military in arms control negotiations has been much more pronounced, which may facilitate a more coherent policy in the search for national security.

WHY NEGOTIATE?

The paucity of arms control agreements reached as a result of meetings numbering into the thousands might raise some question as to why disarmament negotiations have been so pervasive in the postwar world. For an answer to this question one has to make an examination of other motivations for entering into arms control negotiations beyond the narrow objective of reaching an agreement.

One of the major side benefits of negotiating arms control has been the use of such negotiations for propagandistic purposes. Disarmament negotiations are particularly useful for such purposes since virtually no one wants war and everybody wants peace. The tendency to use propaganda themes in disarmament negotiations can be seen from the results of a content analysis of statements made by the United States and the Soviet Union during the pre-1961 debates as summarized in table 1.1.[11] As might be expected, the objectives of peace and security were described as primary goals for both parties. By combining the eight themes coded for each side into a single index, it was found that the resulting propaganda scores for the United States and the Soviet Union moved in the same direction in 18 of 21 rounds of negotiations, producing an overall positive correlation of .56 ($p < .01$). A similar reciprocity was found with respect to the use of hostile themes such as those accusing the other side of lying, bargaining in bad faith, and cheating. In the latter instance the correlation between the hostility scores of the United States and the Soviet Union in the pre-1961 negotiations was .43 ($p < .01$).

A second objective of disarmament negotiations has been to divide the opposition. The Soviet Union has been particularly prone toward presenting proposals specifically designed to appeal to one part of the NATO alliance at the expense of the remaining members. During the 1950s it sought to separate France from NATO by supporting French proposals for banning missiles; also, during the same period, Soviet efforts were directed toward encouraging the Federal Republic of Germany to disassociate itself from NATO with offers of military disen-

Table 1.1 Propaganda Themes Used for
Explaining Disarmament Goals, 1945–60

Goal	USSR (%)	U.S. (%)
Peace	56*	48
Security	41	41
Prevent war	38	25
Tension reduction	35	23
Build confidence	25	20
Economic reasons	19	23
Prevent surprise attack	15	22
Reduce nuclear fallout	7	1

*Percentage based upon number of meetings in which the theme was raised. $N =$ **204 meetings for the Soviet Union and 153 for the United States.**

Source: Lloyd Jensen, *The Postwar Disarmament Negotiations: A Study in U.S.-Soviet Bargaining Behavior*, pp. 244 and 246

gagement in central Europe, combined with promises for the reunification of Germany. The sixties saw Soviet nuclear nonproliferation proposals serving the same function. The SALT negotiations during the following decade led to further suspicions, particularly within the Western alliance, as the two superpowers dealt with strategic arms issues without the active participation of their respective allies. Further efforts to divide the West can be seen in threats issued by Soviet representatives during the disarmament negotiations as in the 1957 threat that "countries which have made their territory available to foreign bases will become the first targets for atom bombs." Similar threats have recently caused some concern in West European countries about the placing of cruise and Pershing II missiles on their territory.

Soviet proposals for banning the bomb, using savings from disarmament for economic development, creating nuclear free zones, and prohibiting the first use of nuclear weapons were all calculated to appeal to Third World nations. The primary purpose of such proposals seemed to be their propaganda value in attempting to portray the Soviet Union as pro-disarmament.

Since the Soviet bloc has been more monolithic than NATO, there has been little prospect for using the negotiations for dividing the Warsaw Pact nations. During the 1950s Polish interest in the military disengagement of central Europe might have been exploited more than it was by the United States, although the Soviet Union seemed to acquiesce to many of the proposals made by Polish Foreign Minister Adam Rapacki. A more promising split that the United States could have exploited was the division between the Soviet Union and Rumania over issues related to nuclear nonproliferation in the 1960s. By the time the United States became cognizant of Sino-Soviet differences on nuclear disarmament issues, the schism between the two communist powers was so deep that it hardly required further encouragement in the form of divisive disarmament proposals.

Proposals might also be designed to take advantage of divisions on disarmament issues among various groups within the adversary's nation. The Soviet Union has long sought to identify with the peace movement in various countries. It was perhaps most successful in this regard with its "ban the bomb" campaigns of the late forties and early fifties. Assertions have also been made that the Soviet Union has been encouraging nuclear freeze groups in the United States and Europe during the eighties. Similar encouragement, however, is not given to its own peace groups that question Soviet policies on disarmament.

A third objective of engaging in disarmament negotiations is to gain information concerning the military capabilities and intentions of the adversary. The disarmament proposals presented by each side provide important clues regarding the weapons systems in which the state has doubts. Many proposals, particularly those emanating from the West, would require extensive inspection of the territory of the adversary, thereby providing not only assurance of compliance with the disarmament scheme but also facilitating the collection of important information concerning the military capabilities and deployments of the other side. American proposals for open skies and for reducing the danger of surprise attack that were introduced in the late fifties are illustrative of proposals that fail to include any provisions for reducing or limiting weapons. These proposals led the Soviet Union to assert that the United States desired inspection without disarmament. With the advent of spy satellites, the need for reconnaissance flights and the exchange of military blueprints as provided in these proposals has ceased to exist.

Finally, an administration may enter negotiations for the primary purpose of reassuring its own domestic public. This appeared to be a major consideration for the Reagan administration, which had developed a hard-line reputation on defense issues. Public opinion polls, showing great concern about increased military spending and the threat of war, placed pressure upon the administration to engage in arms control negotiations. Of even greater moment were pressures emanating from the U.S. Congress demanding that the Reagan administration negotiate more seriously on arms control measures. In June 1983, for example, the House of Representatives approved continued work on the MX only after receiving written assurance from President Reagan that his administration would show greater flexibility in the upcoming disarmament negotiations.

Whatever the motivations for engaging in discussions on disarmament, it is clear that success in such talks comes about only after long and arduous negotiation. Our concern in this book will be with the problems and progress made in Soviet-U.S. disarmament negotiations in the postwar period as we seek to obtain a better understanding of superpower bargaining behavior and the contributions that arms control may provide in the search for national security.

This edition, which is an abridgment of my broader study entitled: *Bargaining for National Security: The Postwar Disarmament Negotiations,* focuses upon four major sets of arms control negotiations in which the United States and the Soviet Union have been involved. These include the nuclear test ban negotiations, the efforts to prevent nuclear proliferation, the Strategic Arms Limitation Talks, and efforts to negotiate nuclear arms control during the 1980s as such issues as intermediate-range nuclear forces, strategic arms reduction, and control of strategic defense systems became the focus of the debate.

2

The Nuclear Test Ban Negotiations

The difficulties of achieving comprehensive solutions to the problems presented by nuclear and conventional armaments had become obvious during the early period of the postwar disarmament negotiations. Whenever negotiations became more serious, there was a tendency to restrict discussion to partial and achievable measures. One such area involved negotiations for a ban on nuclear testing that resulted in the first significant arms control agreement reached in the postwar period—the Limited Test Ban Treaty (LTBT), which was opened for signature in 1963. Efforts to extend this treaty to a comprehensive test ban agreement have proved futile despite hundreds of hours of negotiation since that time, although a Threshold Test Ban Treaty in 1974 and the Peaceful Nuclear Explosions Treaty of 1976 added further restrictions to testing.

Placing limits on the testing of weapons has been viewed as one of the most important moves that can be taken to stop or slow the development of a weapons system. Few decision makers are likely to rely upon a weapon that has not been adequately tested; and, hence, they will not move to the production stage without such testing. Moreover, restrictions on testing can limit the potential power of a weapons system, making it more difficult to increase the accuracy of the destructive capability of the weapon. Finally, limits on testing have often been pressed by states that already have a given weapons system as a way of preventing other states from joining the select company of nuclear weapon states.

Not only may restrictions on testing nip weapons development in the bud, such restrictions also provide the decided advantage of being more verifiable than restrictions on the production, possession, or use of weapons. Once a state has adequately tested a given weapons system, uncertainty arises about whether the state has proceeded to the produc-

14

tion stage. Once produced, a weapons system, particularly one as small as a nuclear warhead, becomes virtually impossible to detect.

EARLY SKIRMISHING

Interest in a nuclear test ban goes back to the mid-1950s as growing public concern was raised about the dangers of nuclear fallout. With the United States entering the thermonuclear age in 1952 and the Soviet Union following suit the next year, there was increased anxiety about the health hazards of nuclear fallout. No longer was one dealing with atomic weapons that could be measured in the low kiloton range, but now such weapons were measured by the megaton with a corresponding increase in radioactive fallout. A fifteen-megaton bomb exploded by the United States in the Bikini Atolls on March 1, 1954, sprinkled radioactive fallout on Marshall Islanders, and a few days later, the Japanese fishing boat, the *Lucky Dragon*, docked with 23 irradiated fishermen aboard, one of whom subsequently died. The public outcry against further atmospheric testing intensified as Prime Minister Jawaharlal Nehru of India called for a separate and immediate nuclear test ban. Support for such a ban was also provided by the pope, Albert Einstein, Albert Schweitzer, and a number of other notables throughout the world.

The Soviet Union was the first to respond in a positive way to such appeals as Nikita Khrushchev announced on February 14, 1955, that "we [the Soviets] are willing to accept certain partial steps—for example, to discontinue the thermonuclear weapons tests."[1] As part of its dramatic policy shift shown in its May 10, 1955, proposals, the Soviet Union suggested ending nuclear tests at the very beginning of the first stage of its comprehensive disarmament plan. The United States response was one of opposition, for it argued that any ban on nuclear testing must be made a part of a comprehensive, safeguarded disarmament agreement. At best, the United States was willing to consider nuclear test restrictions during the second stage of the disarmament process, and a complete ban on testing would not come until the third stage, according to its April 1956 proposals.

The Soviet Union continued to press for a separate ban on nuclear testing in a number of proposals tabled before the onset of the Geneva talks, whereas the United States remained adamantly against such a separation. A U.S. proposal in May 1957 provided that a test ban be linked to a cut-off in the production of nuclear weapons and, in a letter sent to Soviet Premier Bulganin in December, President Eisenhower added agreement on limiting other weapons and providing assurances against surprise attack to the list of conditions for agreeing to a test suspension.

The essentially negative position taken by the United States on the issue of a nuclear test ban during this period reflected deep divisions within the government. Aside from the general reservation that such a ban would interfere with scientific progress, concern was expressed about restrictions that would impede specific weapons programs. Nuclear weapons had become a central part of U.S. military doctrine with the introduction in 1954 of the New Look strategy, which emphasized the threat of massive retaliation should the Soviet Union seek to extend its power in the world. Given the importance assigned to nuclear weapons, some believed that continued testing was necessary to ascertain the effectiveness of existing weapons.

Several new weapons systems were also believed to require testing. As part of its nuclear strategy in the mid-1950s, the United States had decided to emphasize small tactical nuclear weapons that required continued testing to miniaturize nuclear warheads. Smaller weapons would be able to reduce collateral damage and could be used in the battlefield, thus reducing the number of troops needed to balance Soviet conventional superiority. The downsizing of nuclear warheads was also necessary as the world entered the missile age since the throw-weight of such delivery systems was severely limited, particularly when compared to the bomber, which had been the primary vehicle used previously. In addition, the United States was beginning research on an anti-ballistic missile system with its Nike-Zeus system, which would use nuclear warheads to destroy incoming warheads. There was also interest in developing a neutron bomb, which would produce intense radiation but minimize structural damage. But perhaps the scientific dream that raised the most interest among those opposed to a test ban was the possibility of developing a "clean bomb." Apparently, Edward Teller's promise that a thermonuclear bomb that would be 96 percent free of fallout could be developed in four-five years led President Eisenhower to back away from his decision to support a nuclear test suspension in June 1957.[2]

Although Eisenhower and a number of military officials were primarily interested in a clean bomb as a way of reducing collateral damage in nuclear war, thus making such weapons more useful in battle, it was hoped such a device could be used for peaceful explosions involving huge earthmoving efforts such as those required for building harbors, canals, and so forth.

The United States was also constrained during that early period by opposition to a test ban from its allies, Britain and France. It was not until 1957 that the British tested their first thermonuclear device; and, of course, France had yet to test any nuclear devices since its first test did not occur until February 1960.

Still others were concerned that a test ban might diminish support for increasing military budgets or that it might generate additional pressure for disarmament. Henry A. Kissinger, writing in *Foreign Affairs* on the eve of the Geneva Conference on the Discontinuance of Nuclear Weapons Tests in 1958, expressed the fear that such a ban would be the first step in an increased campaign to outlaw nuclear weapons altogether;[3] and the head of the U.S. Atomic Energy Commission, Lewis F. Strauss, argued that such a ban would lead to public complacency, making it difficult to get defense budgets passed by Congress.[4]

Whatever the motivation for the American reticence, the Soviet Union was able to capture the moral high ground as it intensified its advocacy of an immediate test ban. In June 1957 it proposed a two- to three-year moratorium on testing that would be separate from other disarmament measures. The Soviets sweetened the offer by suggesting for the first time that they would be willing to accept on-site inspection. With these important concessions, public support for a test ban was intensified. Nobel laureate Linus Pauling submitted a petition with the signatures of thousands of scientists calling for a nuclear test ban, and a number of religious leaders, including Billy Graham and the pope, were calling for unilateral suspensions of testing to force the Soviet Union to follow suit. American public support for such a ban was also intensifying. The Gallup polls, for example, showed an increase in support for such a ban from 20 percent in April 1954 to 63 percent in 1957.

President Eisenhower responded to these pressures in a June press conference by proposing a ten-month suspension of nuclear tests. Such a limited time was roundly criticized on the grounds that it was meaningless, for it usually took that long to prepare for a new test series. Secretary of State John Foster Dulles supported such a suspension since it would be short enough not to risk the dislocation of scientific personnel should the ban fail to be extended, and it would also provide time to make headway in terms of putting an inspection system into place and to make certain that verification procedures would be adequate.

The pressure intensified the following year when the Soviet Union announced that it was unilaterally suspending all atmospheric testing on March 31 and would continue to adhere to such a ban as long as the United States and its allies refrained from testing. This offer came, however, just after the Soviet Union had completed a long series of nuclear tests and was therefore hoping to stop the United States from conducting similar tests. When the United States announced its own moratorium to begin on October 31, 1958, it likewise was just concluding its most intensive series of tests in history. The United Kingdom, initially hostile to the proposed U.S. test moratorium, agreed to accept it after moving up its own testing program to August 1958 rather than waiting until late fall as initially planned. The pattern of conducting a series of nuclear tests then immediately calling for a test suspension by all parties continued to be used on several subsequent occasions prior to the negotiation of the Limited Test Ban Treaty.

The Soviets' March 31, 1958, moratorium placed considerable political pressure on the United States to respond to the Soviet initiative in some way. The United States, concerned about being upstaged on the test ban issue, proposed in a letter from President Eisenhower dated April 8 that technical discussions be opened to determine the feasibility of an effective verification system. Khrushchev objected to the idea of technical talks, suggesting that agreement on the principle of a test ban must be reached before technical talks on verification could begin. Much to the surprise of the United States, the Soviet Union relented on May 9 by accepting the idea of technical expert talks. Soviet interest in a test ban was apparently much greater than that of the United States at the time, for not only would such a ban prevent the United States from duplicating the recent Soviet test series, but a general test ban could help resolve the problem of nuclear proliferation as the Soviet Union began to worry about the nuclear aspirations of the Federal Republic of Germany and the People's Republic of China. Since the Soviet Union did not share the U.S. interest in developing tactical nuclear weapons, it was less concerned about keeping the testing option open for that reason. Furthermore, the Soviets had considerable interest in slowing the arms race because of the economic costs involved and the need to bolster their domestic economy.

The Conference of Experts, consisting of scientists from the United States, the USSR, and several of their respective allies, met during the summer of 1958 to discuss the verification requirements for a nuclear test ban. The conference proved to be an interesting experiment in international bargaining, as it was composed of academically oriented scientists rather than seasoned diplomats. The American scientists were somewhat at a disadvantage, not only because they lacked the level of diplomatic experience of their Soviet counterparts, but they also failed to receive diplomatic instructions. This was partially due to the failure of Washington to agree upon a negotiating position. It was also probably related to the fact that Washington viewed the negotiations as a scientific exploration of the problems and prospects of verifying a nuclear test ban, not the final word on verification. The Soviet Union saw the negotiations as a process for reaching political decisions on how much verification would be necessary.

In agreeing to the Experts Conference, Khrushchev had proposed an unrealistic demand that the Experts' Report be completed within thirty days after negotiations begin—a tactic often used by the Soviet Union to place pressure upon the United States to reach agreement or be blamed for the failure. President Eisenhower responded by calling for a report within sixty days or as soon as possible thereafter.

The negotiations proved to be quite hectic with sessions often going late into the evenings. These negotiations, as well as subsequent ones dealing with the verification issue, were somewhat impeded by the fact that both sides were reticent about exposing their prized methods of detection. As a result, candid discussion on the requirements and capabilities of verification was often exceedingly difficult. Eventually the scientists were able to agree upon an inspection system that would include some 180 land-based control posts. It was believed that this number would be sufficient to detect underground explosions as low as 5 kilotons in size. The experts also recommended four technical measures for detecting nuclear testing: acoustical waves, electromagnetic waves, radioactive debris, and seismic signals.

The State Department was somewhat displeased that the Experts' Report had agreed upon a single set of control sites rather than leaving the issue for further negotiation. After initial hesitation, President Eisenhower agreed on August 22, 1958, to accept the report as the basis for further negotiation. The Soviet Union in the subsequent Geneva negotiations continued to raise the report to support various positions that it took on the test ban issue.

NEGOTIATING THE LIMITED TEST BAN TREATY

During the nearly five years it took to negotiate the Limited Test Ban Treaty, the positions taken on test ban issues by the two superpowers varied considerably. The United States began the negotiations in the fall of 1958 by insisting that a test ban agreement be linked to progress on other measures of disarmament, particularly a nuclear weapons production cut-off. On January 19, 1959, the United States announced that it would no longer insist upon such a linkage. Apparently, the Defense Department and the Atomic Energy Commission had softened their positions on the issue, perhaps believing that agreement on a test ban treaty was unlikely anyway. It was not until the Reagan administration came into power in 1981 that the United States reversed itself by insisting that a comprehensive test ban agreement be linked to other measures of disarmament.

In June 1961 the Soviet Union began to insist upon linkage as it sought to make the issue of a nuclear test ban conditional upon agreement on general and complete disarmament. The Soviet negotiator, Semyon Tsarapkin, in supporting the shift in policy, argued that the situation had changed in the last two or three years and that a test ban agreement would no longer be very useful. Instead, a verified ban would only provide intelligence gathering in the absence of disarmament.

When the Soviet Union broke the three-year moratorium on nuclear testing on August 31, 1961, yet another form of linkage was suggested when Khrushchev announced that the Soviet Union had resumed testing only to shock the allies into beginning negotiations on Berlin and other German issues. He also repeated the notion that a test ban should be linked to disarmament and hypothesized that the resumption of testing might induce the West to negotiate more seriously about disarmament.

On the eve of the final Moscow negotiations in the summer of 1963, which produced the Limited Test Ban Treaty, Khrushchev was insisting that a test ban be linked to a nonaggression pact between the Warsaw Pact and NATO nations—a proposal that had long been on the Soviet agenda but was equally objectionable to the West. Only after the Soviets dropped this linkage was it possible to conclude the Limited Test Ban Treaty.

Several factors have influenced decisions to link a nuclear test ban with other issues. The early insistence by the United States that a test ban be linked to broader disarmament issues was partially motivated by the desire to retain the moral high ground and to counter the propaganda advantages derived by the Soviet Union's position in calling for an immediate end to nuclear testing. Similarly, the Soviet Union's argument that it had resumed testing in August 1961 only to force the West to negotiate on more meaningful disarmament measures was an effort to minimize the global hostility created by its resumption of atmospheric testing.

Linkage has also been pressed by some as a device to assure that given negotiations are doomed to failure. By making a cut-off in the production of nuclear weapons a condition for supporting a nuclear test ban in the late fifties, the United States was guaranteeing that such an agreement would not be negotiated. The Soviet Union would hardly accept such a proposal at a time when its nuclear stocks were far inferior to those of the United States.

Proposals for linking a test ban to broader disarmament measures may also be motivated by the perception that the other side is more interested than oneself in a nuclear test ban and consequently may pay a price to obtain it. But in this case neither the United States nor the Soviet Union was that interested in a test ban. The exception might have been for brief moments when one party or the other felt itself ahead and wanted to lock in the advantage. The interest shown in a test ban agreement was probably more related to the pressures exerted by an aroused public concerned about the dangers of atmospheric testing.

Linkage may even be supported by those concerned with reaching more significant agreements, believing that measures such as a test ban are largely cosmetic and do little to control the threat of nuclear weapons. If the linkage does not hold some attraction for the adversary, such an approach will do little to further the cause of disarmament. Instead, it might be preferable, as some disarmament proponents have suggested, that agreement on small issues such as a test ban be reached in order to build the trust that is necessary for obtaining agreement on more controversial issues or to gain experience and reassurance regarding verification.

Positions also changed over time regarding whether a test ban should be comprehensive or partial. The Soviet Union up to the present time has generally favored a comprehensive test ban that would include weapons testing in all environments—atmospheric, outer space, underwater, and underground. The United States has often opposed a comprehensive solution largely on the basis that tests in certain environments, particularly those conducted underground, could not be adequately verified. Thus any restrictions should be limited to those explosions that would be verifiable.

The United States was the first to offer the possibility of a partial test ban agreement when Eisenhower proposed in a letter to Khrushchev, dated April 13, 1959, that the United States would support a comprehensive test ban only if the Soviet Union would change its position with respect to procedures for on-site inspection, eliminate its veto requirement, and enter into early discussion of procedures for detecting high altitude testing. If the Soviet Union were unwilling to make such changes, the president proposed that a first step be taken by suspending atmospheric tests up to 50 kilometers while political and technical problems were being resolved.

The Soviet Union rejected the partial approach suggested by Eisenhower, perhaps in the belief that it would benefit the United States more than the Soviet Union. It was assumed that the United States would have more to gain from testing in the nonrestricted environments since the United States had a greater interest in tactical nuclear weapons than did the Soviet Union and such tests are most suitable for testing underground.

With the recognition that some tests would not be readily verifiable with existing means of verification or that the verification procedures required would be so onerous as to be unacceptable to sovereign nations, the United States and the Soviet Union eventually agreed that the more difficult tests to detect could be restricted through the process of an unverified moratorium, at least in the short run. The two states differed, however, in how long that moratorium could last while the parties sought to improve verification procedures and to negotiate a comprehensive test ban treaty. The Soviet Union insisted upon a four- to five-year moratorium, whereas the United States wanted it limited to one- to two years.

Verification

As in so many arms control negotiations, verification became the major obstacle to agreement. The ability of the Geneva Experts Conference to reach a consensus on the verification requirements for a nuclear test ban agreement suggested that perhaps these negotiations would not be as vituperative as earlier disarmament negotiations. Yet despite the fact that both the United States and the Soviet Union ultimately accepted the Experts' Report as the basis for the test ban talks beginning in October 1958, verification issues continued to plague the negotiations.

As in the case of negotiations for a comprehensive plan of disarmament, the United States continued to place far more emphasis upon verification procedures than did the Soviet Union. Under early U.S. plans the international control organ would have been required to be "installed and working effectively" prior to the institution of the nuclear test ban.

The priorities of the Soviet Union were just the opposite as it sought to obtain an agreement on the principle of a test ban prior to discussing control procedures. It was not until November 1958 that the Soviet Union accepted a control system as an integral part of the test ban agreement. Prior to that time it had insisted upon a separate protocol dealing with the control system.

A partial explanation for the alleged failure of the Experts Conference to evaluate verification capabilities accurately may have been related to a general lack of data on the problems involved in the detection of underground tests. Most nuclear tests after all had been conducted above ground prior to 1958. With the flurry of tests that began just prior to the opening of the Geneva Conference on the Discontinuance of Nuclear Weapons Tests, the United States was able to collect new data that led to a reassessment of verification capabilities. The U.S. series, Hardtack II, revealed that the minimum yield for safely detecting an underground test using the Geneva Experts' formula was 20 kilotons rather than the 5 kilotons previously estimated. Although a 20-kiloton level would have assured the detectability of virtually any test above the size of the Hiroshima bomb, many experts felt this was insufficient.[5] In presenting the evidence for the Hardtack II series in January 1959, the United States argued that the restoration of the 5-kiloton level would require 10 times as many on-site inspections annually or a control network of some 500 stations.[6] The Soviet Union rejected this contention, arguing that the United States was basing its conclusions on a single shot, the 5-kiloton Logan test.

Although the Hardtack II results led the United States to assert that the Geneva Experts' assessments were inadequate, a more serious attack on the Geneva system resulted when the United States raised the possibility of decoupling underground nuclear explosions in order that such tests would not register so high on seismological instruments and might even escape detection altogether. The idea of decoupling, which was introduced by Albert Latter in 1959, suggested the possibility of digging a large hole underground in which a nuclear device could be exploded. The large cavity in effect would lessen the shock to the surrounding earth and thus be less detectable. In fact, Latter's suggestion that the decoupling effect could be as high as 300 would have meant "that a 100 kiloton explosion would not even be detected and located by the experts control system."[7]

U.S. scientists were clearly divided on Latter's decoupling theory. Many felt that to dig a large enough hole to muffle a nuclear explosion would be a difficult and costly task. To do so without being detected, as would be required if one wanted to test surreptitiously, would be a virtual impossibility. To dispose of the excavated materials would be a huge undertaking.

The theory of decoupling was applied in the Cowboy series of experiments (December 1959–March 1960), which used data extracted from chemical explosions to suggest a decoupling factor of 120. Soviet scientists referred to experiments that showed a decoupling factor of only 2, but U.S. scientists were able to demonstrate fallacies in the calculations. Whatever the proper assessment, the argument of decoupling assumed a less significant role in subsequent debates on a comprehensive test ban.

In seeking to ascertain the number of on-site inspections required, the United States wanted that number to be determined on a scientific basis rather than based upon a political compromise as proposed by the Soviet

Union. The United States preferred a sliding scale in which the number of on-site inspections would be related to the number of suspicious events during any given year. Prime Minister Harold Macmillan supported the notion of an annual quota for inspections in his effort to get the United States and the Soviet Union to compromise on the issue.

In May 1959, the United States accepted the idea of an annual quota for on-site inspections as long as a Soviet veto would not be applicable. Debate over the next few years revolved around the question of how many on-site inspections would be allowed annually. The United States began by demanding twenty such inspections per year, whereas the Soviet Union was willing to accept three at most. In May 1961, the United States accepted a sliding scale for on-site inspections on Soviet territory that would range from twelve to twenty per year. Subsequent moves resulted in further reductions so that on the eve of agreeing to the Limited Test Ban Treaty in 1963 the United States was insisting upon only six such inspections annually. At the same time, the Soviet Union was proposing a limit of only two or three, reversing a position it had held for several months that would have denied any on-site inspections on Soviet territory.

Despite all of the energy exerted in debating the issue of on-site inspection and control posts, Swedish scientists, among others, raised questions as to whether such procedures could be effective even if allowed. Congressional hearings on the Limited Test Ban Treaty revealed that the digging of just one hole to find radioactive debris as uncontestable evidence of a test explosion would take as much as fifty-five days after an explosion occurs.[8] The costs of an effective system also raised questions as even the more limited Experts' proposals for a control system would have cost into the billions.

In April 1962 the eight nonaligned states in the Eighteen Nation Disarmament Committee sought to simplify verification requirements by proposing that the inspection system be based upon existing national networks of observation posts. After all, over 7,800 seismological stations already in existence throughout the world would be able to monitor underground explosions. Research was also demonstrating that many nuclear explosions could be distinguished from earthquakes because of the differences between the two in the initial shock waves.[9]

When evaluating the costs and complexities of the test ban verification system, it should be remembered that the number of control posts and on-site inspections being discussed was related to a ban that would cover only the larger underground tests. Concerned about the problems of detecting low-yield underground tests, the United States in February

1960 proposed placing the threshold on underground explosions at 4.75 on the Richter scale. It was estimated that any test above the size of that exploded at Hiroshima would register at least 4.75 or better. A month later the United States agreed to the notion of a unilateral moratorium on tests below the 4.75 threshold while negotiations and research would continue in an effort to reduce that threshold, leading ultimately to the abolition of all underground testing. The Soviet Union was quick to accept the 4.75 threshold level with a moratorium on testing below that level but insisted the proposed Experts' Report provided sufficient verification capabilities for all tests, both above and below the threshold. In August 1961, the United States indicated a willingness to eliminate the 4.75 threshold entirely if the Soviet Union would agree to increasing the number of control posts and on-site inspections. This overture, however, became the victim of the Soviet Union's resumption of nuclear testing announced a day or so after the U.S. proposal was tabled.

The fact that the United States was beginning to be more conciliatory on verification issues, following the hard line it had taken in the years 1959–62, was related in large measure to the significant progress that was being made in research to improve verification procedures. Initially, such efforts were insignificant, raising questions about the United States' seriousness about a nuclear test ban. Prior to 1960 the United States had spent only a total of 20 million dollars on the problem of nuclear test detection—an insignificant amount considering how seriously the United States took the verification issue in the debates.[10]

Beginning in 1960, research into the problems of verification was considerably bolstered with the establishment of the VELA program. During FY 1960 and 1961, over $50 million had been appropriated for the program with $59 million designated for FY 1962 alone. On the basis of research conducted under these programs, it was discovered that the sensitivity of seismographic equipment could be increased by a factor of five or ten by placing the equipment in deep holes rather than at the surface. Research also indicated that the number of shallow earthquakes in the Soviet Union was far fewer than had been previously thought, reducing the number of suspicious events requiring investigations. It was further discovered that underground explosions conducted in alluvium produced deep cavities that would be detectable from the air.[11] This discovery was significant since such tests were the most difficult to detect with seismological equipment. Increasing the number of control posts and placing them closer to areas where earthquake activity occurs would also increase detection prospects. The development of tamper-proof detection systems or "black boxes" also improved the prospects of verification with limited damage to Soviet sensitivities about national sovereignty. In December 1962, Premier Nikita Khrushchev agreed that three such stations could be placed upon Soviet territory.

Progress on detection techniques was such that the United States felt it could make a number of concessions on verification procedures to be used. For example, President Kennedy announced on August 27, 1962, that a substantial reduction could be made in the number of control posts required and, more importantly, from the perspective of Soviet sensitivity to its sovereign rights, these posts could be manned by Soviet nationals with international supervision.

By 1963, improvements in verification procedures led to estimates that stations located outside the territory of the USSR would be just as effective in detecting Soviet underground tests as the verification system proposed in the 1958 Experts' Reports.[12] As noted earlier, the Experts insisted that a number of control posts be situated on Soviet territory as well as externally located. Because of these improvements it was reported that President Kennedy and Prime Minister Macmillan, during talks in Bermuda in 1962, regretted that the United States had made so much of the possibility of clandestine underground testing.

Although most of the attention in the nuclear test ban negotiations was given to the problems of detecting underground nuclear explosions, verification of testing in other environments was not without controversy. Concern about possible evasion of high-altitude testing restrictions led President Eisenhower on May 5, 1959, to make continued U.S. participation in the negotiations dependent upon an early discussion of the problems involved. As a result, Technical Group I was formed at the Geneva Conference to evaluate verification requirements for a high-altitude test ban. During these talks, the Soviet Union accepted all but one of the eleven verification procedures proposed, several of which would take advantage of the then developing technologies of outer space satellites. In its final report, Technical Group I recommended the placement into orbit of 5 or 6 large satellites able to detect radiation from nuclear explosions in space.[13] Progress was such that the United States representative in Geneva admitted in the spring of 1962 that larger nuclear explosions could be detected by national verification means. He also pointed out that detection capabilities were considerable with respect to outer-space and underwater testing, but doubts remained on the ability to detect underground tests.[14]

Despite this optimism the fact remains that the VELA system launched in 1970 was not completely reliable. A White House panel was unable to reach an airtight conclusion on whether South Africa had exploded a nuclear device over the Atlantic Ocean in 1979.[15] The Defense Intelligence Agency claimed there had been a nuclear explosion, but others were not so certain.

The Moratorium on Testing

The fact that a test ban agreement could be negotiated at all is in no small measure related to the unilateral moratorium on further nuclear testing that both sides had accepted by the fall of 1958 and continued to adhere to until the Soviet Union resumed testing on September 1, 1961. Once into the moratorium, pressure was exerted upon both parties not to be the first to break it. Indeed, each side had pledged that it would not resume testing until the other side did. The Soviet Union persisted in honoring its unilateral moratorium after the French exploded their first atomic bomb in February 1960 despite the fact that it had made continued adherence to the ban contingent upon observance by *all* Western states.

The United States was the first to blink on the moratorium as the Eisenhower administration was pressed by various domestic interests to renew testing, given the slow progress of the talks. Among those taking such a stand was Nelson Rockefeller, who was preparing for a run for the presidency in 1960, John A. McCone, the chairman of the Atomic Energy Commission, and Senator Clinton P. Anderson, the chairman of the Joint Committee on Atomic Energy. On August 26, 1959, President Eisenhower announced that the U.S. moratorium would be extended to the end of the year. In so doing, he was merely extending it two months beyond the initial one-year moratorium that was to have expired on October 30th. In agreeing to such a limited extension, Eisenhower was communicating his frustration that more progress had not been made on negotiating a test ban. He was unwilling to support the British position that the moratorium should continue as long as negotiations were in progress. On December 29, 1959, President Eisenhower went a step further by announcing that the United States considered itself free to resume nuclear weapons testing but added that it would "not resume nuclear testing without announcing our intention in advance of any resumption."[16] The chief British negotiator, Sir Michael Wright, has criticized this position by suggesting that it created the worst of all possible worlds. The United States would lose whatever security benefits might be gained by resuming testing and, at the same time, would be subjected to world criticism, allowing the Soviet Union "to claim that the West was the first to speak of resuming."[17]

Despite the announcement that it no longer felt itself bound by the moratorium on nuclear testing, the United States made no immediate effort to prepare test sites, nor did it provide any budgetary allocations for nuclear testing. The Atomic Energy Commission finally declared on March 16, 1960, that it would prepare for underground tests in New Mexico in 1961 and Dwight Eisenhower, after leaving the presidency, noted that he would have resumed nuclear testing following the 1960 presidential election had Richard Nixon won.[18]

During this period, the Soviet Union continued to give assurances that it would live up to the moratorium. On August 11, 1959, Premier Khrushchev pledged not to be the first to resume nuclear testing. He continued to reassure the United States on this score by promising President Kennedy as late as the Vienna summit in June 1961 that the Soviet Union would not resume nuclear testing until the United States did. In making the promise, it may well have been that the Soviet Union had anticipated that the United States would be the first to break the moratorium. Support for such a viewpoint could be found in the changing climate of opinion on the subject in the United States. The Joint Chiefs of Staff in February 1961 had asked for a resumption of testing if agreement were not reached on a test ban within sixty days, and Gallup polls were showing a 2 to 1 majority favoring the unilateral resumption of testing by the United States.

The Kennedy administration appeared to be more predisposed than the previous administration toward reaching agreement on a nuclear test ban treaty as reflected in the substantial number of concessions it made in the March 21, 1961, proposals. The Soviet Union was not responsive to the U.S. overture, perhaps because it had already made the decision to resume nuclear testing.

When the Soviet Union resumed testing on September 1, 1961, the immediate U.S. response was an offer to ban all atmospheric testing, but the Soviets were given only a week to react. Since the Soviet Union had just begun its largest test series ever, involving a total of fifty atmospheric tests within a period of sixty days, the response, as might be expected, was *nyet*. As a result, the United States resumed its own testing on September 15, albeit underground. The following month, Prime Minister Macmillan sought President Kennedy's agreement for a two-month moratorium on atmospheric testing, but Kennedy rejected the proposal. According to some insiders, the reason for this decision was premised on the belief that the Soviet Union would be more inclined to negotiate an end to the arms race once it realized that the West would not stand idle and let the Soviet Union benefit militarily without a response.[19]

Despite the importance of extended moratoria for creating the appropriate environment for negotiating a test ban, it has been argued that the effect of breaking any such moratorium is decidedly against a democracy. It would be virtually impossible for a democracy to break a test ban as abruptly as the Soviet Union did, for the time and effort required for preparing nuclear weapons tests would undoubtedly be leaked in the democratic society. Also democratic states appear to be more concerned about the impact of adverse domestic and international opinion than do their more authoritarian counterparts. Because of this disadvantage and disappointment with the turn of events, President Kennedy declared in an address to the nation on March 2, 1962, that "we know enough now about broken negotiations, secret preparations and the advantage gained from a long test series never to offer again an uninspected moratorium."[20]

Such reservations did not prevent President Kennedy from announcing in his American University commencement address on June 10, 1963, that "the United States does not propose to conduct nuclear tests in the atmosphere so long as other states do not do so. We will not be the first to resume."[21] This statement, along with other conciliatory gestures made in the speech, set the tone in making it possible to conclude negotiations on the Limited Test Ban Treaty 55 days later. Premier Nikita Khrushchev is reported to have told U.S. negotiator Averell Harriman that the American University speech was the "best speech by any President since Roosevelt."[22]

The United States decision to initiate another uninspected moratorium, despite having been caught off guard by the Soviet resumption of nuclear testing in September 1961, was made as a result of the feeling that the Soviet Union had not gained that much militarily. According to data reported by the U.S. Atomic Energy Commission, the United States made up for the Soviet encroachment by exploding more than twice as many weapons as the Soviet Union during the two years following the Soviet resumption of testing.[23]

The Third Party Role

The success of the negotiations resulting in signing the Limited Test Ban Treaty in the summer of 1963 was also partially due to the role played by third parties. The United Kingdom lobbied the United States vigorously on occasion in an effort to get the latter to be more responsive to Soviet concessions on test ban issues. Rather than serving simply as a negotiating partner to the United States, the British often sought active mediation between the superpowers.

The British position on the test ban issue, however, was initially hostile. This was particularly true prior to its first hydrogen bomb test in 1957 after which the United Kingdom became an eager advocate of a test ban agreement. The British government had greater domestic pressures affecting its arms control policies than did the United States, given the strong anti-nuclear attitudes of large segments of the British population. Sensitivity to those public attitudes was heightened in 1959–60 due to the fact that Prime Minister Harold Macmillan was coming up for reelection. The British also had more to fear from nuclear weapons in the late fifties and early sixties than did the Americans since the number of intercontinental-range ballistic missiles capable of hitting U.S. soil was extremely limited at the time. Consequently, Britain, at closer range, was more of a nuclear hostage to the Soviet Union than was the United States.

In his role as mediator between the superpowers, Macmillan visited Moscow in February 1959 at which time he sought to break an impasse on the inspection issue by proposing a quota system for on-site inspection. Efforts to press the United States to be more forthcoming can be seen in Macmillan's last-minute flight to the United States in the spring of 1960 to lobby for U.S. acceptance of the principle of an annual quota for on-site inspections. Apparently, this particular trip was not completely necessary for the United States was already becoming more conciliatory on the issue. The CIA head, Allen Dulles, and others had concluded that the United States was ahead in nuclear technology and therefore could lock in the U.S. advantage by becoming more responsive to Soviet positions for the sake of agreement.[24]

After Kennedy assumed the presidency, Macmillan continued to press the testing issue, trying first at the Nassau December 1961 meeting to dissuade Kennedy from resuming atmospheric testing. In March 1963 it was Macmillan who wrote Kennedy suggesting that he meet directly with Khrushchev on the issue of arms control. Although rejecting Macmillan's suggestion for a summit meeting, the president did agree to the idea of a high-level conference, and on June 8 the Soviet premier accepted, setting the stage for the negotiation of the LTBT in Moscow.[25]

Other third party pressures for a nuclear test ban came from the nonaligned countries in the Eighteen Nation Disarmament Committee. Among the more significant initiatives taken by these eight states was a memo dated April 16, 1962, which sought to provide a compromise on verification issues. The memo called for an inspection system based primarily upon existing national observation posts. By using the 7,800 existing meteorological and geological land stations, the need for creating new control posts, particularly on Soviet territory, would be largely negated. It was also largely pressure from the eight neutral states in 1962 that caused the Soviet Union to accept the notion of two to three on-site inspections per year.

Although the Limited Test Ban Treaty was negotiated primarily during tripartite negotiations involving the United States, the Soviet Union, and the United Kingdom, the treaty itself was opened to signature by all states. By 1987, the LTBT had become one of the most universally accepted arms control agreements with around 120 signatories. With the exception of France and the People's Republic of China, virtually all important states are members. Furthermore, no state has exercised the rather easy requirements for withdrawal, which involves only a three-month notice.

EVALUATING THE LIMITED TEST BAN TREATY

Any evaluation of the Limited Test Ban Treaty, which was signed in Moscow on August 5, 1963, must be mixed. As the first significant arms control agreement in the postwar world, it represented somewhat of a breakthrough. The treaty symbolized a period of improved relations between the United States and the Soviet Union, and it was hoped that the LTBT would provide the beginning of a series of more significant arms control agreements. The nearly universal adherence to the treaty raised some hope that the problem of nuclear spread would be minimized since so many threshold nuclear states were included among the signatories. India, having ratified the LTBT, was forced to test underground as it did in 1974 or violate the treaty. In conducting its one underground test, India took great pains to assert that the test was a "peaceful nuclear explosion."

The treaty helped minimize a potential health hazard by eliminating the dangers of nuclear fallout from atmospheric explosions. This was not an insignificant achievement, for research had indicated serious health hazards, particularly since strontium 90 threatened to damage uncounted numbers of children because of contamination of milk supplies. The 1958 atmospheric tests alone were expected to double the amount of this dangerous chemical in the soil by 1960, and the areas most at risk would be in the northern hemisphere.[26]

Secretary of Defense Robert McNamara supported the Limited Test Ban Treaty because he believed it would freeze U.S. nuclear superiority.[27] It was felt that the extra costs imposed by underground testing would dilute limited Soviet military resources. Even more important, a partial test ban would impede Soviet development of an ABM system that could be more effectively tested in the atmosphere than underground. It was also believed that since the Soviet Union preferred larger nuclear devices than did the United States, the former would be at a disadvantage, for underground testing is not as desirable a testing environment for the very large nuclear device.

On the negative side of the ledger, the treaty did not stop nuclear testing, in fact, such testing increased significantly after the treaty was opened for signature, albeit underground. Data in table 2.1 comparing the number of nuclear tests for the five nuclear powers reveal that more tests per year were conducted after the treaty was signed in 1963 than before it was opened for signature. The number was especially high for the United States. Soviet testing accelerated somewhat in 1978, while U.S. tests have remained somewhat stable since 1975. British testing virtually ceased after 1963, making a comeback after Margaret Thatcher assumed power in 1979. France and China have not ratified the LTBT and have engaged in active testing programs that included atmospheric tests until 1974 for France and until 1980 for China. It remains to be seen whether the current lull in Chinese testing that began in 1985 will continue.

A partial explanation for the increase in testing by the United States is related to the fact that the Joint Chiefs of Staff were able to obtain agreement from the president to increase the number of tests if the chiefs would agree to support the Limited Test Ban Treaty. Without their support, it would have been difficult, if not impossible, to obtain Senate approval for ratification of the treaty. Perhaps it can be assumed that the Soviet military received similar concessions for they also had initially been extremely hostile to the treaty.

Had the LTBT provided for an inspection system, it might have been judged more successful in contributing to the control of the U.S.-Soviet arms race. For many proponents of arms control, the precedence of establishing an inspection system on Soviet territory at times seemed to be more important than the objective of stopping further nuclear testing. It might even be argued that arms control advocates, preoccupied with establishing the precedence of on-site inspection, played into the hands of those who sought to use verification concerns to defeat all efforts to obtain a comprehensive test ban. It was perhaps a case where demanding the best was the enemy of the good. The Soviet Union after all was willing to accept limited on-site inspection and unmanned seismic stations in 1963—procedures that would have provided considerable assurance against evasion for all but the smallest underground nuclear devices.

Table 2.1 Known Nuclear Test Explosions

Time Period	U.S.	USSR	Britain	France	China
July 1945–Aug. 1963	331	166	23	8	0
Aug.-Dec., 1963	14	0	0	1	0
1964	29	6	1	3	1
1965	29	9	1	4	1
1966	40	15	0	6	3
1967	29	16	0	3	2
1968	39	13	0	5	1
1969	29	15	0	0	2
1970	33	13	0	8	1
1971	15	20	0	5	1
1972	15	22	0	3	2
1973	12	14	0	5	1
1974	12	20	1	7	1
1975	17	15	0	2	1
1976	15	17	1	4	4
1977	12	18	0	6	1
1978	16	27	2	8	3
1979	15	29	1	9	0
1980	14	21	3	13	1
1981	16	21	1	12	0
1982	18	31	1	6	0
1983	17	27	1	7	2
1984	17	27	2	8	2
1985	15	8	1	8	0
1986	14	0	1	8	0
Total	813	570*	40	149	30

*The Stockholm International Peace Research Institute and the Swedish National Defense Research Institute reported 18 additional Soviet tests between 1956 and 1958. Sixteen more tests were reported by the French Ministry of Defense between 1963 and 1977.

Source: Based upon data from Natural Resources Defense Council as reported in Michael R. Gordon, "The Arms Race Shows No Signs of Slowing Down," *New York Times*, March 23, 1986, p. E3. Robert S. Norris of the NRDC kindly supplied the figures for 1986.

Whether the Limited Test Ban Treaty has been instrumental in stopping the spread of nuclear weapons to other states is uncertain. The treaty allows its signatories to test nuclear devices as long as the tests are conducted underground as was India's nuclear explosion in 1974. The added cost of testing underground cannot be considered a sufficient deterrent to any state that is determined to develop nuclear weapons.

Moreover, testing itself may not be essential for the development of primitive nuclear devices. Since 1945 every state that has tried to detonate an atomic bomb has succeeded on the first attempt, at least as far as publically available information shows.[28]

It has also been suggested that the Limited Test Ban Treaty did a disservice to the cause of disarmament by taking the issue of nuclear testing off the front pages of newspapers and television. After the test ban was put into effect, there was less need for the public to be concerned about the environmental hazards of testing. By going underground, the dangers had been reduced considerably. The incentive for extending the test ban was somewhat diminished, particularly since the main selling point for stopping nuclear testing had been the danger of nuclear fallout. The LTBT may also have dissipated the public and political forces favoring disarmament in general, for testing was to become a less visible symbol of the dangers of nuclear war.

THE THRESHOLD TEST BAN TREATY

The fact that more than a decade elapsed before the United States and the Soviet Union could agree upon further restrictions on nuclear testing provides some evidence of just how the Limited Test Ban Treaty had taken away the momentum for restricting nuclear testing. The Threshold Test Ban Treaty (TTBT), signed by the United States and the Soviet Union at the 1974 Moscow summit, did little to restrict U.S.-Soviet testing since the threshold at 150 kilotons was placed so high. Tests above that level were unnecessary, for extrapolations can be made from smaller tests that allow accurate design judgments to be made for more powerful nuclear devices. Besides, the larger devices are more likely to vent, threatening health hazards, and if the resulting radiation drifts beyond national borders, there would be a violation of the Limited Test Ban Treaty.

Although little pressure for restricting underground nuclear testing came from U.S. and Soviet domestic interests, third parties had begun to make the issue of a comprehensive test ban the central arms control issue. Interest in extending the test ban was particularly intensified during the debates on the Nuclear Nonproliferation Treaty during the sixties. A number of nonnuclear weapon states felt that they were being discriminated against by being asked to give up the nuclear weapons option while the existing nuclear weapon states could continue to expand their nuclear armaments. A comprehensive test ban came to be viewed as one of the most important first steps that the superpowers could take to show that they too were serious about restricting nuclear weapons. Also, unlike the NPT, such a treaty would place equal obligations upon both nuclear and nonnuclear weapon states.

To support their case, the nonnuclear weapon states called attention to the Preamble of the Limited Test Ban Treaty, which obligated the parties to continue negotiations in an effort to end all nuclear weapons tests. These states also referred to article 6 of the Nuclear Nonproliferation Treaty, which demanded that progress be made on controlling the arms race by the superpowers. The SALT I agreements were regarded by these states as largely cosmetic since they did not reduce existing weapons systems.

It was the Soviet Union that sought to keep alive the issue of a comprehensive nuclear test ban, perhaps recognizing the propaganda value of doing so. Often, for example, the issue of a comprehensive test ban treaty would be at the top of the list of priorities that the Soviet Union presented in agenda debates before the Eighteen Nation Disarmament Conference in Geneva.

In February 1974, the Soviet Union began another offensive in favor of a comprehensive test ban treaty. Rebuffed by the United States, which believed that testing was necessary to improve its nuclear arsenal and regarded a comprehensive agreement as nonverifiable, the Soviet Union suggested the possibility of establishing a quota that would allow so many tests annually. When this too was rejected, Brezhnev proposed during Henry Kissinger's visit to Moscow in March 1974 that a "threshold" limit be placed upon underground tests. Kissinger was willing to discuss this proposal since the Soviet Union was more dependent upon high-yield weapons than the United States, and these would be the sorts of tests that would be disallowed under a threshold test ban.[29]

During subsequent expert discussions in Moscow, the United States was concerned to keep the threshold high. In particular, Kissinger was afraid that a low threshold would alienate France and particularly China by placing extraordinary global pressure upon them to desist from their weapons testing programs. As a result, he pressed for a 200-kiloton threshold, but eventually compromised on a 150-kiloton level.

Unlike the Limited Test Ban Treaty, which took years to negotiate, the Threshold Test Ban Treaty was completed in a matter of weeks. The final details were finished at the Moscow summit meeting toward the end of June. Also, in contrast to the LTBT, this treaty was negotiated and signed only by the United States and the Soviet Union.

Political objectives rather than arms control objectives seem to have provided the primary impetus for this treaty. Chief among these was the desire to produce a U.S.-Soviet agreement that could be signed at the Moscow summit in June–July, 1974. President Nixon was under great pressure to have an international political success in view of the Watergate scandal, which resulted in his resignation only weeks after his return from the summit.

The TTBT also may have been viewed as a sop to the nonnuclear weapon states which were to meet the following year in the First Review Conference on the operation of the Nuclear Nonproliferation Treaty. The failure of the superpowers to comply with article 6 calling for progress toward arms control was certain to be high on the agenda. At least, the superpowers might argue that the Threshold Treaty was a step in that direction.

The United States might have viewed the effort as a way of reducing the advantages that the Soviet Union gained from propagandizing in support of a comprehensive test ban agreement. Just as the LTBT served to lessen the intensity of the cry for a ban on nuclear testing, the Threshold Test Ban Treaty might diminish pressure for a ban on all tests.

Since the TTBT provides only a partial ban, it has some of the weaknesses of the Limited Test Ban Treaty. The chief limitation is that underground nuclear testing is still allowed. A threshold of 150 kilotons has to be regarded as quite trivial, particularly since most U.S. weapons tests have been below 10–15 kilotons, with many less then 2 kilotons. Seismic data show a similar pattern for the Soviet Union. Just as in the case of the earlier treaty, Defense Department support for the Threshold Test Ban was held hostage to agreement to accelerate testing and $100 million appropriation was used for this purpose.

The acceleration of testing, even above the 150 kiloton level, was made possible by virtue of the fact that the TTBT was not to go into effect until March 31, 1976. The basic reason for this delay was to allow time for the negotiators to agree upon how peaceful nuclear explosives were to be handled. The United States was concerned that such explosions could be used to provide information that could be invaluable for military purposes. After all, there is little, if any, difference in the mechanisms for peaceful or warlike nuclear explosions. Both can wreak considerable damage.

PEACEFUL NUCLEAR EXPLOSIVES

Concern has been expressed by both the United States and the Soviet Union about the need to allow peaceful nuclear explosions that, unless exempted, would violate the test ban agreements. Article 1 of the LTBT prohibits nuclear explosions that cause "radioactive debris to be present outside the territorial limits of the State under whose jurisdiction or control such explosion is conducted." Even without such legal restrictions, radioactivity would have to be reduced to a minimum or the consequences might mean considerable damage to the environment as well as a real threat to life. As a result, enthusiasm for peaceful nuclear explosions has had its ups and downs over the years depending upon the degree of optimism concerning the prospects of developing relatively radioactive-free nuclear explosions.

The hypothetical benefits of peaceful nuclear explosions have long been recognized and include the use of such explosions for mineral extraction and the building of storage facilities, harbors, canals, highways, and landslide dams. Research has also suggested the possible use of nuclear explosions for distilling seawater, separating isotopes, generating thermal power from the heat inside the earth, and even for producing hydroelectric power by creating land depressions into which seawater can flow.[30]

The drafters of the LTBT were aware of the treaty's restrictions upon the use of nuclear explosives for peaceful purposes. In fact, it was because of this concern that the number required to amend the Limited Test Ban Treaty was changed during the negotiations from two-thirds to a majority for the explicit purpose of facilitating a future amendment allowing peaceful nuclear explosions near the surface.[31] Few treaties can claim such undemanding amendment requirements. President Kennedy, in a letter designed to gain Senate support for the Limited Test Ban Treaty, promised the Senate leadership that the "United States will diligently pursue the development of nuclear explosives for peaceful purposes by underground tests within the terms of the treaty, and as and when such developments make possible constructive uses of atmospheric nuclear explosions for peaceful purposes, the United States will seek international agreement under the treaty to permit such explosions."[32]

At the time of the signing of the Limited Test Ban Treaty, U.S. optimism about the utility of peaceful nuclear explosions was in decline. Because of the perception that there would not be a positive payoff for peaceful nuclear explosions (PNEs) for some time, Averell Harriman, in negotiating the Limited Test Ban Treaty for the United States, sought to relinquish the peaceful nuclear explosions option in return for Moscow's agreement to include a withdrawal clause in the treaty. The interest in research on peaceful nuclear explosives, dubbed Project Plowshare, continued to lose support, and by 1978 the plowshare program had disappeared entirely from the budget.

Soviet interest in peaceful nuclear explosions proceeded in the opposite direction. In 1959, Seyom Tsarapkin, the Soviet delegate to the Geneva Conference on the Discontinuance of Nuclear Weapon Tests, objected vehemently to allowing nuclear explosions for peaceful purposes. He regarded such explosions as fraught with harmful consequences for humanity as well as a stimulus to the nuclear arms race.[33] The fact of the matter is that a peaceful nuclear explosive cannot be distinguished from one that could be used to kill people.

In the seventies, it was the Soviet Union which was interested in allowing peaceful nuclear explosions as it began to envision huge earth-moving projects that would perhaps be feasible physically and monetarily only if nuclear explosives were used. Among these were proposals for diverting rivers and building harbors. Given such interests, the Soviet Union has tested a hundred or so PNEs since the late 1960s, whereas the United States has not tested any since 1973.[34]

It was against this background that the Peaceful Nuclear Explosion negotiations began in Moscow in October 1974. Six rounds were held over the next 18 months, resulting in an agreement in April 1976. With its mammoth earth-moving projects in mind, the Soviet Union wanted to allow peaceful explosives as high as 400 kilotons and expressed interest in having as many as 20 simultaneous explosions of bombs with a total yield of 3 megatons.[35] A compromise was reached in the final treaty, which limits simultaneous explosions to 1.5 megatons.

For the first time in any arms control agreement, the Peaceful Nuclear Explosions Treaty provides for on-site inspection on Soviet and U.S. soil as observers from the other side are permitted anytime several peaceful devices total over 150 kilotons. By agreement, they may even be allowed when the explosion is expected to be in the 100-150 kiloton range. The PNE Treaty also enables these observers to place instruments down into the hole where the nuclear device is emplaced in order to get a more accurate reading. As part of the verification procedure, extensive amounts of information must be provided about *all* PNEs of any yield, before and after the explosion.

Following the successful negotiation of the Peaceful Nuclear Explosions Treaty, both the PNET and the Threshold Test Ban Treaty were submitted to the U.S. Senate for consideration. Although in 1974 the TTBT had been politely received, albeit with no great enthusiasm, by 1976 the picture had changed. The détente of the Nixon era was over with President Gerald Ford even excising the term *détente* from his campaign rhetoric. An American presidential election year was hardly the time for pressing a controversial arms control agreement with the Soviet

Union. Even the traditional supporters of arms control agreements failed to be supportive and instead criticized the high thresholds that were established by the treaties. Rather than being the precursor to a more comprehensive test ban, these treaties were viewed largely as the death knell for such an agreement. When Carter assumed the presidency in 1977, the two nuclear testing treaties remained on the shelve because of the new administration's interest in negotiating a comprehensive test ban.

The failure to ratify the TTBT and the PNET, while at the same time living up to the obligations imposed by the treaties, has had some serious disadvantages from the perspective of U.S.-Soviet security interests. Chief among these is the opportunity to obtain more information about the testing programs of the adversary. The Threshold Test Ban Treaty, for example, provides for the exchange of geological and geophysical information and for the exchange of data on two previous tests so that the seismometers used in the verification process can be calibrated. It would also require that the parties identify their test sites and that they agree not to conduct tests elsewhere. As already pointed out, the Peaceful Nuclear Explosions Treaty provides for on-site inspection which would help establish the precedent and experience for this type of verification on Soviet soil. Only by gaining experience with such procedures can their weaknesses be recognized and the means for improvements be realized.

CARTER AND THE TEST BAN ISSUE

During the first two years of the Carter presidency considerable progress was made on the issues dividing the United States and the Soviet Union with regard to a comprehensive test ban treaty. In his first letter to Leonid Brezhnev, which was written within days of the presidential inauguration, President Jimmy Carter urged that negotiations for a comprehensive test ban be undertaken. The initial Soviet response was positive as the Soviet Union agreed to voluntary on-site inspection in March 1977. Tripartite negotiations, which included the United Kingdom, were inaugurated in June of that year and lasted until November 1980. Early in these negotiations, the Soviet Union made a number of concessions to the U.S. position, including a willingness to accept a moratorium on peaceful nuclear explosions (later clarified as a three-year moratorium, but with prospects for renewal). The Soviets also accepted the U.S. proposal for a treaty of indefinite duration. But most importantly the Soviet Union was no longer insisting as it had in 1975 that all nuclear weapon powers be included in a comprehensive test ban;

such a requirement would have doomed the treaty to failure, given the attitudes of France and China on the issue.

While initially enthusiastic about a comprehensive test ban, the Carter administration began backing off from some of its own proposals, partially because of a divided administration in which Zbigniew Brzezinski, the national security advisor, James Schlesinger, the secretary of energy, and the Joint Chiefs of Staff were all opposed to such a ban. In fact, Brzezinski has written in his memoirs that he went along with internal and external discussions on the issue simply because President Carter badly wanted a comprehensive test ban, whereas he felt that both a SALT and a comprehensive test ban treaty would overload the legislative system. Brzezinski was willing to go along with his commander in chief only if some testing were allowed.[36]

The first of several retractions occurred in May 1978, when the United States retreated from its proposal for a comprehensive ban of unlimited duration. The United States now wanted a treaty limited to five years. The Soviet Union accepted the U.S. change. In September, the United States, because of internal pressure to allow at least some testing, proposed permitting small nuclear "experiments." It was difficult, however, for the administration to define exactly what threshold would be used for the permitted tests. At the same time, the Carter administration again changed its position with regard to the issue of duration, proposing that the treaty be limited to three years. More serious, however, was the demand that after three years the treaty be renegotiated and ratified rather than merely extended if no one disapproved.

Retractions also occurred in 1979 as the United States position hardened even further. For example, the United States demanded that the seismographs to be positioned on Soviet territory be manufactured in the United States and that real-time satellite readings be provided from the seismic stations. U.S. negotiators were also under instructions not to accept the preambular hortatory language found in earlier treaties that called for ambitious disarmament goals.

The United Kingdom began to assume a harder position in 1979 as well. Great Britain, in view of its smaller geographical area, began to balk at the number of unmanned stations that would be placed upon its territory. While the United States was able to get Britain to change its position on this issue, other differences led Brezhnev and Carter to agree at the June 1979 Moscow summit conference that they would go ahead with a comprehensive test ban without Britain if necessary.

Despite these retractions, considerable progress had been made toward a comprehensive test ban treaty when the trilateral negotiations were recessed in November 1980. According to what had been agreed, the ban would rely upon automatic national seismic detection stations on the territory of the three powers: ten each for the two superpowers and a lesser number for the United Kingdom. Voluntary on-site inspection would be utilized, based upon challenges and responses. If the parties failed to agree, the argument could be taken to the United Nations Security Council. A consensus had further developed that there would be a moratorium on peaceful explosions, during which time further studies would be conducted on ways to allow such explosions without providing military advantages.[37]

REAGAN AND THE TEST BAN ISSUE

The Reagan administration came into power with a generally hostile attitude toward arms control. During the presidential campaign, Ronald Reagan had declared the SALT II Treaty to be "fatally flawed," and he was no more supportive of the test ban agreements. The new administration made no effort to revive the trilateral talks on a comprehensive test ban treaty that had recessed in November 1980. It also demanded that the Threshold Test Ban Treaty and the Peaceful Nuclear Explosion Treaty be renegotiated before ratification would be considered. The primary concern has been the verifiability of the treaties as violations of the Threshold Treaty have become part of the litany of alleged Soviet violations of various arms agreements. President Reagan in his February 1985 report to Congress on Soviet arms control violations noted that a number of Soviet tests "constitute a likely violation of legal obligations under the Threshold Test Ban Treaty. . . ."[38] The Soviet Union has also accused the United States of repeated instances of exceeding the 150-kiloton limit.

Soviet compliance with the 1963 Limited Test Ban Treaty has likewise been challenged by the Reagan administration, which has called attention to the fact that radioactive fallout from underground tests has drifted beyond Soviet borders in violation of the treaty. Richard Perle complained of almost 200 such instances in the last 23 years, but prior to the Reagan era these alleged violations were not challenged. At least 100 U.S. tests since 1964 have also released radioactive gases, but since the Nevada test site is not as close to the national border as those of the Soviet Union, the Limited Test Ban Treaty, for the most part, was not violated.[39]

Concerned about such violations, the Reagan administration proposed in February 1983 that formal talks be undertaken to develop on-site verification procedures for the Threshold Test Ban Treaty, which does not include any such provisions. Those negotiating the treaty had believed on-site inspection was unnecessary to obtain a better reading of the magnitude of underground explosions. The administration's proposal would have required that American experts be able to observe the placement of sensitive sensors in any Soviet testing cavity where the detonation is expected to be in excess of 75 kilotons. Even prominent Republicans were upset with the harsh stance on verification taken by the Reagan administration. Senator Charles Percy, while chairman of the Senate Foreign Relations Committee, threatened to hold up the nomination of Kenneth Adelman as chief of the Arms Control and Disarmament Agency if he did not get action on the Threshold Test Ban Treaty.[40]

By proposing the renegotiation of two existing test ban treaties, the administration hoped to divert attention from the issue of a comprehensive test ban. In this way, it could claim to be interested in a comprehensive ban if such a ban could be made verifiable. It could also expect the Soviet Union to reject any effort to renegotiate the existing treaties, given the latter's interest in a comprehensive test ban treaty. Such a treaty in turn would render the Threshold Test Ban Treaty and the Peaceful Nuclear Explosions Treaty superfluous.

In the summer of 1983 the Reagan administration admitted for the first time that its refusal to engage in negotiations for a comprehensive nuclear test ban was related to a desire to continue underground nuclear tests for national security reasons. In a written response to the House Appropriations Committee, the Arms Control and Disarmament Agency noted: "While a CTB continues to be a long-term U.S. objective, nuclear tests are specifically required for the development, modernization and certification of warheads, the maintenance of stockpile reliability and the evaluation of nuclear weapons effects."[41] Among the administration's proposals for a substantial military buildup was a plan to build seventeen thousand new nuclear warheads over a period of six years. Continued testing was viewed as essential to the program. A more critical objection to negotiating a total ban came as a result of the decision in March 1983 to pursue the Strategic Defense Initiative, which would entail a space-based defense system. Although many of the defensive weapons envisioned in this program would involve conventional components, one of the key defensive systems required development of an X-ray laser powered by a small nuclear explosion. The first of such experiments was conducted December 28, 1985, under the code name Goldstone.

The United States, in opposing even to negotiate on a comprehensive test ban, found itself at some variance with most of its allies and virtually isolated on the issue globally. In December 1982 it was the only state to vote against a UN resolution requiring that all nuclear testing be outlawed; the resolution carried, 111 to 1, with 35 abstentions. Two years earlier only the United Kingdom joined the United States in voting against a UN resolution calling for multilateral negotiations on a comprehensive test ban.

There would seem to be a number of advantages for supporting a comprehensive test ban, not the least of which is that such a ban would be more in line with the overwhelming demand of other states. Some twenty resolutions calling for the prohibition of nuclear testing have been adopted by the UN General Assembly during the period 1975–84. The average vote on these resolutions was 121 states in favor.[42] Many states in ratifying the Nuclear Nonproliferation Treaty explicitly referred to the need to make further progress on a comprehensive test ban and other disarmament measures as a condition for their continued adherence to the treaty. During the three Review Conferences that have been held on the Nuclear Nonproliferation Treaty to date, the issue of a comprehensive test ban has been the disarmament measure most frequently mentioned.

A second advantage of a comprehensive test ban lies in its ability to restrict the qualitative arms race. The failure to limit Soviet testing allows the Soviets to make improvements on the weight to yield ratio of nuclear weapons. With their advantage in terms of throw-weight, further refinements in the size of Soviet nuclear warheads will only allow Soviet missiles to carry considerably more destructive payloads. It has also been suggested that a test ban might inhibit Soviet ability to field a cruise missile force as efficient and as sophisticated as that of the United States. The problem is that with each month's delay in negotiating such a ban, the Soviet Union may catch up with the United States in terms of weapons design.

Third, a comprehensive test ban would remove the major loophole in existing test ban treaties, which allows underground testing to continue. India, in exploding its underground nuclear device in 1974, used such a loophole as it asserted that it was merely developing a peaceful nuclear device. For a test ban to aid in stopping the further spread of nuclear testing, it needs to be comprehensive. For some states, lacking unpopulated territories, conducting underground is the only place they can test anyway, given the hazards of radioactive fallout.

Fourth, some of the verification difficulties in determining compliance with a high threshold such as that allowed in the TTBT can be minimized by a treaty that bars all tests. It is more difficult to ascertain the precise yield of an underground test than it is to determine whether or not an event occurred at all. Of course, the problem remains that some of the very smallest of nuclear explosions may not be detected, as will be discussed subsequently. But the question remains whether or not tests of such low magnitude provide any important military advantages. According to Leslie Gelb, experts generally agree that cheating at very low levels of one kiloton to five kilotons would not allow the development of new strategic weapons.[43]

How valid then is the position of the Reagan administration that the 1974 and 1976 treaties and the proposed comprehensive test ban treaty are not in the national security interests of the United States? As noted earlier, the first reservation raised by the administration for not ratifying the two treaties or engaging in comprehensive test ban talks was related to the alleged nonverifiability of nuclear testing programs. However, considerable progress has been made over the years in improving detection capabilities. At present, it is difficult to find any scientists, including even those opposed to a ban on underground testing, who will not admit that, with a few seismic stations on Soviet territory, it is possible to detect any explosion above 10 kilotons. In fact, respected seismologists Lynn R. Sykes and Jack F. Evernden have asserted that with fifteen such stations, strategically placed, the only explosions "with a significant likelihood of escaping detection" would be those of less than one kiloton.[44] This assessment would apply to decoupled explosions from underground cavities as well.

A number of procedures have been developed to help distinguish earthquakes from nuclear explosions, including instruments capable of pinpointing where an event occurs and at what depth. Because of the costs and difficulties of digging deep holes to explode weapons without the other side detecting the excavation, any event deeper than fifteen kilometers is most certainly an earthquake. Also, the first waves of earthquakes and nuclear explosions, as measured by seismological equipment, are quite distinct.

Verification potential has also been improved by the October 1985 offer by India, Argentina, Greece, Mexico, Sweden, and Tanzania to monitor a comprehensive ban on underground tests with seismic devices on their own soil and to implant devices near nuclear test sites in the Soviet Union and the United States.[45]

Since the probability of detection is relatively high and since it requires several such tests to feel completely confident with a new nuclear weapon, it is unlikely that a state would want to take much of a risk of being caught. States presumably sign treaties because they perceive that doing so is in their national interest, and they do not want to give other states an excuse for withdrawing from a treaty. The gains to be derived by exploding a few, very small nuclear devices would seem to be hardly worth the risk of discovery.

Verification becomes problematic if one is attempting to establish whether or not a state is violating a high threshold such as that established by the Threshold Test Ban Treaty. Determining whether the United States or the Soviet Union has surpassed the 150-kiloton limit is difficult, particularly as these two states attempt to push the limits. As pointed out earlier, the Soviet Union has been accused of surpassing the 150-kiloton limit on more than fourteen occasions. Recent assessments made by scientists selected by the Department of Defense, however, indicate that the estimates of the magnitude of such explosions should be reduced by at least 20 percent. The primary reason for recommending such a reduction is related to the fact that the Nevada test site is more geologically active than the Soviet test sites making seismic waves emanating from the latter somewhat stronger for a given explosive magnitude. If such a reduction were made, most, if not all, of the Soviet tests could be regarded as complying with the Threshold Test Ban Treaty.[46] In April 1986 the Central Intelligence Agency decided to adjust its mathematical multiplier downward by 20 percent, but the administration was quick to argue that a number of Soviet tests would still have been in violation.[47]

That the inadequacy of verification capabilities was not really the major reservation to a comprehensive test ban on the part of the Reagan administration is suggested by the fact that little was being spent to improve seismic research and no interdepartmental review was undertaken for two years despite improvements in verification capabilities.[48] Even if a foolproof inspection system were feasible, it is unlikely that the administration would support a comprehensive test ban in view of its belief that continued testing is necessary to U.S. national security interests. As noted earlier, a number of tests are viewed as necessary for modernizing the American nuclear force. Several of the newer delivery systems, however, already have available warheads as in the case of the cruise, the MX, and the Midgetman missiles; the Trident can use existing MK 12A warheads. Although a comprehensive test ban might interfere with the development of the Trident II missile, the X-ray laser, and smaller yield warheads, each of these particular systems has been criticized because of its probable effects on the stability of the nuclear deterrent system. The Trident II has been viewed as a first strike weapon due to its hard-kill capability, and concern has been expressed about reducing the yield of nuclear weapons that will make their use more probable. Finally, many scientists have opposed the development of the X-ray laser for reasons that will be examined in chapter 5.

In the past, continued testing has been seen as necessary to improve the yield to weight ratios of nuclear warheads. According to Wolfgang Panofsky, director of the Stanford Linear Accelerator, however, the technological limits in this area have essentially been reached.[49] After all, given present efficiencies, it would not require much more than a small suitcase to transport a nuclear device with the destructive capacity of the Hiroshima bomb.

Nuclear testing has been viewed by the Reagan administration and some scientists as essential for ascertaining nuclear stockpile reliability. Nuclear weapons are fabricated from chemically active materials that deteriorate in unexpected and unpredictable ways, making periodic testing of stockpile weapons necessary. In an effort to make the case for the need for reliability testing, the Reagan administration released data in March 1986 showing that a large percentage of Polaris warheads would have failed during the 1960s because of deterioration and design problems, and similar instances were found during the 1970s with respect to Poseidon and Minuteman warheads.[50] However, it is not clear that test explosions are necessary to discover such problems as several respected scientists have argued that most such testing is done by disassembling and reassembling a warhead's parts. They note that all of the components can be tested one by one just as is done in building the weapon initially.[51]

The former director of the Los Alamos National Laboratory, Donald Kerr, has suggested, however, that the reason little proof testing has been done in the past is that stockpile and design problems are often corrected by adding an experiment to a test that is part of the continuing program. Such would be precluded in a comprehensive test ban, making direct proof tests more important, particularly since the expected lifetime of a stockpile is typically between fifteen and twenty-five years.[52]

Whether or not proof testing is necessary for assuring the reliability of stockpiled weapons largely boils down to how the weapons are designed. During Glenn Seaborg's tenure as head of the Atomic Energy Commission (1961–71), nuclear weapons were designed on the assumption that a comprehensive test ban agreement would be negotiated. At some time after that period, design policy was changed so that more sophisticated and efficient designs were emphasized, thereby making reliability testing necessary.[53] By returning to a more simple design policy, it would be possible to remanufacture weapons that have been proof tested many years earlier.

Finally, even if a comprehensive test ban were to make the reliability of existing nuclear weapons questionable, Bruce Russett and Fred Chernoff have suggested that this might actually be a virtue rather than a liability. If both sides lost some of the certainty about whether their weapons would work "they might hesitate to launch an attack that could misfire. By this reasoning, deterrence is strengthened by any factor that contributes to a prospective attacker's lack of confidence that everything will work according to plan."[54] Such a view, however, is not universally accepted as seen by a 1986 letter from Deputy Secretary of Defense Frank J. Gaffney, Jr., to Congressman Ed Markey. According to Gaffney, the Russians would worry whether their arsenals were still in working order and might get edgier if reliability testing were disallowed.[55]

The latest rationale for continued testing was presented by George H. Miller of the Lawrence Livermore National Laboratory who argued in February 1987 that continued testing is necessary not so much to develop new weapons for the Strategic Defensive Initiative but rather to study the possible threat of the Soviet Union using X-ray lasers to defeat a space-based defense system. The purpose of continued testing, according to this view, would be to provide information critical for developing a counterdefensive system directed against the X-ray laser.[56]

Despite U.S. reservations about a separate comprehensive test ban treaty, political initiatives taken by the Soviet Union in 1985–86 have placed considerable pressure on the United States to respond more favorably to proposals for a comprehensive test ban. In August 1985 Gorbachev announced that the Soviet Union would institute a six-month unilateral ban on nuclear testing, which was subsequently extended to March 31, 1986. Gorbachev went even further on March 13, 1986, when he announced that the unilateral ban would remain in effect until the United States resumed its nuclear testing.

The United States response to the March initiative by Gorbachev was to conduct yet another underground test later that same month. But despite the U.S. resumption of underground testing, Gorbachev, on the heels of the Chernobyl nuclear disaster in May, extended the ban until August 6, the forty-first anniversary of the bombing of Hiroshima, subsequently making January 1, 1987, the date on which the Soviet Union's unilateral moratorium on testing would end. The Soviet moratorium remained in effect until the United States exploded its first underground test in February 1987, whereupon the Soviet Union, as promised, announced it was no longer bound by its nineteen-month unilateral moratorium. At the same time, the Soviets indicated they would resume the moratorium if the United States would stop its tests even though the latter had conducted twenty-six nuclear tests during the Soviet moratorium.

In late July 1986, the United States and the Soviet Union, partially in response to increasing domestic and international pressures favoring a comprehensive nuclear test ban, met for the first time on the test ban issue since President Reagan came into office. In agreeing to the meeting, Gorbachev indicated a willingness to consider President Reagan's four-year-old proposal to have specialists from both countries discuss better monitoring of underground nuclear testing. The Soviet Union also accepted the offer of the private U.S.-based Natural Resources Defense Council to set up sealed seismographic instruments at three sites in the Soviet Union and agreed in principle to a May 1986 U.S. Geological Survey proposal to establish an experimental network of up to eighteen seismic monitoring stations on Soviet territory.[57]

In view of the various Soviet concessions, it is doubtful that U.S. arguments that verification problems make it impossible to negotiate a comprehensive test ban treaty will be able to stem the growing tide of opinion favoring such a ban. Perhaps some temporizing might be done if the United States were to agree to ratify the Threshold Test Ban Treaty, which would be a positive, though limited, step. Such a move would at least meet the administration's interest in testing new devices as well as checking the reliability of existing stockpiles. At the same time, U.S. ratification would be viewed by arms-controllers as just another cosmetic move to give the illusion of progress.

CONCLUSION

A possible ban on nuclear testing has been a prominent issue on the arms control agenda since the late 1950s, particularly among those who saw it as a way to slow the spread of nuclear weapons to additional states. Primary concern was initially focused upon the possible health hazards of continued atmospheric testing, but once this problem was solved with the signing of the Limited Test Ban Treaty in 1963, which prohibited atmospheric testing, public interest in the test ban issue dissolved. But because testing underground was still allowed by the treaty, more tests were actually conducted before, rather than after, the signing of the treaty.

Efforts to negotiate a comprehensive test ban as envisioned by provisions in the LTBT have been largely unsuccessful. The 1974 Threshold

Test Ban Treaty established a limit of 150 kilotons on all underground nuclear tests, but most of the tests conducted underground have been somewhat below that level since it is possible to extrapolate from smaller tests. The Peaceful Nuclear Explosions Treaty of 1976 provided procedures for exploding peaceful nuclear devices in order that such explosions would not be used as a ruse for testing. This treaty established for the first time the important precedent of on-site inspection on Soviet territory. The current lack of interest shown in peaceful nuclear explosives, however, has rendered that treaty relatively unimportant.

Neither the Threshold Test Ban Treaty nor the Peaceful Nuclear Explosions Treaty has been ratified. Upon assuming office, President Carter withdrew the two treaties from Senate consideration, hoping instead to negotiate a comprehensive test ban that would make the treaties superfluous. They remain unratified to date as the Reagan administration opposed further restrictions upon nuclear testing. Initially the reason given was that the treaties were not verifiable, but subsequently Reagan advisors have argued that nuclear testing is necessary as long as the world must rely upon nuclear deterrence for its security. The primary reason for desiring continued nuclear testing is related to a plan to produce some seventeen thousand new nuclear warheads and to keep open the option to test nuclear components to be used in the Strategic Defense Initiative. Many in the Reagan administration also believed testing to be necessary to determine the continuing reliability of existing nuclear stockpiles.

Despite the dismal prospects for a comprehensive test ban, a number of advantages might be gained if such an agreement could be negotiated. A comprehensive test ban would be popular with most other states in the world and may even be the price that will have to be paid to assure continued adherence to the Nuclear Nonproliferation Treaty. Additionally, such a ban could aid in restricting the qualitative arms race; close a critical loophole in present treaties; and reduce the difficulties of ascertaining whether a given underground explosion has surpassed some artificial threshold.

Improvements in verification procedures, Soviet acceptance of on-site inspection, the unilateral moratoriums on nuclear testing announced by the Soviet Union in 1985 and 1986, as well as congressional opinion have also exerted considerable pressure on the United States to resume negotiations on a comprehensive test ban treaty. But as long as the current administration or any subsequent one believes testing to be essential to develop new nuclear devices or to ascertain the reliability of existing ones, progress cannot be expected regardless of the advances in verification technology.

Thirty years of negotiating on the nuclear test ban issue have provided a number of lessons of relevance both to the problems of negotiating within governments and between governments. Since nuclear testing involves a highly technical area, scientists as well as the military have been able to play a particularly important role in the negotiations. It was conservative scientific opinion that was apparently critical in influencing President Eisenhower initially to oppose any test ban moratorium, and scientists at national testing laboratories were influential in leading President Carter to retract a number of concessions related to a comprehensive test ban. Promises have also had to be made to the military in both the United States and the Soviet Union to get them to acquiesce to the various treaties that have been negotiated, often allowing them to increase the amount of testing in return for their acceptance of various restraints upon the size and location of testing.

The positions taken by the United States and the Soviet Union on the issue of nuclear testing have also been affected by the pressures of other states in the international system. The nuclear testing issue has often been made the litmus test for U.S.-Soviet seriousness about arms control and disarmament. Nonaligned states pressed hard for a nuclear test ban during the negotiations that resulted in the Limited Test Ban Treaty in 1963. Britain's role as a participating mediator between the United States and the Soviet Union during these negotiations should also not be underestimated.

Public concern about the dangers of nuclear fallout provided additional pressure leading to the 1963 partial test ban. Once the danger was taken from the headlines, mass public concern about the nuclear test ban became minimal. Occasional public protests against continued underground testing have developed subsequently, but nothing to compare with the massive concern expressed during the late fifties and early sixties.

The desire to gain military advantages and to keep technological options open have also been important factors that help explain the positions taken by the United States and the Soviet Union in the test ban negotiations. A common feature of these negotiations has been the tendency of one side or the other to propose a ban on further testing following its own successful series of tests, apparently in an effort to lock in the technological advantages gained and to prevent the other side from doing the same. The desire to keep technological options open has been shown by the efforts of both sides to at least allow some testing to continue.

It is because of such technological uncertainties as well as concerns about the verifiability of a nuclear test ban that the United States and the Soviet Union have shown a tendency to engage in approach-avoidance bargaining behavior during the test ban negotiations. On at least two occasions the United States and the Soviet Union were close to agreement on a test ban treaty only to have one or the other party back off due to uncertainty about the implications of the treaty for its national security interests. Most of the provisions for a test ban treaty had been agreed to by both parties in 1960, but the Soviet Union subsequently began to make a number of retractions, culminating eventually in its decision to resume nuclear testing in September 1961. Similarly, the two had come close to agreement on a comprehensive test ban in 1978, only to find the Carter administration backing away with a number of retractions from its previous position. The pressures are such that one can expect that the issue of a comprehensive nuclear test ban will remain on the agenda, but the ambivalences about the security implications will continue to impede a total ban.

3

Nonproliferation of Nuclear Weapons

Concern has been expressed from the beginning about the dangers of the proliferation of nuclear weapons. Early predictions about when the Soviet Union would join the nuclear club were generally far off the mark. President Truman, for example, is reported to have thought that the United States would be able to retain its nuclear monopoly for ten to twenty years, but it took the USSR only four years to duplicate the American feat.[1] The United Kingdom followed suit in 1952; France, in 1960; and China, in 1964.

During the sixties, predictions about the number of states likely to become nuclear weapon states generally measured in the dozens. President Kennedy in 1963 speculated that some twenty five countries would have nuclear capability by the mid-1970s.[2] Despite such dire predictions, only India with its 1974 underground test has been added to the list of five powers known to have tested a nuclear device.

This chapter explores the reasons for the concern about the spread of nuclear weapons and includes an analysis of the efforts to control such spread. The United States and the Soviet Union, as the largest nuclear power states, have assumed prominent roles in the unending struggle to stop the spread of nuclear weapons, often pursuing nonproliferation policies in concert with each other. As a result of such cooperation, one of the most significant arms control agreements of the postwar world was opened for signature in 1968—the Nuclear Nonproliferation Treaty. The nonproliferation regime has also been strengthened over the years by agreements regulating nuclear suppliers, a more active nonproliferation role played by the International Atomic Energy Agency, and the signing of a number of bilateral and regional restrictions upon nuclear spread.

52

THE EFFECT OF NUCLEAR SPREAD ON SECURITY

It has been commonplace to argue that the spread of nuclear weapons will add to the insecurity of all nations. As spread occurs, there are more chances for accidental war or war by miscalculation, increased probabilities of irresponsible or irrational leaders obtaining control of nuclear weapons, and increased opportunities for nuclear blackmail. Yet these arguments have often fallen upon deaf ears as national leaders assess the utility of nuclear weapons in terms of prestige, a larger voice in world and alliance affairs, and the opportunities to enhance security by controlling the nuclear strike option. There is also the fear that no nuclear weapon state would risk possible annihilation to protect the non-nuclear state from nuclear blackmail or massive conventional strikes, let alone a nuclear attack.

It may well be that in some instances the prophets of doom have exaggerated the destabilizing effects of nuclear spread and that a world of five nuclear powers, two of whom have overkill capabilities, is already sufficiently terrifying and dangerous. One study, for example, argues that dissemination has already occurred and that since the distribution of nuclear power is dangerously unequal, the acquisition of nuclear weapons by additional countries might help stabilize power relationships.[3] Kenneth N. Waltz likewise minimizes the dangers of nuclear spread as he argues that such spread to American allies has complicated Soviet calculations and consequently strengthened deterrence. He argues further that small nuclear forces can have a similar deterrent effect regionally. Nuclear weapons may even dampen regional arms races, for less military capability is needed if the primary objective is merely to deter a regional adversary. All that is required is the ability to inflict unacceptable damage.[4]

To a certain degree there may be a grain of truth in such views. If nuclear deterrence is largely a matter of being able to communicate the credibility of a probable nuclear retaliation to a first strike, then having nuclear capabilities in the hands of the potential attack victim should be more credible than relying upon the nuclear force of an ally. Indeed, French President Charles DeGaulle's major concern with the United States was that the latter would not risk nuclear war in case Western Europe was struck massively with conventional force. Having a small nuclear force in the territory of the potential victim and controlled by that victim so that it need not rely entirely upon the superpower to initiate the nuclear strike is viewed as one way of making certain that nuclear weapons will be used if they are believed necessary for defense. By having this triggering potential, it is hoped that the nuclear threat will be made more credible and hence able to deter the threatened attack.

A crucial aspect in evaluating the relative dangers inherent in nuclear spread relates to whether or not such spread is limited to responsible leadership. It is perhaps erroneous to assume that small powers desiring nuclear status are the only ones that are likely to behave irresponsibly, yet there might be something to the notion that the smaller, developing state has less to lose and will therefore be less constrained in its use of nuclear weapons. Pressures of internal instability with which many of these states appear to be plagued might also tend to induce rash international behavior to redirect internal frustration. But even assuming that irresponsibility is as likely to arise in any political system, whether developed or underdeveloped, it is a statistical fact that the more national decision-making units having control over nuclear weapons, the greater are the chances that one of them might behave in an irrational and irresponsible fashion.

Even the most mature and responsible leadership, as long as it has nuclear weapon capability, is going to be tempted to use that capability if it becomes engaged in a war of attrition or possible defeat. A most humane leader can sometimes be convinced of the utility of using nuclear weapons if confronted with the dangers of certain defeat or if such an option would appear to reduce unacceptable levels of bloodshed among one's own citizens. It should be remembered that it was the United States that was the first and fortunately thus far the only state to use nuclear weapons, apparently with little concern for the moral issues involved.

As nuclear weapons spread to less wealthy nations, protection against accidental firings is likely to be deemphasized. The smaller nuclear power, having sacrificed extensively to develop a nuclear capability in the first place, simply cannot afford the luxury of multiple protection for its nuclear striking power. It will be less likely to contribute the necessary funding to develop an invulnerable retaliatory capability through the hardening of underground silos or through mobility by using train cars or naval vessels. As a result, any such striking force will be "soft" and hence provocative since the state with unprotected missiles can hardly afford the luxury of delayed response. Dangers of war by miscalculation and hasty reaction to nuclear accidents are increased under such circumstances.

EARLY PROPOSALS FOR PREVENTING NUCLEAR SPREAD

The effort to negotiate a nuclear nonproliferation treaty in the midsixties was by no means the first time that the issue of stopping the spread of nuclear weapons has been raised in disarmament negotiations. In a sense, the history of the negotiations since World War II has been very much motivated by the desire to prevent additional nations from obtaining nuclear weapons. Among the many proposals that have been made for slowing the spread of nuclear weapons have been those for a nuclear production ban, nuclear test bans, nontransfer agreements, nuclear free zones, plus a variety of measures to make independent nuclear capability less necessary as far as nonnuclear states are concerned.

The earliest postwar proposals sought to tackle the problem of nuclear spread by prohibiting the further production and possession of nuclear weapons by all national governments. The Baruch Plan, introduced in 1946 by the United States, would have placed nuclear weapons and technology under the control of the International Atomic Development Authority. The Gromyko Plan, presented by the Soviet Union as an alternative to the Baruch Plan, called for immediate destruction of all nuclear weapons that were then a monopoly of the United States. As a nonnuclear power, the Soviet Union felt it could not allow its security to be determined by an international control organ certain to be dominated by the West. Security could not be guaranteed until the Soviets also acquired nuclear weapons. Prior to that they could only hope that the West would not violate the agreement.

When it became clear that the Baruch Plan had little chance for success, the United States began to emphasize Atoms for Peace in 1953. These proposals would have diverted some fissionable materials to peaceful purposes, but the proposals had little relevance for nonproliferation and disarmament in general because of their limited scope. The Atoms for Peace proposals emphasized the positive aspects of nuclear energy in terms of its advantages for economic development. Both superpowers began courting developing nations with optimistic promises concerning the future of atomic energy for peaceful purposes. The current threat of nuclear proliferation is in no small measure attributable to the competition between the United States and the Soviet Union in providing nuclear reactors and information on the peaceful atom to Third World countries during the mid-1950s.[5]

Apparently in developing the Atoms for Peace program, little attention was given in the United States to the arms control implications of providing fissionable materials and nuclear technology to nonnuclear weapon states. The U.S. Atomic Energy Commission, for example, was informed of the proposal only after the fact. Soviet Foreign Minister V. M. Molotov recognized the potential dangers when he asked Secretary of State John Foster Dulles what in the world the United States had in mind in proposing to allow stockpiles of weapons grade material to spring up all over the world.[6] Despite reservations, the Soviet Union could not allow the United States to be the sole beneficiary of the goodwill of developing countries, which had been sold on the economic miracles of peaceful nuclear energy.

The Atoms for Peace proposals became the basis of the International Atomic Energy Agency, which was established in 1957 to deal with peaceful nuclear activities and to serve as a clearing house for the exchange of peaceful fissionable materials and technology under international control. From the perspective of reducing the dangers of nuclear proliferation, the most important function of IAEA was its inspection obligations designed to assure fissionable materials would not be used for weapons purposes. The IAEA was somewhat slow in assuming such responsibilities in part because of the hostility toward verification demonstrated by the Soviet Union and other states. It was 1961 before the safeguards system was instituted. Even then its inspection activities were limited to smaller reactors, because agreement to include reactors with outputs above 100 megawatts-thermal was not reached until 1964. States would be subject to safeguards only if they received assistance from the IAEA or if they requested safeguards. Consequently, significant amounts of fissionable materials were not covered. As late as 1966 Sterling Cole, the first director general of the IAEA, noted that "not a single nuclear power plant capable of producing by-product weapon material has come under Agency control" except for psychological gestures or demonstration and test purposes.[7]

Other direct forerunners of the nonproliferation proposals are found in the various plans calling for "atom free zones," which were a prominent feature of the disarmament debates in the midfifties. Most such plans for denuclearization of a region have dealt primarily with central Europe, Africa, and Latin America; but proposals have also been made involving the Balkans, the Adriatic and Mediterranean areas, the Middle East, Scandinavia, and Asia and the Pacific. The Soviet Union began hinting of the possible denuclearization of central Europe as early as 1956, but the most fully developed plans were presented by the Polish foreign minister Adam Rapacki on October 2, 1957. The Rapacki Plan would have provided for a ban on the production and possession of nuclear weapons in both East and West Germany as well as in Czechoslovakia and Poland. A modification of the plan in November 1958 would have covered the reduction of conventional weapons in the area as well—a stance designed to appeal to the NATO membership, which had long been concerned about Soviet conventional superiority in central Europe.

The official U.S. position taken on these proposals was highly negative, not only because of concern over the lack of inspection and enforcement procedures, but also because of the fear that the implementation of such proposals would force the Federal Republic of Germany out of the Western alliance system. Chancellor Konrad Adenauer of the Federal Republic was opposed to considering any such proposals and the United States deferred to him on the issue.

Although nuclear free zone proposals continued to be made, it was not until 1967 that success was obtained with the signing of the Treaty of Tlatelolco which provided for a nuclear free zone in Latin America. Some twenty-two states now embrace this agreement which prohibits both the production and transfer of nuclear weapons into the region. In July of 1964 the Organization of African Unity declared its readiness to undertake a nuclear nondissemination treaty for the continent of Africa but has yet to follow through on such a treaty. In 1986 thirteen South Pacific nations, including Australia and New Zealand, signed the South Pacific Nuclear Free Zone Treaty. The treaty participants asked the five nuclear weapons states to ratify protocols which would forbid nuclear testing in the area as well as prohibit states from using or threatening to use nuclear weapons in the region. Despite the fact that the protocols would not interfere with ongoing activities such as the passage of nuclear warships, the Reagan administration rebuffed the treaty as did France, which wanted to be able to continue testing in the area. Both China and the Soviet Union, on the other hand, agreed to sign the protocols.

Pressure for a more global nonproliferation agreement began to develop with the 1958 Irish draft U.N. resolution, which called for the creation of a committee to study the dangers of nuclear dissemination. This resolution was not brought to a vote. The Irish government was back the following year with a similar resolution, which was passed unanimously except for thirteen abstentions. Two additional resolutions sponsored by the Irish delegation were adopted in 1960 and 1961.

Despite the considerable support rallied behind the notion of nonproliferation as evidenced by the General Assembly votes, the Ten Nation Disarmament Committee and its successor in 1962, the Eighteen Nation Disarmament Committee, failed to discuss the issue for several years. Instead, general and complete disarmament (GCD) became the main topic of debate with the Soviet Union presenting such a plan in 1959 and the United States tabling its first general and complete disarmament plan during the following year. Both proposals for GCD provided for the nonproliferation of nuclear weapons during the first stage of the proposed three-stage plan.

Support favoring a nonproliferation treaty developed briefly when President John F. Kennedy asked Ambassador Averell Harriman to raise the issue of nonproliferation at the 1963 Moscow meetings in which the Limited Test Ban Treaty was negotiated. Khrushchev, however, refused to discuss the issue of China and proliferation while the United States did not want to press the issue given West German and French anxieties.[8]

In a unilateral move with some implications for the proliferation problem, President Johnson announced in April 1964 that the United States would reduce the production of U-235 (weapons-grade uranium) by 40 percent and plutonium production by 20 percent over a four-year period. Premier Khrushchev responded by announcing that the USSR would not proceed with the construction of two large nuclear reactors intended for the production of plutonium. Although such actions promised to reduce the total supply of fissionable materials, the significance of these moves as a precursor of nuclear arms reduction was minimal. The cutbacks after all were primarily a response to extensive nuclear stockpiles on both sides. Nevertheless, the initiative demonstrated the possibilities of unilateral and reciprocal constraints upon armaments.

THE NUCLEAR NONPROLIFERATION TREATY

Impetus for a broadly based nuclear nonproliferation treaty was provided by nearly unanimous resolutions passed in 1965 in both the General Assembly and the United Nations Disarmament Commission, calling for the Eighteen Nation Disarmament Committee to give priority to negotiating such a treaty. Progress was slow primarily because of differences between the United States and the Soviet Union on the issue of the Multilateral Force (MLF). In 1964 the United States had proposed the creation of MLF, which would have provided for some twenty-five surface ships loaded with nuclear weapons to be placed under NATO control. These ships would be manned by citizens of at least three NATO countries, each of which would have a veto over the use of those weapons. The Soviet Union was particularly concerned that the Federal Republic of Germany, which was to play a central role in MLF, would thus be able to get its finger on the nuclear trigger.

The Soviet Union's initial proposal for a nonproliferation treaty presented in September 1965 contained several provisions that not only would have prevented MLF but would have made allied nuclear consultation extremely difficult, if not impossible.[9] According to former U.S. Arms Control and Disarmament Agency Director William C. Foster, the Soviet plan was so broad that it would even deny consultation between

NATO allies in preparation for their defense against possible nuclear attack.[10]

Whereas the Soviet proposal sought to restrict nuclear sharing in any form, the United States attempted to legalize such a process by arguing its legitimacy on the basis of individual or collective self-defense. In a draft treaty tabled at the Eighteen Nation Disarmament Conference on August 17, 1965,[11] the United States proposed restricting only the number of decision makers having control over the use of nuclear weapons. Since, under the multilateral force proposals being debated at the time, the United States would retain a veto over the use of nuclear weapons, it was argued that there would be no increase in the number of decision-making units with control over the use of nuclear weapons.

After the United States decided in the fall of 1966 not to press the issue of a multilateral force, some progress in the arms talks was achieved. The United States and the Soviet Union began to cooperate in their search for solutions to prevent the spread of nuclear weapons. Their cooperation on the issue was such that the nonnuclear weapon states began to accuse them of forming a condominium against those states not having nuclear weapons.

In August 1967 the United States and the Soviet Union, as cochairpersons of the Eighteen Nation Disarmament Committee, tabled identical texts of a draft Nonproliferation Treaty. These drafts were essentially complete except for provisions related to verification, which were added in January 1968. Although other states were able to discuss the draft treaties presented by the two superpowers, it was clear that such states could do little to change the basic content. Despite the many reservations expressed by nonnuclear weapon states in ENDC meetings and subsequently in General Assembly discussions on the proposed treaty, the final document essentially followed the draft outlines provided in 1967 by the superpowers.

Perhaps the most fundamental change between the jointly sponsored 1967 Draft Treaty and the Final Treaty was the insertion of article VI, which obligated the nuclear weapon states to pursue negotiations for nuclear arms reductions. The nonnuclear weapon states were particularly disturbed that the NPT did nothing to restrain what they referred to as vertical disarmament on the part of the nuclear weapon states while restricting horizontal nuclear proliferation among states. If nonnuclear weapon states were to forego the nuclear option, they wanted the existing nuclear powers to at least begin to reduce their nuclear arsenals. Further differences had to do with changing the duration of the treaty, which would be limited to twenty-five years rather than unlimited as previously proposed. Review conferences would be held every five years, allowing the nonnuclear states to monitor whether the superpowers were living up to their obligation to do something about existing nuclear weapons.

The heart of the Nuclear Nonproliferation Treaty, which was opened for signature on July 1, 1968, is found in its first two articles. The first article provides that each nuclear weapon state not transfer nuclear explosives or otherwise assist a nonnuclear weapon state in developing such weapons. Article II places obligations on the nonnuclear weapon state not to receive or manufacture nuclear explosive devices. The third article, dealing with verification, requires that states party to the treaty individually or collectively negotiate safeguards agreements with the IAEA. Articles IV and V were designed to reassure nonnuclear weapon states that they would be able to enjoy the peaceful uses of nuclear energy and nuclear explosions without discrimination. Nuclear weapon states are obligated under these articles to provide not only technological assistance but also material assistance to nonnuclear weapon states.

Having successfully negotiated the Nonproliferation Treaty, the United States and the Soviet Union were confronted with a number of problems in helping to assure a viable nonproliferation regime. The fact that so many states continued to have serious reservations about the treaty, as shown by the debates as well as the reservations that many states attached after signing the treaty, did not augur well for the goal of preventing the spread of nuclear weapons. A content analysis of the 1968 General Assembly debate on the NPT revealed that 62 percent of the eighty-seven speakers raised questions about the security implications of the treaty. Another 44 percent thought the measure should be linked to broader disarmament while 41 percent expressed concern about how the treaty might affect the peaceful uses of energy.[12]

Many speakers expressed concern that the treaty would not obtain universal support, for a number of states made it clear that they had no intention of ratifying the NPT. Among these were the nuclear weapon states, China and France, although the latter announced that it would behave as if it were a member. More significantly, a number of so-called nuclear threshold states with the technological and economic capability of eventually producing nuclear weapons held out on ratification. In fact, as late as January 1987, almost two decades after the treaty was opened for signature, states like India, Pakistan, Brazil, Argentina, South Africa, and Israel were still refusing to ratify the NPT. Even among the nuclear threshold states that have ratified the treaty, a number of reservations are attached to their signatures. This is particularly disquieting since the requirements for withdrawing from the treaty are so undemanding. All that is required is three months advance notice by the state desiring to relinquish its obligations. The long list of reservations makes it questionable whether the treaty will be renewed when it expires in 1995.

THE SAFEGUARDS SYSTEM

The implementation of the Nonproliferation Treaty required that safeguards agreements be negotiated with the International Atomic Energy Agency, which was to serve as the primary organization verifying compliance with the treaty. Considerable delay occurred in completing these safeguards agreements as the majority of states involved failed to meet the required eighteen-month to two-year deadline. Such delays in applying safeguards raised questions about the possibility that fissionable materials might have been stockpiled during the five years and possibly longer between the time that the NPT was opened for signature and the time in which most safeguards were put into operation.

Even with the IAEA safeguards system in place a number of reservations have been raised about its efficacy in guaranteeing that fissionable materials will not be diverted to weapons purposes. Among the complaints leveled against safeguard procedures are the lack of real-time monitoring of plant operations; the refusal of certain states to accept inspectors of particular nationalities; the lack of money for an expansion of the numbers of inspectors; and the need for an increase in remote monitoring equipment commensurate with expanded global numbers of plants and throughput of materials.[13] In testimony before the Senate Foreign Relations Committee in 1981 a former inspector argued that IAEA inspectors have limited or no access to certain kinds of materials; are occasionally denied access to areas they are required to inspect; are rarely able to make "surprise" visits; and are overwhelmed by reporting or analysis backlogs.[14] The IAEA admitted that same year that it was unable to carry out full safeguards functions in Pakistan and India.[15] It was the fear of just such safeguards deficiencies that led Israel to attack the Iraqi Osirak research reactor in 1981, despite the fact that the facility was under IAEA inspection.

In attempting to evaluate the effectiveness of the IAEA safeguards system, it should be remembered that even national and corporate control systems do not have a perfect record in accounting for fissionable materials used in nuclear facilities. A Department of Energy audit for an eight-month period in 1980–81 revealed that 55.6 pounds of plutonium could not be accounted for—enough material for a half dozen bombs. In 1977 another federal study found that a cumulative total of more than 8,000 pounds of highly enriched uranium and plutonium had disappeared since the beginning of the nuclear era.[16]

With the development of the fast breeder reactor, the dangers of illegal diversion are likely to be compounded because of the capability of these reactors to produce more fissionable materials than they consume. It is anticipated that a breeder reactor will be able to produce two plutonium-239 nuclei for every one that is burned, which means that the reactor will be able to double its plutonium stock over the period of a decade. Unless effective controls can be established forcing the return of this excess plutonium to the control agency, substantial numbers of bombs could be produced by states that are not yet members of the nuclear club. The difficulty of safeguarding global plutonium supplies, which had more than doubled during the period 1975–80, has been underscored by Victor Gilensky, a member of the Nuclear Regulatory Commission. In a speech at MIT, Gilensky concluded that "separated plutonium is not safeguardable by any means now available to us—we cannot count on warning in time to head off an illicit weapons effort."[17]

The question naturally arises as to how much potential diversion can be allowed with states still feeling secure. Since existing nuclear weapon stockpiles have grown to such proportions and threaten to grow substantially more, it would seem that any evasion of the IAEA system would not be as destabilizing on a global basis as it might have been in an earlier day. Proliferation within a particular conflict region might be quite another matter. At any rate, support or nonsupport of the NPT revolves around the problem of balancing risks. Reservations concerning the effectiveness of any inspection system need to be balanced against the perceived dangers inherent in the failure to put a disarmament measure into operation. Support for an effective inspection and control system also needs to be balanced against the fears that the inspection system will be too onerous in terms of both costs and threats to sovereignty.

Considerable controversy has raged over the question of where to apply IAEA controls. The treaty was viewed as creating a considerable imbalance of obligations as far as the nuclear and nonnuclear states were concerned. Inspection was to be applied only to current nonnuclear states, but the United States and the United Kingdom agreed in December 1967 to have similar controls placed upon all of their peaceful nuclear activities. In February 1983 the Soviet Union announced that it would place some of its peaceful nuclear power plants under IAEA safeguards, and China unexpectedly followed suit in September 1985. Since

France earlier had indicated that it would allow similar inspections of its plants and would act as if it were a member of the treaty, all five nuclear weapon states now accept safeguards applied to some of their peaceful nuclear facilities. Although such actions helped to redress some of the imbalance, the nuclear weapon states are still free to designate which plants are to be considered peaceful ones and which ones are outside the control system.

The Indian representative in viewing the efforts to control peaceful nuclear activities while disregarding warlike nuclear activities suggested that it was "like an attempt to maintain law and order in a society by placing all its law abiding citizens in custody while leaving its law-breaking elements free to roam the streets."[18] Arguments raised against gun control laws in the United States have been strikingly similar.

In addition to the controversy over whether or not to exempt the nuclear weapon states from the inspection system, debates arose over the issue of which nuclear activities should be inspected in order to guarantee that the nonnuclear state was complying with the treaty. Some states preferred that controls be established only at crucial points in the nuclear fuel cycle and that even these controls should be as automated as possible. Other states believed that controls should be applied to the entire fuel cycle including uranium enrichment plants, reactors, fabrication plants, and reprocessing plants.[19]

SECURITY ASSURANCES

In an effort to generate support for the Nonproliferation Treaty, the Soviet Union and the United States sought to reassure those states that were hesitant to support the treaty that their security interests would be taken into account. The treaty itself did little to satisfy the security concerns of the nonnuclear weapon states as the United States and others believed that security guarantees should be negotiated separately from the treaty. A major reason for this strategy was the recognition that it would take considerable time to negotiate such an agreement. No blank article was left as was the case with article III concerning safeguards in the 1967 United States and Russian NPT proposals, presumably because of the contention that the United Nations provided a basic formula for peace and security or at least as much of an obligation as the United States and the Soviet Union were willing to accept.

The preferred security guarantee sought by the nonnuclear states was a negative one in which the nuclear weapon states would agree not to use nuclear weapons against nonnuclear weapon states. More than half of those states showing concern about the security issue suggested a nuclear-use ban as a desirable option. Whereas the United States has been skeptical of such guarantees because of the lack of enforcement procedures, the Soviet Union has frequently favored use bans throughout the history of the postwar disarmament negotiations. In 1966 the Soviet Union expressed its support for such a guarantee within the framework of a treaty to halt nuclear spread but subsequently supported the U.S. position of deferring the issue.

During the debates on the treaty, the United Arab Republic proposed an amendment incorporating the Soviet proposal that nuclear weapon states would not undertake to "use or threaten to use nuclear weapons against any non-nuclear weapon state party to this Treaty which has no nuclear weapons on its territory." This would have meant that a state like the Federal Republic of Germany, albeit a nonnuclear weapon power, would not be protected by the security guarantees since United States nuclear warheads are stationed on its soil.

The debates on the security guarantees indicated a number of serious reservations concerning the use of the United Nations as the protector of security interests. Although the UN resolution providing such guarantees was passed by a vote of 10 to 0, the five states that abstained (Algeria, Brazil, India, France, and Pakistan) made it clear that they were most disillusioned with the resolution. Nations both within the Security Council and outside of it viewed the resolution as inadequate because of the veto and the fact that not all of the permanent members of the Council were expected to sign the treaty. India was also critical of the fact that the resolution and the individual guarantees offered by the United States, the United Kingdom, and the Soviet Union were contingent upon a state's signing the NPT. This the Indians regarded as actually against the spirit of the UN Charter, which was designed to apply to all members and even to nonmembers if there is a threat to world peace.

Several states would have preferred that Security Council guarantees be written directly into the treaty. Perhaps part of the motivation for keeping the treaty and the guarantees separate was related to the desire to get agreement on the NPT first. It would then be possible to resolve the issue of security guarantees—an issue that was recognized from the beginning as a sensitive one that might preclude any chance of agreements. Reservations were also raised concerning the meaning of the word *aggression* as used in the UN resolution. Would the guarantee apply to the threat of aggression or to protection from conventional attack? Furthermore, if assistance were required, it was not at all clear how much and what kind would be provided.

Should the Security Council fail to act on behalf of the victim of aggression as has often been the case as a result of the use of the veto, both the Security Council resolution and the guarantees of the three nuclear weapon states provide the right of individual and collective self-defense in accordance with article 51 of the United Nations Charter. This article, however, fails to protect a state against nuclear blackmail since an attack need actually have occurred. A state must also be a part of an alliance system before it can feel reasonably confident that article 51 of the UN Charter will be activated on its behalf. Yet even members of alliance systems might have some concern for their security in view of the flagrant violation of Czech sovereignty by the Soviet Union in August 1968. The Czechoslovakian crisis raised questions in the minds of many of the representatives of the nonnuclear states regarding the extent to which nuclear weapon states could be trusted either in terms of desisting from attack or defending the victim in the event of armed aggressioin. As a result, the crisis was used by a number of states to justify their procrastination in signing and ratifying the treaty.

Because of the continuing pressure from nonnuclear weapon states, the United States, the United Kingdon, and the Soviet Union added additional guarantees during the UN Special Session on Disarmament in 1978 when they agreed not to use nuclear weapons against any state that had renounced the acquisition of such weapons. The Soviet Union excepted any state that had nuclear weapons on its soil, and the United States indicated that the nonnuclear weapon state must not be engaged in an armed attack or be allied with a nuclear weapon state. The Russian formula was directed against states like the Federal Republic of Germany while the U.S. position made it clear that the West might use nuclear weapons against a Warsaw Pact state if an attack came from the East. In 1982 Brezhnev went a step further in the Second UN Special Session on Disarmament when he announced that the USSR ''assumes an obligation not to be the first to use nuclear weapons.'' He added that ''in the formulation of its policy, the Soviet Union will naturally take into account how the other nuclear Powers act. . . .''[20]

With respect to positive guarantees, representatives from the United Kingdom and Canada argued during the NPT debates that stronger security assurances could not be given except under military alliance with nuclear powers. The general reluctance in the United States to provide even limited security guarantees beyond current alliance commitments to nonnuclear states was demonstrated most vividly by the fact that almost a third of the United States Senate voted for the Ervin amendment, which would have made Senate approval contingent upon the understanding that no commitments to defend smaller nations from nuclear aggression be undertaken.[21] Even though the proposed amendment was defeated, such moves were hardly likely to inspire confidence in what were already regarded as totally inadequate security guarantees by many nonnuclear states.

The Nixon Doctrine, which stressed that Asian states must take greater responsibility for their own defense and cannot expect the United States to intervene on a massive scale on their behalf, reduced confidence in alliances with the United States. Japan and Australia were particularly concerned about the seeming withdrawal of the United States from Asia and were shocked by the failure of their ally even to consult them concerning changing U.S.-Chinese relations. Additional questions about the reliability of the United States as an ally arose with the collapse of South Vietnam in 1975 and the fall of the Shah of Iran in 1979. President Reagan raised similar sensitivities among West European allies when he claimed that it would be possible to keep a nuclear war on the European continent limited to a tactical exchange.[22]

Despite uncertainties about alliances, it might still be assumed that states belonging to formal alliances would be less likely to be concerned about receiving security guarantees or some other form of assurance than those that do not have such protection. Since presumably allies of nuclear powers are more apt to enjoy the protection of the nuclear umbrella, one would expect that they would be less concerned about giving up the nuclear option and less insistent about obtaining formal guarantees from the nuclear powers. Thus it was possible for the Australian delegate to suggest calmly that "if States become parties to the treaty and if they are subsequently threatened, their recourse would be to seek support by a larger Power or combination of Powers."[23] On the other hand, the nonaligned state cannot be as certain of such support, hence the very real concern about security guarantees. The content analysis of the final General Assembly debate noted above found that 90 percent of the thirty nonaligned states participating in the debates expressed reservations about security guarantees, whereas only 51 percent of the fifty-seven nominally aligned states raised the question of security. A chi-square test indicated this relationship to be significant at the .001 level. Similar support suggesting that nonaligned states were more likely to be concerned about the treaty than aligned states was found as 78 percent of the nonaligned states ($N = 40$) indicated general dissatisfaction with the treaty either verbally or by voting against it or abstaining during the Assembly debates as constrasted to only 30 percent of the nominally aligned ($N = 61; p < .001$).[24]

THE PEACEFUL ATOM

Since nuclear energy can be used for both weapons or peaceful purposes, a number of states raised questions about how the Nuclear Nonproliferation Treaty might affect the use of the peaceful atom. Several states were particularly interested in the possible negative effect of the treaty upon the competitive position of nuclear energy as a fuel source. Among questions posed were the following: Will international safeguards make such fuels noncompetitive? Will adequate fissionable supplies be guaranteed at a reasonable price? Will the nuclear powers share nuclear technology or would they assume an exploitive monopolistic position? These questions seemed to take on even greater urgency with the 1973 OPEC oil embargo and the subsequent spiralling of oil prices.

Attitudes about the competitive position of nuclear energy have fluctuated over the years with considerable optimism being shown during the midfifties as a result of the publicity surrounding the Atoms for Peace program. There followed a period of considerable pessimism as the nuclear weapon states were slow to convert their nuclear stocks to peaceful purposes, and experts were beginning to conclude that nuclear power was not competitive with other energy sources. Studies presented at the Third and Fourth International Conferences on the Peaceful Uses of Atomic Energy in 1964 were somewhat more optimistic since it was discovered that fissionable materials had a longer life than expected.[25] New technologies such as breeder reactors and the development of the less expensive centrifuge process for enriching uranium added to the optimism. The sharply increasing prices of oil during the seventies meant that nuclear energy might become more competitive.

Counterbalanced against these optimistic assessments were increasing reservations about the environmental hazards of nuclear energy, which reached a peak with the Three Mile Island nuclear accident in 1979. The Soviet nuclear reactor accident at Chernobyl in 1986 served only to heighten anxiety about the peaceful uses of nuclear energy. At the same time, increasing construction costs and long delays in building nuclear reactors further contributed to the pessimism. The hopeful assessments about nuclear energy suffered an additional blow when the United States, during the Carter administration, decided not to proceed with the Clinch River breeder reactor while attempting to discourage other states from developing similar facilities on the grounds that such reactors would contribute to the proliferation problem. Breeder technology had seemed so promising because it would produce more plutonium than it would consume. Although this would contribute to enlarging the fuel supply and providing less expensive nuclear energy, it would also increase the danger of plutonium being diverted to weapons purposes.

The effect of the treaty on the use of nuclear explosions for large earth-moving projects was also cited as an issue of concern by more than a quarter of the participants during the 1968 General Assembly debates on the Nonproliferation Treaty. The language of the treaty is most restrictive on this issue because of the fact that it is impossible to distinguish a peaceful nuclear explosion from a nuclear weapon explosion as discussed in the previous chapter. The superpowers sought to retain control over the technology of peaceful explosions while guaranteeing that they would share that technology with nonnuclear weapon states under international supervision. Accordingly, article V of the NPT requires that the potential benefits from any peaceful applications of nuclear explosives be made available under international control and at the lowest possible cost to nonnuclear weapon states that are party to the treaty.

As indicated in the previous chapter, assessments of the potential of peaceful nuclear explosions have fluctuated over the years. In the late 1950s the Soviet Union wanted to prohibit all nuclear explosions, peaceful or otherwise, whereas the United States had an active peaceful explosions research program underway with its Plowshare program. U.S. interest in peaceful nuclear explosions began to decline in the midsixties, so much so that by 1978 the Plowshare program had disappeared entirely from the federal budget.[26]

While U.S. interest was declining, the Soviet leadership began to show greater optimism about the potential of nuclear explosions for large earth-moving projects. During the Peaceful Nuclear Explosions Treaty negotiations in the midseventies, the Soviets asserted that they would like to conduct peaceful explosions as high as 400 kilotons in clusters up to 3 megatons. At the top of the Soviet list was a project that would divert the waters of at least one northbound river into the southbound Volga.[27]

Despite these fluctuations in optimism about the peaceful uses of nuclear energy, many states still believe in its potential and, as a result, continue to oppose any aspect of the NPT which they fear will interfere with the peaceful atom. The treaty has not yet provided the signatories with the anticipated advantages of the peaceful atom, and, according to one assessment, "non-parties could be argued to have had the bulk of the help offered in this area."[28] The preference shown to nonsignatories has occurred largely as a result of the desire on the part of the nuclear weapon states to appease those states that are viewed as the most likely proliferators. Such a policy, however, is likely to erode existing support for the treaty.

In addition to attempting to reassure nonnuclear weapon states about economic and security concerns, both the United States and the Soviet Union have from time to time exerted direct pressure upon various states in an effort to reduce the danger of proliferation. Such pressure was used against Euratom in 1967 as the U.S. Atomic Energy Commission indicated that restrictions would be placed on the American export of fissionable materials if Euratom did not comply with the IAEA regarding reexport.[29] Veiled threats were also made to India in President Johnson's Food for Peace message to Congress delivered on February 2, 1967, wherein the president suggested that those states that spend vitally needed resources on ''unnecessary military equipment'' can no longer take food supplies for granted.[30] However, India refused to sign the treaty. The reported demand made by a former U.S. assistant secretary of defense that Israel sign the NPT in return for the shipment of Phantom jets was likewise unsuccessful.[31]

Pressure of this sort decreased considerably, for the Nixon administration assumed a much more ambivalent posture on the question of nuclear spread, leading the Japanese to question whether the United States cared any longer about limiting the number of nuclear powers.[32] This seeming lack of concern about the proliferation problem was perhaps partially related to a preoccupation with other issues such as Vietnam as well as the desire not to antagonize U.S. allies. At any rate, the failure of the Nixon administration to press the nonproliferation issue partially explains why it took almost two years before the Nuclear Nonproliferation Treaty came into effect with the required forty ratifications in addition to those of the United States, the Soviet Union, and the United Kingdom.

It took the Indian underground nuclear explosion in 1974 to force the Nixon administration to realize that it should be more sensitive about the dangers of nuclear proliferation. It was at that time that the U.S. Atomic Energy Commission, in an effort to reduce weapons-grade fissionable materials, announced that it would accept no new contracts for the enrichment of natural uranium. Anxiety about the further spread of fissionable materials to other regions led the United States in 1974 to invite the Soviet Union, Britian, West Germany, France, Japan, and Canada to discuss the prospects of creating a Nuclear Supplier Group that would regulate the shipment of fissionable materials. In 1978 the Supplier Group, which had increased in size to some fifteen states, agreed upon guidelines that required that certain nuclear technology, equipment, and material could be transferred only if the recipient nation agreed to apply IAEA safeguards to the item supplied and would use such materials only for peaceful purposes.

Fear of nuclear proliferation was intensified in 1975 when France and the Federal Republic of Germany decided to sell important components of the nuclear fuel cycle to several threshold states that had refused to ratify the Nuclear Nonproliferation Treaty. Germany agreed to provide Brazil with enrichment services and facilities while France planned to supply Pakistan and South Korea with plutonium reprocessing plants capable of producing weapons grade materials. Under pressure from the United States, France decided in 1978 not to provide the components needed to complete the plutonium reprocessing plant it was helping Pakistan build.[33] Similar pressures against West Germany by the Carter administration may help explain the German announcement in June 1977 that it was establishing a formal ban on any future export of nuclear reprocessing technology.[34] Germany, however, did not renounce its nuclear arrangement with Brazil, and Pakistan, having lost the assistance of France, decided to construct a uranium enrichment plant of its own by relying upon overseas purchases of parts and technology from commercial suppliers. Direct pressures upon the threshold states themselves, enabled the United States to persuade South Korea and Taiwan not to proceed with their respective plans for constructing reprocessing plants.

While the Soviets had a more cavalier attitude about the dangers of proliferation during the early postwar years than did the United States, the Soviets soon changed their position. As early as 1960 "the Soviet Union pressed for the strictest possible safeguards on nuclear exports, while the U.S. government favored looser controls."[35] It was also at the insistence of the Soviet Union that strict safeguards were applied to the nuclear programs of the East European satellites. The IAEA safeguards system for East Germany, for example, has been regarded as a model safeguards agreement. By 1967 the Soviet Union was endorsing IAEA inspection for all nonnuclear weapon states.[36]

The Soviet Union has generally sought to influence the proliferation policies of other states by utilizing less publicized techniques as it did in pressuring India to accede to safeguards in exchange for heavy water supplies.[37] Similarly, the Soviets delayed nuclear plant construction in Cuba until an IAEA safeguard agreement was negotiated in 1980.[38] In 1977 the Soviet Union alerted the United States to the fact that South Africa was preparing a nuclear test site. After confirming the information, the United States successfully pressed South Africa to desist from its nuclear plans.[39]

The Soviet Union held a long series of ad hoc negotiations with the United States on the subject of nuclear proliferation beginning in 1977. These talks were resumed in December 1982 with the Reagan administration. Although the START and INF talks fell victim to the U.S. deployment of intermediate-range nuclear forces in Europe the following year, talks on nonproliferation continued to be held.

THE NONPROLIFERATION POLICIES
OF CARTER AND REAGAN

In evaluating possible approaches to controlling the proliferation of nuclear weapons, the contrasting approaches of the Carter and Reagan administrations are instructive. For the Carter administration the problem of proliferation was essentially a technical one in which an effort was made to establish international control over the entire nuclear fuel supply. The Reagan administration, on the other hand, saw the problem as a political one in which the effort should be one of guaranteeing a nuclear fuel supply in order to discourage nonnuclear weapon states from developing their own fuel cycles that would not be under U.S. or international control.

The Carter administration, unlike its predecessor, supported congressional efforts to pass the Nuclear Nonproliferation Act (NNPA) in 1978. Going beyond previous U.S. policy, the NNPA mandates that two years after passage any recipient of U.S. nuclear exports has to apply comprehensive safeguards to the entire fuel cycle whether or not that state is a member of the Nuclear Nonproliferation Treaty. This required that existing bilateral supply agreements be renegotiated, placing considerable strain on U.S. relations with various states that were disturbed by the breaking of contractual relationships.

If all supplier states had followed the United States lead, the danger of proliferation could have been reduced. But, with the exception of Canada, few states established such requirements. This worked to the benefit of other nuclear suppliers as recipients preferred the less onerous safeguard requirements. France, for example, replaced the United States as a supplier of fissionable materials to India since the latter was unwilling to accept the new American safeguard demands. Although the Reagan administration opposed certain aspects of the Nuclear Nonproliferation Act, it has chosen not to amend the act for fear that the debate over the issue would further reduce confidence in the constancy of the United States as a supplier nation.[40]

The Carter administration believed in treating all nonnuclear weapon states alike as far as nuclear controls were concerned, whereas the Reagan administration proposed making distinctions that would give preferential treatment to the advanced industrial states and those states that were not regarded as likely proliferators. Since plutonium production was seen as a major problem with respect to the dangers of nuclear proliferation, Carter proposed denying plutonium reprocessing plants to both domestic and international commercial interests. The Carter decisions to cancel the breeder reactor and to close the Barnwell reprocessing plant were reflective of the administration's desire to create a nuclear technology less dependent upon plutonium as the fuel source. The Reagan policy was based on a willingness to provide reprocessed plutonium, but not the reprocessing facilities, to nonnuclear weapon states. Reliance on this approach would help ensure that production facilities would remain under U.S. control. It was felt that a restrictive policy would only force nonnuclear weapon states to build their own reprocessing facilities.

The Carter administration attempted to educate other states about the dangers of a plutonium-based fuel cycle as it pressed for a 1978 conference referred to as the International Fuel Cycle Evaluation (INFCE). It was hoped that a general dialogue involving some 66 supplier and consumer states would aid in developing a consensus in support of an effective nonproliferation regime—an objective that the United States, given its declining influence, could not achieve alone. After three years of discussion, most states remained unpersuaded on the issue of the dangers of plutonium reprocessing and showed more concern about the problems and uncertainties of supply than about proliferation dangers. The environmental hazards of plutonium storage and the proliferation potential of enriched uranium, which is used in some reactors, were viewed by the INFCE as more serious problems.[41] The Reagan administration remained unconvinced about the dangers of plutonium as it reactivated the Clinch River breeder reactor, recommissioned the Barnwell reprocessing plant, and substantially increased the production of plutonium.

It was the policy of the Carter administration to exert strong pressure upon other states in order to discourage them from exporting sensitive nuclear technology and material to nonnuclear weapon states. As a result, the administration assumed an active role in pressing the Suppliers Group to adopt a trigger list of items that would be subject to international control. The Reagan administration was more concerned about the possible negative reactions of allies and others who would be disturbed by such restrictions. Accordingly, it sought to modify the trigger list through bilateral negotiation. Reagan was also interested in minimizing certain restrictions in order to aid the U.S. nuclear industry, which was suffering a severe economic decline in view of numerous slowdowns and cutbacks of nuclear reactor orders throughout the world, and particularly within the United States itself. Billions of dollars in potential nuclear exports were at stake, which would only go to foreign competitors if restrictions were not removed. In support of more relaxed controls, the Reagan administration argued that with the increased mastery of nuclear technology throughout the world, the ability of any one country to control proliferation had diminished considerably.[42]

As part of its strong nonproliferation policy, the Carter administration complied with the requirements of the Glenn-Symington amendment to the 1961 Foreign Assistance Act when in early 1979 it cut off all aid to Pakistan. According to this amendment, both economic and military aid are to be denied any country that delivers or receives enriched or reprocessing technology without full safeguards. It had become obvious by that time that Pakistan was intent upon developing the bomb as it continued to reject verification over critical nuclear facilities and materials. In contrast, the Reagan administration in 1981, as part of its effort to bolster security in the Persian Gulf, asked for a waiver of the amendment and subsequently instituted a five-year program of economic and military aid to Pakistan.[43] Four years later, President Reagan sought a similar exception to the Glenn-Symington amendment with regard to nuclear exports to Argentina, but the House Committee on Foreign Affairs rejected the request.[44]

There is evidence that President Reagan may have become somewhat more sensitive to the dangers of proliferation. For example, the president warned Pakistan in a letter dated September 12, 1985, that Pakistan risked losing American military assistance if it continued its nuclear weapons development program.[45] However, this did not stop the president from asserting in November 1986 that Pakistan "does not possess a nuclear explosive device"—a proclamation that was necessary in order to continue the $600 million economic and military assistance program to Pakistan. This assertion was made despite a Defense Intelligence Agency report that Pakistan detonated a high explosive device in September as part of its continuing efforts to build an implosion-type nuclear weapon.[46]

Denial of military assistance to a country may have a negative impact upon the goal of discouraging nuclear proliferation in view of what has been called the "dove's dilemma." It is argued that providing a state with the military assistance that the state deems essential for its national security will actually have the effect of making the state less likely to seek the nuclear option. This was the rationale used by the Reagan administration in providing conventional arms aid to Pakistan. To the extent that such conventional armaments are used only for deterrence and defense, such use can also be seen as contributing to peace and security in the region. But conventional arms aid can also lead to regional arms races as experience with arms aid to South Asia has demonstrated over the years.

Despite its strong stance against nuclear proliferation and a 298 to 98 House vote disapproving the action, the Carter administration persisted in a 1980 plan to send nuclear fuel shipments to India. In undermining its own anti-proliferation policy, the administration showed that it was more concerned about the threat of the Soviet Union to South Asia, following the 1979 Afghanistan invasion, than it was about the dangers of proliferation.

Both economic and security interests led the Reagan administration to negotiate a thirty-year nuclear assistance pact with the People's Republic of China, which was signed by the president during his trip to China in April 1984. Objections were raised to this pact by virtue of the cavalier attitude assumed by China about the proliferation problem. Prior to the 1980s China even hinted that further spread of nuclear weapons would be useful in undermining imperialism. The danger of Chinese re-exports of nuclear technology and fuels to other potential proliferators concerned many experts, particularly since reports suggested that China had provided inadequately safeguarded nuclear assistance, to such potential proliferators as Pakistan, Iran, Brazil, South Africa, and Argentina.

The Reagan administration delayed submitting the U.S.-China nuclear assistance pact to Congress as required by law. More than a year was spent trying to obtain greater security assurances from China, assurances it was reluctant to provide. Since China decided to join the IAEA and to accept agency safeguards over its nuclear export program, some, but not all, congressional opposition was overcome. Despite lobbying by influential senators on both the right and the left, Congress was unable to muster the necessary votes to defeat the agreement, and it automatically went into effect in January 1986. The potential $25 billion return for the U.S. nuclear industry was apparently too much of an incentive to ignore.

CONCLUSION

The experience of the United States and the Soviet Union in negotiating nuclear nonproliferation has shown that even when the two superpowers agree on an arms control issue, they are not always able to obtain the support of other states. Part of the problem in generating a consensus on nonproliferation policy is related to the fact that states of different sizes and technologies have varying economic, political, and security interests. All cannot agree that proliferation to additional states, particularly to themselves, is destabilizing. Furthermore, to the extent that atomic energy promises economic benefits, many states are unwilling to accept a nonproliferation regime that might interfere with the peaceful atom.

The United States and the Soviet Union were ultimately successful in negotiating the Nuclear Nonproliferation Treaty in 1968 that, even though it now has more adherents than any other arms control agreement, may not remain viable in the long run in light of the many reservations appended by the signatories as well as the refusal of several nuclear threshold states to join. Criticism of the treaty has been extensive at the three review conferences held thus far, and the viability of the treaty beyond its expiration date of 1995 must remain in doubt.

Subsequent efforts have been made by both the United States and the Soviet Union to strengthen the nonproliferation regime, including the exertion of pressure upon states to ratify the NPT, the development, in concert with other members of the Nuclear Supplier Group, of a trigger list of nuclear materials and technology requiring safeguards, and efforts to strengthen the International Atomic Energy Agency, which applies safeguards for the NPT.

Of the postwar governments, the Carter administration adopted the most stringent nonproliferation policy. Believing that plutonium presented the greatest danger to proliferation, the administration sought to reduce global dependence upon such fuel. Among its actions were efforts to encourage the development of nuclear reactors that would not require plutonium, efforts to restrict the reprocessing of spent fuel rods, and an attempt to stop the development of breeder reactors that have the capability of producing more plutonium than they consume. The Reagan administration reversed these policies and went a step further with its decision to distinguish in its nuclear supply effort those states it believed to be likely proliferators from those which were not so regarded. The Carter policy had been one of applying similar restrictions to both.

The debate on how best to achieve the objective of a nonproliferation regime continues. Some see the solution as one of restricting nuclear technology and materials whereas others favor allowing states to develop their own nuclear facilities but under international safeguards. By refusing as a supplier to cooperate, the danger is that a nonnuclear state may choose to use both legal and illegal means to develop its own nuclear capability for which there would then be no control. Furthermore, the new nuclear state may exacerbate the proliferation problem by becoming nuclear suppliers themselves.

Though answers are by no means easy, the problem is such that even during periods in which arms talks on other issues have been disrupted and relations seriously strained between the United States and the Soviet Union, the two superpowers have continued their periodic meetings to deal with the issue of proliferation. Such cooperation has not been without its costs as other states accuse the superpowers of exploiting the atom not only for military purposes but also for economic gains.

Perhaps the clearest lesson to be learned from the many debates on the subject of nuclear proliferation is that the positions that states take on issues that have decided military, political, and economic implications will be dictated by what they perceive to be their national interests. Unlike so many other areas of arms control, this is an area where the objectives of the United States and the Soviet Union coincide, often in opposition to the interests of the nonnuclear weapons states. As long as this identity of interests between the United States and USSR is recognized, progress can be made in controlling the spread of nuclear weapons, but when one or the other or both seek to exploit the situation for temporary economic or political gain, the results can be disastrous as when both states during the 1950s sought to gain the favor of the developing world by exaggerated claims about the potential of peaceful nuclear energy.

Domestically, the nuclear power industry has taken an avid interest in the proliferation issue. Possible international restraints on nuclear energy facilities tend to be resisted by the nuclear industry as do constraints on the export of nuclear technology, fuel, and components. At stake are billions of dollars in sales and construction contracts. Whereas the American public appears much less concerned about the proliferation problem than they do about nuclear testing in the atmosphere, their elected representatives in recent years have been quite active on the issue. In 1978 Congress passed the Nuclear Nonproliferation Act, which sought ever greater restrictions on nuclear sharing with nonnuclear weapon states. Congress has also fought with various U.S. presidents in an effort to restrain activities that threatened the nonproliferation regime, opposing President Carter on the shipment of nuclear fuels to India in 1980 and President Reagan in his attempts to build a breeder reactor and to place greater reliance upon plutonium production.

The political advantage of generating goodwill by providing nuclear assistance to other countries versus the security concerns of the military and intelligence agencies over such acts has often pitted foreign offices against the military and other security agencies. For the most part the Soviet Union has been more resistant to nuclear sharing than the United States, but this may be partially due to the primacy that the Soviet military enjoys in the arms control area.

4

The Strategic Arms Limitation Talks

Although the atomic explosions at Hiroshima and Nagasaki in 1945 were generally welcomed in the allied countries as a way of saving lives and ending the war, it was soon clear that these weapons could also threaten the future of the world. Many experts on the subject were aware that the secrets of the bomb would not remain a monopoly of the United States for long and that efforts to control these highly destructive strategic weapons should begin as soon as possible.

PRE-SALT NEGOTIATIONS

When the United Nations Atomic Energy Commission began its deliberations on June 14, 1946, the United States tabled its first strategic arms control plan in the postwar period—the so-called Baruch Plan named after the head of the U.S. delegation Bernard Baruch. The plan provided for complete control of atomic weapons development from the mining of fissionable materials to the production of the completed weapon itself. The plan remained the cornerstone of United States strategic disarmament policy until the fall of 1955, when a reservation was placed upon all past U.S. disarmament proposals.

It has been suggested that the Baruch Plan was a generous offer to the Soviet Union since the United States, as the only nuclear weapons state at the time, was demonstrating a willingness to turn over all nuclear weapons and their development to an international control organization. The proposal for a variety of reasons was not seen by the Soviet Union to be within its national security interest. First, acceptance of the plan would foreclose the possibility of the Soviet Union's ever developing its own nuclear capability, while, at the same time, forcing it to accept the fact that the United States had unlocked the secret to the atomic bomb and could just as easily withdraw the nuclear facilities from international control. Second, since the control organ would be subject to the supervision and direction of the United Nations, the Soviets would be placed in the position of a permanent minority on all decisions related to the operation of the control organ. At the time, the Soviets could count on only about five votes in the United Nations General Assembly in contrast to about forty-five for the United States. Soviet interest would not be protected by the right of veto—a procedure that was explicitly eliminated under the Baruch proposals. Third, the nuclear facilities themselves would be located geographically at positions closer to the territory of the United States and its allies than to the Soviet Union, making it easier for the former state to commandeer those facilities should the United States perceive such action to be within its national interest.[1]

These factors, combined with a distrust of the United States dating back to U.S. efforts to reverse the outcome of the Bolshevik revolution as well as American hostility toward communist ideology, led the Soviet Union to counter with a simplistic proposal of its own that called for the abolition of all nuclear weapons within a period of three months. The plan, named after the Soviet representative Andrei Gromyko, failed to include provisions for verification and enforcement, providing only that the parties to the convention would, within six months, pass legislation requiring severe penalties for violations.

Given the extreme positions taken by the two protagonists, it was inevitable that little progress would be made on the issue of nuclear disarmament. The Soviet Union, for the reasons noted, was hardly in a serious negotiating mood prior to exploding its own nuclear device in August 1949, several years earlier than many U.S. nuclear experts predicted. With the entry of the Soviet Union into the nuclear club, another issue came to complicate the search for nuclear disarmament—concern about the past Soviet nuclear production. By the early fifties, American scientists and politicans were beginning to ask how one would be able to determine the number of nuclear weapons in Soviet stockpiles. Concealing such weapons would be a relatively simple matter, according to most scientists. Robert J. Oppenheimer, the father of the atomic bomb, had asserted, for example, that the only way that one could verify whether or not a nuclear bomb was hidden in a wooden box would be to use a screwdriver.[2] To locate any nuclear weapons that the Soviet Union would choose to hide was a virtual impossibility, particularly since the Soviets refused to allow on-site inspection. After August 1953 the threat of past nuclear production took on a more ominous tone as the Soviet Union exploded its first hydrogen bomb only nine months after the United States entered the thermonuclear age.

Since the problem of past nuclear production was such a serious one in the minds of American decision makers, the United States nuclear policy in 1953 began to emphasize "Atoms for Peace." As outlined in a speech to the United Nations on December 8, 1953, President Eisenhower proposed a program to develop the peaceful use of atomic energy. The plan called for joint contributions of fissionable materials from both American and Soviet stockpiles to an International Atomic Energy Agency. The plan, however, was not a disarmament program, for the amounts to be diverted were expected to be small. In some respects the emphasis upon the peaceful atom served only to exacerbate the spread of nuclear weapons as pointed out in the preceding chapter. At the same time, these proposals provided the basis of the International Atomic Energy Agency, potentially the most important agency for guaranteeing the peaceful use of atomic energy as far as nonnuclear weapon states are concerned.

The diversion from nuclear disarmament policy reflected the growing disenchantment of United States decision makers with the Baruch Plan. Although the plan remained American policy until 1955, statements were increasingly being made to the effect that the United States would continue to support the plan only until a better one could be devised.

Due to the growing disenchantment of the United States with its own nuclear disarmament proposals, the Soviet Union in late 1954 and particularly in its May 1955 proposals accepted a number of suggestions being made by the West with respect to the control of both conventional and nuclear weapons. These included acceptance of the notion of dealing with the control and reduction of weapons in stages, the elimination of the requirement of a use ban as a precondition for nuclear disarmament, and the creation of ground inspection control posts. On September 19, 1955, the Soviet Union went so far as to agree that it would consider aerial inspection in the final stage of the disarmament scheme. But the concession came too late, for the United States had only a few days earlier placed a reservation upon its own disarmament proposals, including the Baruch Plan.

Just as the growth of technology led to a severalfold increase in the destructiveness of nuclear weapons within the span of a few years, the technological revolution also affected the means of delivering those weapons. Bombers were developed that had intercontinental range, but perhaps even more critical from the strategic standpoint was the development of missiles.

Although Hitler had used V-2 rockets against Britain in World War II, the development of long-range missiles was fairly slow in coming. There was the recognition prior to the development of the hydrogen bomb that long-range missiles would be unable to carry the heavy payload of nuclear weapons. After all, the bomb dropped on Nagasaki, quite appropriately dubbed the ''fat man,'' weighed some ten thousand pounds and measured sixty inches in diameter yet yielded only fourteen kilotons of destructive power.[3] Subsequent refinements have meant that similar amounts of destructive power can be packed into an attaché case. Nor did the United States anticipate the Soviet Union's rush to develop intercontinental missiles capable of carrying nuclear warheads. In October 1948 the Joint Chiefs of Staff estimated that it would be 1977 before the Soviet Union would have such a capability.[4] As it happened, the Soviet Union was able to launch its first intercontinental ballistic missile (ICBM) two decades earlier than the time predicted. That the Soviet Union was able to catch the United States by surprise was related to the fact that the Soviets started their program in 1946 and continued it to completion, whereas the United States did not initiate a serious and persistent program until 1954.[5]

While rockets and missiles were still under development, there were few references in formal U.S. and Soviet disarmament statements and proposals to controlling these weapons. In one of the few early comments regarding the issue, the Soviet delegate on June 8, 1954, informed the Disarmament Subcommittee meeting in London that rocket weapons should not be forgotten; President Eisenhower in a letter to Soviet Prime Minister Bulganin dated August 4, 1956, noted that he favored ''elimination of the growing threat of nuclear weapons and new means of delivery.''[6] Although the Soviet Union, prior to the launching of Sputnik, indicated a willingness to regulate missiles and rockets, its stance became tougher in 1958 as it sought to extract an agreement to liquidate foreign military bases and to prohibit nuclear weapons as the price for even discussing limits on missiles and space vehicles.[7] The United States, which was behind in the missile race at the time, proposed after Sputnik to place limits upon the production, but not the testing, of missiles in an effort to forestall all-out Soviet deployment of such weapons. The Soviet Union was particularly critical of these proposals since they dealt only with the control of ICBMs not other means of delivery such as intermediate-range ballistic missiles (IRBMs) and bombers in which the United States had the advantage given its overseas bases and substantial number of bombers.

Rather than deal with the basic problem of the production and possession of nuclear missiles, attention in 1958 was directed toward the issue of banning nuclear weapons from outer space. The Soviet Union again sought to link such a ban with its concern to abolish all foreign bases but was unsuccessful in this effort.[8] The linkage was later dropped, leading to the successful negotiation of the Outer Space Treaty which was opened for signature in 1967.

Reflective of the general retreat from nuclear disarmament in United States arms control policy was the increased concern expressed about the dangers of surprise attack, particularly on the part of United States negotiators. Sophisticated delivery systems served only to enhance such a danger. Although the United States was successful in getting the Soviet Union and its allies to the bargaining table to discuss the issue in November 1958, the resulting Surprise Attack Conference was a complete disaster. The two sides failed to communicate in these debates as the West spoke largely in favor of inspection and control procedures to reduce the dangers of surprise attack, whereas the Soviet Union and its allies argued that the only way to reduce such dangers would be through nuclear disarmament.

The effort to negotiate seriously about the control of strategic weapons suffered its greatest setback in the fall of 1959 when the Soviet Union introduced its first plan for general and complete disarmament (GCD).[9] Designed as it was to abolish all conventional and nuclear weapons in the short period of four years, the presentation of the plan could hardly be regarded as any more than a propaganda ploy on the part of the Soviet Union. Assertions that states could retain those weapons necessary to their internal security and the liberalizing of the four-year deadline hardly made these proposals any more palatable or realistic. Nevertheless, in order not to lose the propaganda battle, the United States was forced to respond in kind as it, along with its allies, introduced its first general and complete disarmament proposal in March 1960. Unlike the Soviet plan, no explicit deadlines for reducing weapons to a level consistent with internal security were included. The Western plan called for a number of actions to be taken as rapidly as possible such as the prohibition of weapons of mass destruction in space, international observance of missile launchings, and cessation of the production of fissionable materials for weapons purposes. Reduction of existing weapons was simply cited as an ultimate goal, and a number of joint U.S.-Soviet studies were proposed for seeking to obtain such an objective.

When the Kennedy administration came into power in 1961, more serious attention was given to the issue of arms control and disarmament. The Arms Control and Disarmament Agency was created, greatly expanding the number of government personnel working on these issues. New initiatives were undertaken with respect to efforts to control strategic weapons. Most significant of these was the McCloy-Zorin talks, which produced an agreed statement of principles dated September 20, 1961.[10] The statement reaffirmed the commitment of the two sides to general and complete disarmament; but, as desired by the United States, the required reductions would be completed in stages. Sufficient verification that all requirements of a given stage had been met would have to be assured before progressing to the next phase of reductions.

Modifications continued to be made in the GCD proposals by both sides over the next three years. In April 1962 the United States matched the specificity of Soviet proposals for GCD by presenting a treaty outline that called for the completion of general and complete disarmament in three stages over a period of nine years. For its part, the Soviet Union began to hint of greater flexibility in its proposed four-year schedule for GCD.

That the Soviet Union was using its GCD proposals for propaganda purposes and perhaps to split the Western alliance system is evidenced by its September 1962 proposals. These would place a ban on the production and possession of missiles in the first stage rather than delaying complete abolition to the third stage as provided in the initial Soviet plan for general and complete disarmament. In so doing, the Soviets were complying with the preference of France to give the highest priority to controlling missile development and production. The reversal in staging may also have been related to changing Soviet perceptions of the military balance. When presenting its first GCD proposal, the Soviet Union thought itself to be ahead in the missile race and wanted to retain that advantage as long as possible by delaying the abolition of nuclear missiles to the last stage. By 1962, it was clear that the United States was in the superior position, making the abolition of missiles in the first stage a highly desirable option from the Soviet perspective.

A slight concession was made to the U.S. position in September 1963 when the Soviet Union conceded that a ''nuclear umbrella'' for the two superpowers could remain into the third stage of general and complete disarmament. But the proposed umbrella would consist only of ICBMs, not SLBMs in which the United States had a considerable qualitative and quantitative advantage.

Although the last formal proposals for general and complete disarmament were made in 1964, references to the goal have continued to be made from time to time during the disarmament negotiations. Whenever the negotiations have taken a more serious tone, they have tended to focus upon partial measures of disarmament such as a nuclear test ban or nuclear nonproliferation.

The control of strategic weapons also was introduced as one of several options of partial arms control measures. In January 1964, for example, the United States proposed a verified freeze on the character and numbers of strategic nuclear offensive and defensive vehicles. The proposal was quickly rejected by the Soviets not only because of the verification provisions but also because of the fact that the Soviet Union was far behind the United States in terms of both the quantity and quality of missiles. The Soviet leaders responded to this gap by sending missiles to Cuba in the fall of 1962 in a desperate effort to obtain short-term security.

In January 1964 the United States presented yet another one-sided proposal when it suggested scrappping medium-range bombers. The plan would have removed some 80 percent or more of the total Soviet air fleet capable of delivering nuclear weapons, but it would merely have phased out the B-47—a bomber that the United States was planning to replace with the B-52.

It was also in January that the United States proposed halting the production of fissionable materials, taking advantage of the fact that its nuclear stockpile was substantially larger than that of the Soviet Union. Three months later these proposals were made more concrete when President Johnson unilaterally announced that the United States would close one separation plant and reduce the production of fissionable materials. The move led to private negotiations between the United States, the Soviet Union, and the United Kingdom during which unilateral pledges were made to reduce the production of fissionable materials. In these pledges the United States agreed to cut its production of U-235 by 40 percent over a period of four years and plutonium production by 20 percent. The Soviet Union promised similar substantial reductions and agreed not to proceed with the construction of two large atomic reactors which had been planned.

Subsequent unilateral reductions of delivery vehicles by the United States seem not to have had the same results in terms of stemming Soviet delivery capabilities. On April 26, 1965, Adlai Stevenson announced to the United Nations that by mid-1966 the United States would have inactivated or destroyed more than 2000 B-47s, it would have reduced the number of B-52s, and it would forego the construction of some Minutemen missiles that had been planned.[11] A month later Secretary of Defense Robert McNamara indicated that at least half of the existing B-52s would be phased out by 1970.[12] Former American arms negotiator

William C. Foster expressed concern over the failure of such announcements to be linked with demands that the Soviet Union make similar reductions.[13]

Concern about controlling strategic weapons was considerably heightened by the progress being made on the anti-ballistic missile (ABM). Although the United States had begun ABM development with its Nike-Zeus system in the mid-1950s, the Soviet Union surpassed the United States in the early 1960s, first with the installation of the Tallinn system around the Estonian capital and then with the Galosh system encircling Moscow. As early as 1963 Soviet leaders were boasting about having solved the missile defense problem. Such bravado was particularly disconcerting for, if true, an effective Soviet ABM system could neutralize the United States nuclear deterrent.

Instead of responding to Soviet ABM developments in kind, Secretary of Defense Robert McNamara chose to emphasize a buildup in offensive capability. Of greatest significance was the decision to proceed with the development of the multiple independently targeted reentry vehicle (MIRV). It was reasoned at the time that an accelerated competition for anti-ballistic missiles would be particularly destabilizing since such competition would increase the incentives for the state falling behind to initiate a preemptive nuclear strike before an effective ABM system could be put into place by the other state. What is critical is not whether such a system could be built but rather whether one or both parties felt that it could be built.

In December 1966 the United States responded to the ABM threat by calling for U.S.-Soviet talks limited to the question of defensive missile systems. As might be expected, the Soviet Union responded in January 1967 by insisting that the proposed talks also include offensive weapons rather than be limited to the ABM, in which it felt superior.

Positions on ABM controls gradually changed, for by late 1967 most United States intelligence analysts agreed that the Tallinn system had no ABM capability and could not be easily upgraded.[14] The Soviets themselves became less enthusiastic about the Galosh system, and they decided in the same year, largely because of the system's relatively poor performance, to curtail by one-third the originally planned 96 ABM missile system around Moscow.[15]

Pressures began to mount in the United States to develop an ABM system to replace the then defunct Nike-Zeus system. Acquiescing to these pressures for fear of the electoral consequences, Secretary of Defense McNamara announced the creation of the Sentinel ABM system on September 18, 1967. In his announcement McNamara took special pains to reassure the Soviet Union that the system was not meant to be one capable of defending against a massive nuclear missile strike. Instead, it would be designed to defend only against a limited strike involving either the accidental firing of a few missiles or a launch from China or some other country lacking sophisticated nuclear missile delivery systems.

The sensitivity of the Soviet Union to United States ABM developments is further illustrated by the June 27, 1968, announcement made by Andrei Gromyko that the Soviet Union was ready to begin negotiations on strategic arms limitations. It was not entirely by coincidence that this statement was made three days after the United States Senate defeated an amendment that would have denied funds for the deployment of the Sentinel ABM system.

President Johnson, vilified for his role in Vietnam and concerned about his image in history, was particularly interested in holding talks on strategic arms limitation at the highest level before retiring from the presidency in January 1969. As a result, a summit meeting to discuss these issues was scheduled for September 30, 1968. Soon after an agreement to hold the summit talks was reached, the entire effort fell victim to the Soviet invasion of Czechoslovakia on August 21, and the SALT effort was delayed until the arrival of the Nixon administration.

THE STRATEGIC ARMS TALKS

It was not until November 17, 1969, that the Strategic Arms Limitation Talks got underway in Helsinki, Finland. The delay of several months was due to the desire of a new administration to have sufficient time to develop its disarmament policy—a process that requires intensive discussion and debate within the government as well as between allies. In addition, President Nixon believed that the Soviet Union was more interested in the SALT talks than the United States. This impression was conveyed by Foreign Minister Gromyko who, on the very day of the inauguration, invited the Nixon administration to hold such talks as soon as possible. Given such perceptions, the new administration was determined that the Soviets would pay a price, and that price was the controversial linkage policy that demanded that settlement on a wide variety of political disputes such as Vietnam and the Middle East would have to be reached first. Unfortunately, the willingness of the Soviet Union to make such trade-offs was found not be great, for some elements in the Soviet Union appeared to be interested in the talks only as a way of dividing the West. Ultimately, the United States was forced to drop its linkage requirements and to negotiate limitations on arms on their own merits.

Ten years and hundreds of meetings were spent negotiating strategic arms control during the SALT period. Although the results have not been overly impressive, several agreements related to the control of nuclear weapons were reached. These included two SALT agreements signed by Richard Nixon and Leonid Brezhnev in May 1972. The first involved a five-year interim offensive arms agreement that froze United States and Soviet ICBM and SLBM levels as of July 1972. The second and more significant was an Anti-Ballistic Missile Treaty that limited each side to two ABM sites, one around its capital and the other to protect one ICBM missile site. A year later this agreement was modified so that each side would be allowed to retain only one site located either around its capital or at a missile site. The United States subsequently chose to place its ABM site situated in North Dakota into mothballs, and the Soviet Union has not extended its Galosh ABM system around Moscow to the levels allowed in the revised agreement. The SALT process also produced agreement in 1971 on measures to reduce the danger of accidental nuclear war as well as an agreement on improvements in the hot line between Moscow and Washington, making use of the latest satellite technology. In 1973 the two states also signed an agreement on procedures for preventing nuclear war. The SALT process culminated in 1979 with the signing of the SALT II Treaty, which called for some reduction in nuclear delivery systems, but this treaty was never ratified, having been withdrawn from Senate consideration by President Jimmy Carter following the Soviet incursion into Afghanistan in December 1979.

Defensive Weapons Control

In any arms control negotiation one of the most complex issues is that of which weapons should be covered. Such was certainly true of the strategic arms talk. Of particular concern in the early phases of the SALT negotiations was the issue of offensive vs. defensive weapons. The linkage between the two is a very real one affecting the stability of the nuclear deterrent itself. Failure to control the development of the anti-ballistic missile system, for example, might stimulate an offensive missile race in the effort to assure each state of its ability to penetrate the defenses of the other. The threat of the adversary's producing an effective ABM system became the main rationale for developing the MIRV system. By releasing independently targeted missiles a short time before hitting their target, the MIRV would make it far more difficult for any ABM system to intercept incoming missiles. Not only would there be the danger of an offensive arms race, involving both MIRVed and unMIRVed weapons systems, there could be the costly threat of a defensive arms race as well.

Traditionally, the Soviet Union has been more defense-minded than the United States, spending a ratio of about 3 to 1 for defense compared to 1 to 1 for the United States.[16] Such an approach is to be expected for a state that has suffered numerous military invasions in the past, culminating in the loss of some 20 million lives during World War II. The United States, on the other hand, has never been subject to such an invasion. Despite preoccupation with defense, the Soviet Union became concerned about the ABM developments of the United States and the possible neutralization of its own offensive capability. Gradually the Soviet Union began to revise its position, which held that the ABM was an instrument of peace since its purpose was defensive, not offensive. By the time the SALT talks had begun, control of the ABM had become a Soviet priority.

It was not until the second round of SALT I, which began in Vienna in March 1970, that the United States presented its first ABM proposals. It offered the Soviet Union the option of either zero ABMs or one site to protect the national command authorities (NCA) in Moscow and Washington. In making this proposal, the United States was hopeful of inducing the Soviet Union to accept various alternative offensive arms limits that were made at the same time. Not only did the alternative ABM proposals fail to provide a sufficient incentive for the Soviet Union to agree to offensive weapons control, but the Soviet Union also selected the least desirable ABM option, from the American perspective, when it quickly accepted the national command authorities proposal over the zero option. Whereas NCA would have satisfied U.S. Defense Department interests in continuing research and development efforts on the ABM, it was soon recognized that it would be difficult politically for Congress and the administration to build an ABM site limited to Washington. Such might be perceived in the American hinterland as a selfish effort on the part of the politicians to save their own skins while caring little about the rest of the country. As a result, the United States began to back away from its own proposals by asking for an imbalance in ABM sites favoring itself. Kissinger sought to deflect the embarrassment of the United States' rejecting its own proposals after they had been accepted by the Soviet Union by joking that the Soviets had simply chosen the wrong option and would have to choose again. Subsequently, the

United States retreated from the zero option when it proposed in March 1971 that the United States be given four ABM sites around various missile fields while allowing the Soviet Union to retain only its Galosh system around Moscow. Later, the United States proposed a 3 to 1 then a 2 to 1 ratio favoring itself before agreeing in March 1972 to two ABM sites each. The last proposal, however, was made conditional upon Soviet acceptance of limits on submarine-launched ballistic missiles. Although the Soviet Union agreed to an SLBM freeze in April, it refused to accept U.S. proposals for a special clause in the ABM Treaty that would allow withdrawal if a more complete offensive weapons limitation agreement was not reached within five years.[17] Ultimately, the United States had to be content with a unilateral threat of withdrawal if progress was not made on strategic arms limitations. The ABM Treaty in article XI required only that active negotiations be continued on the subject.

The final treaty signed between Nixon and Brezhnev on May 26, 1972, met the Soviet objective of equality and more importantly, from the Soviet perspective, it required that one site must be around the capital; both could not be used to protect missiles as the United States preferred. Although research and development on the ABM could continue under the treaty, each party agreed not to develop, test, or deploy ABM systems or components that were sea-based, space-based, or mobile land-based. The ABM Treaty also prohibited MIRVed and rapid reload ABM capabilities and, according to Agreed Statement D appended to the treaty, future exotic ABM systems were to be subject to discussion and possible amendment.

Offensive Weapons Control

Soviet views on the control of offensive weapons fluctuated considerably during the SALT negotiations. They had rejected out of hand American proposals made in the mid-sixties for a nuclear weapons freeze since a freeze at that time would have placed them in a position of permanent inferiority. As the seventies approached, the strategic weapons gap was beginning to close. Whereas its growing offensive nuclear weapons capabilities encouraged the Soviet Union to think more seriously about strategic arms control and particularly about the possibilities of a freeze, the fact that the United States was not adding to its ICBM stockpiles after reaching the number of 1054 such vehicles in 1967 meant that the U.S. had limited leverage in inducing the Soviet Union to accept an offensive weapons agreement. The United States hoped that Soviet interest in an ABM agreement would be a sufficient inducement for the

Soviet Union to accept an offensive weapons agreement; and, as a result, the United States throughout SALT I rejected the Soviet preference for an ABM Treaty only.

Despite the stabilization of U.S. missile numbers, the offensive arms race continued. The United States conducted its first MIRV tests in August 1968. Since MIRV was the only ongoing American offensive missile system in the early days of SALT, it would have been necessary to place that system on the negotiating table if any progress toward arms control was to be achieved. The United States was reluctant to do so; and when it finally introduced the possibility of MIRV controls, President Nixon insisted that any agreement on the issue must include on-site inspection—a requirement that would guarantee that the proposal would be rejected. Also, the Soviets were not interested in pressing the MIRV issue since it was not until 1973 that they tested their first MIRV vehicles, some five years after the United States. Soviet reticence to deal with this issue is reminiscent of their abrupt rejection of the Baruch Plan at a time in which they did not have the atomic bomb.

Forward-Based Systems

Controversy also revolved around the issue of what constitutes a strategic weapon. The United States regards its triad of weapons—the ICBM, SLBM, and long-range bombers—as strategic weapons. Shorter-range missiles and bombers stationed overseas are not considered part of the strategic capability of the United States even though many such weapons are capable of delivering nuclear warheads to Soviet territory. While the nuclear forces of the United Kingdom and France, which are not inconsiderable, were viewed by the Soviets as a strategic threat to their territory, such weapons have not been calculated as part of the U.S.-Soviet strategic balance. The Soviets, throughout SALT raised the issue of these forward-based systems, demanding their abolition or some compensation in terms of being allowed additional strategic weapons.

Proposals to ban forward-based systems go back to Soviet suggestions for banning all foreign bases. Since the Soviets had few such bases and, until Cuba, none in close proximity to U.S. territory, the United States had little incentive for accepting such proposals. As the range of delivery systems increased with the development of the ICBM, foreign bases became less important to American defense, leading the United States by the mid-sixties to remove its intermediate-range missiles (Thor and Jupiter) from Western European territory. Nevertheless, in an effort to show support for Europe, thousands of U.S. nuclear warheads remain in Europe, some of which could be used on strategic missions.

The United States persisted in its efforts to keep forward-based systems out of the SALT talks. The Soviets were just as insistent that they be included. Occasionally, the latter would hint at compromise on the issue if there was adequate compensation. In August 1970, for example, the Soviet Union proposed that it be allowed higher ceilings of ICBMs and SLBMs than the United States. By the following May, the Soviets had tacitly dropped the FBS issue when they agreed to support an interim offensive missile freeze plus an ABM Treaty. At the same time, they issued a warning against possible increases in British and French nuclear forces. In a unilateral statement made at the signing of the Interim Offensive Arms Agreement in May 1972, the Soviets indicated that if the United States, the United Kingdom, and France collectively exceeded the freeze levels on submarines and SLBMs, the Soviet Union would increase its own numerical limits.

During the SALT II talks the Soviet Union in July 1973 requested additional missile launchers to compensate not only for FBS but also for the Chinese nuclear threat, which the Soviets perceived to be primarily directed toward them. Two months later they were asking for the withdrawal of all nuclear forces from abroad. This demand would have affected thousands of nuclear warheads for the United States while having little or no effect upon the Soviet capabilities. In February 1974 the Soviet Union hinted that it might drop its insistence on counting FBS when and if all other issues are resolved. At the November 1974 Vladivostok meetings, during which agreement was reached on equal aggregates of 2,400 strategic delivery systems, the Soviet Union officially dropped its insistence upon including FBS in the strategic calculation. Less than two months later it was again asking some compensation for FBS. Although no action was taken on FBS in the SALT II Treaty, the United States and the Soviet Union signed a joint statement of principles that would allow either party in subsequent negotiations to raise any issue related to the further limitation of strategic arms. For the Soviet Union this meant forward-based sytems.

The Issue of Equivalence

A second major factor complicating negotiations on the control of strategic weapons has been that of determining the equivalence of weapons systems. The offensive force structures of the two sides are substantially different, influenced as they are by differing geopolitical requirements and disparities in weapons technology. Since the force structures of the two sides are highly asymmetrical, it is virtually impossible to obtain agreement upon comparable reductions in a given weapons system. For example, the Soviet Union has 70 percent of its strategic capability in the form of land-based ICBMs compared to 30 percent for the United States. Efforts to establish numerically comparable levels of missiles are impossible to achieve in a given category. The solution in SALT I was simply to freeze missile launchers at 1972 levels, giving the United States a total of 1,710 strategic missiles compared to the Soviet's 2,350.

The United States could justify its acceptance of lower levels of missiles by virtue of the fact that its ICBMs and SLBMs were more accurate. Under the 1972 Interim Agreement, the United States would be able to MIRV each missile, effectively increasing the number of strategically deliverable nuclear warheads severalfold. Soviet ability to catch up was limited, because it had not even tested the MIRV when the Interim Agreement was signed in 1972 while the United States had begun MIRV deployment two years earlier. Although the Soviet Union would eventually be able to emulate the United States as it has done on every other weapons system, the five-year period for the Interim Agreement was viewed as sufficient time for negotiating a follow-on comprehensive offensive weapons agreement to deal with the inequalities. Other factors such as the superior number of American long-range bombers, the existence of British and French nuclear capabilities, and U.S. forward-based systems meant that the imbalanced missile freeze was not necessarily to the disadvantage of the United States. In addition, the United States had not planned to add to its number of missiles during the five-year period anyway. Nevertheless, the Interim Agreement, limited as it was to strategic missiles, gave the appearance of providing the Soviet Union a strategic advantage over the United States. This alleged inequality led Senator Henry Jackson in the fall of 1972 to press through an amendment that required that any future agreements on strategic arms must be based upon equivalence. Asserting such a principle is far simpler than determining at what level of arms such equivalence is achieved.

During SALT II the formula developed for providing the appearance of equivalence was based on the notion of equal aggregates. Under this scheme a state could retain, within a range, its own preferred mix of ICBMs, SLBMs, and long-range bombers, each of which would count as one unit. At the Vladivostok summit meeting between Brezhnev and Ford in 1974, an overall aggregate of 2,400 vehicles was accepted by both parties. Ultimately this was to be reduced in the 1979 SALT II

Treaty to 2,250 each. SALT II also provided a sublimit of 1,200 MIRVed missile launchers of which 820 could be ICBMs. In addition, 120 heavy bombers could be loaded with air-launched cruise missiles, providing a total of 1,320 multi-warhead delivery vehicles.

While the concept of equal aggregates was an ingenious solution for dealing with diverse weapons systems, determining equivalence remains difficult at best. The meaningfulness of equal numbers is affected by the probable survivability of the various systems. In this regard, the United States has the advantage with its greater emphasis upon SLBMs rather than the more vulnerable land-based ICBMs. Its superior bomber force is also less vulnerable than the ICBM, which constitutes the bulk of Soviet strategic forces, since some bombers can be kept in the air all the time or can be in the air within minutes in case of a real or imagined attack.

Comparing relative numbers of SLBMs also may not provide an accurate assessment of relative strength, for the United States is able to have far more submarines on active duty at any one time. Because of the lack of overseas bases, it has been estimated that customarily the Soviet Union has only 11 percent of its SLBMs at sea in contrast to 50 percent for the United States.[18]

Other complications in ascertaining strategic equivalence relate to the performance capabilities of the weapons themselves. The Soviet Union has alway emphasized missiles capable of carrying heavier payloads. On the other hand, Soviet missiles have generally been less accurate and their nuclear warheads less compact than those of the United States. With the greater payload capability, the Soviet Union with its SS-18 is able to deliver nuclear warheads up to 25 megatons in size compared to about 5 megatons for the United States' largest missile. There was even some concern that the SS-18 might be able to carry as many as 30 MIRVed warheads, each with almost as much explosive power as the warheads placed on the U.S. Minuteman III, which has been fitted with only three MIRVs. The end result is a huge imbalance in missile throw-weight capability between the United States and the Soviet Union. One estimate provided by the Congressional Research Service in 1982 placed U.S. ICBM throw-weight at 2,220,330 pounds compared to 9,954,100 pounds for the Soviet Union.[19]

Despite the imbalance in nuclear missile throw-weight, the United States has had the advantage in terms of numbers of warheads. When the SALT II Treaty was signed in 1979 the United States had an estimated 9,200 strategic nuclear warheads compared to 5,000 for the Soviet Union.[20] This advantage was due not only to rapid progress in U.S.

MIRVing activities but also to the higher payload capability of bombers that constitute a substantially higher proportion of the U.S. nuclear deterrent system.

The air-launched cruise missile (ALCM) limits in the SALT II Treaty would also seem to provide advantages to the United States, whose technology in this area is superior to that of the Soviet Union. Whereas the SALT II Treaty limited MIRVing to fourteen warheads on SLBMs and ten on ICBMs, the treaty allows an average of twenty-eight cruise missiles on each bomber. Although the United States agreed to place no more than twenty cruise missiles on each B-52, which was designed to carry the cruise missile initially, similar limits will not apply to deployments of cruise missiles on other heavy bombers as long as the average limit of twenty-eight is not exceeded. SALT II left open the option of sea- and ground-launched cruise missiles, at least after the initial three-year term of the protocol, which would have expired December 31, 1981, had the treaty been ratified.

As one grapples with the issue of equivalence, the question arises as to whether or not it makes much difference what the precise numbers are given the huge nuclear weapons arsenals available to each side. Since both sides have overkill capabilities does it make any difference whether one has the capability of killing everyone once or dozens of times? The fact of the matter is that only about two hundred sites in the Soviet Union are useful targets for nuclear weapons. A single Trident submarine carries enough nuclear warheads to destroy virtually all of those targets. This is not to say that some redundancy in weapons systems is not desirable, nor does it mean that there are no psychological or political advantages to having superior numbers of weapons, particularly as related to less sophisticated publics and political leaders. But in an age of overwhelming overkill one has to question any drive toward nuclear superiority, as did Henry A. Kissinger on July 3, 1974, when he asked rhetorically: " . . . what in the name of God is strategic superiority? What is the significance of it politically, militarily, operationally at these levels of numbers? What do you do with it?"[21]

Qualitative vs. Quantitative Limits

Perhaps the most important restraint that could be placed upon strategic weapons is that of limiting qualitative developments. Yet placing restrictions upon technological development is difficult not only because of the problems involved in verifying research and development but also because once a given weapons system is identifiable to outside observers, too many vested interests have come into existence, making a change in course difficult. There is also the concern of any state to be on the cutting edge of technology combined with a general unwillingness to accept technological constraints, particularly out of fear that the other side will not live up to similar obligations. Nevertheless, if qualitative controls are to be effective, they almost of necessity must be in place before a weapons system is fully tested.

No state is likely to produce or to rely upon weapons that have not been adequately tested. According to former Secretary of Defense Harold Brown, the number of tests required before a weapon can be considered reliable ranges between twenty and thirty.[22] Restrictions upon testing can therefore provide one of the best means for impeding technological development. Unfortunately, the point in which a test ban might have slowed strategic weapons development significantly has long passed as more and more sophisticated strategic weapons have entered the arsenals of the superpowers. The missile age might have been forestalled had restrictions been placed upon missile testing during the 1950s. The MIRV might have been stopped had the United States and the Soviet Union agreed to forego MIRV testing during the late sixties and early seventies. A number of experts were urging that the United States postpone its MIRV tests to determine whether a ban on such testing might be negotiable, but the Nixon administration chose to push ahead with the testing and production of the MIRV as a bargaining chip. The vulnerability that the United States feels at present with respect to the survivability of its ICBMs is related in no small measure to the fact that testing has been allowed to continue to the point that the Soviet Union now has ICBMs capable of hitting within a few hundred feet of target.

Despite the difficulties involved, there was some effort during the SALT negotiations to place qualitative constraints upon the development of weapons systems. The Interim Offensive Arms Agreement attempted to place certain limitations upon the modernization of ICBMs by disallowing "significantly increased" silo measurements. An agreed interpretation at the time placed these limits at 10–15 percent, limits believed to provide an adequate restraint upon substantial increases in missile size. With such restrictions on silo size, the U.S. negotiators hardly expected that the Soviet Union would be able to increase the volume of a missile by 50 percent as the Soviets did when they replaced the SS-11 with the SS-19. Such a fete was accomplished by more efficient use of silo space and better missile propellant. At the same time, Secretary of State Henry A. Kissinger was quick to point out that the current size of U.S. missile silos would allow the United States to emplace heavy missiles in existing silos and thus to move toward equality of throw-weight if it chose to do so.[23]

The Interim Agreement did not place any limit on the size of SLBMs or the size of the submarines carrying them. The United States was interested in producing the Trident submarine system, which would considerably increase the size and capability of both SLBMs and submarines. Since the agreement did not include restrictions on bombers, research and development, or the MIRVing of missiles, the United States would still be able to increase its offensive capability considerably.

The Anti-Ballistic Missile Treaty similarly pays more attention to quantitative restrictions than to qualitative ones. Research and development of ABM systems based upon new technologies such as lasers are not prohibited by the treaty. At most, the parties are only expected to discuss possible limitations upon future exotic ABM systems that might be developed.

The SALT II Treaty included some important limitations upon qualitative improvements not found in the Interim Agreement, which permitted almost unlimited modernization of missile forces. SALT II, prior to its expiration in 1985, would have permitted only one new ICBM missile system each for the United States and the Soviet Union. Limits were also placed upon how many reentry vehicles (RVs) could be emplaced upon each missile, allowing SLBMs to have up to fourteen independently targeted nuclear warheads and the ICBM to have as many as ten, the number designated for the MX missile. Such a restriction was viewed by many to represent a victory for the United States, particularly since it was believed that the giant Soviet SS-18 might be able to carry as many as thirty or so RVs.

The SALT II Treaty did little to limit the testing of weapons systems. Although the United States favored restrictions upon the number of missile tests that could be conducted, the final treaty required only that advance notice be given of certain tests. Additional restrictions were placed upon the testing of sea- and ground-based cruise missiles as well as mobile ICBMs only during the period covered by the protocol. Even had SALT II been ratified, it would not have impeded qualitative developments in those areas although some opponents of the treaty, interested in keeping all cruise and mobile missile options open, were fearful that the protocol provisions might be extended.

SALT II did provide an outright ban upon two weapons systems— fractional-orbital ballistic missiles (FOBs) and the emplacement of missiles on surface ships. The United States was particularly concerned about the Soviet development of a missile that would allow the Soviet Union to place a nuclear warhead into partial orbit (thereby not violating the 1967 Outer Space Treaty) and then direct the warhead to a U.S. target. Such a device would enable the Soviet Union to send a nuclear device the long way around the earth, striking the United States from the south. The Soviet Union, on the other hand, appeared the more anxious to restrict missiles from surface ships because of Soviet comparative weaknesses in that area.

Although efforts had been made to restrict the range of air-launched cruise missiles during the SALT II negotiations, the Soviet Union ultimately agreed not to impose any limits upon their range as Foreign Minister Gromyko conceded that the United States could send them around the earth if it wished. On the other hand, there was great concern about the range of the Soviet Backfire bomber, which some felt had intercontinental range and therefore should be included in the SALT limits. Although it was generally accepted that the Backfire could fly one-way suicidal missions against the United States, a return flight would require refueling in the air. Despite many reservations, the Backfire bomber was excluded from the SALT ceilings. The Soviet Union in a separate letter from Brezhnev indicated that it would not increase the capabilities of Backfire nor would it increase the production rates of the bomber beyond the current thirty per year.

The SALT process has done little to restrict the quantitative arms race, particularly since the MIRVing process allowed the superpowers to increase substantially the number of strategically deliverable nuclear warheads. In terms of numbers of missiles, the Interim Agreement was successful in establishing a freeze on the number of missile launchers, and the SALT II Treaty went further by placing limits that, for the first time, would require the reduction of offensive weapons systems. Under the SALT II ceilings, for example, the Soviet Union would have been required to dismantle a total of 250 missiles.

One of the possible consequences of any effort to establish quantitative limits on weapons systems is that such limits might only stimulate a qualitative arms race—the kind of arms buildup which the United States has generally emphasized. The Soviet Union, on the other hand, traditionally has concentrated upon increasing its quantity of arms to make up for the lack of technological equality. Older weapons frequently have not been retired as new ones come on line, leaving the Soviet Union with many antiquated, less effective liquid-fuelled missiles. The SALT I agreements by allowing modernization of existing weapons forced dismantlement of the old weapon as each new unit came on line. Such a change in the direction of the arms race may not be entirely beneficial, for qualitative arms races are generally more expensive than quantitative ones. Qualitative arms races may also be more destablizing because of the fear that the other side might achieve a major scientific breakthrough which could undermine the deterrent threat.

Verification

Perhaps no issue has impeded progress toward strategic arms control more than that of concern about verification. In a world filled with suspicion how can anyone trust the other side to live up to its end of the bargain? The problem of verification was highlighted during the 1930s when Nazi Germany proved itself effective in evading the arms control limitations established by the victorious powers in the Versailles treaty. Verification became a central issue during the debate over the Baruch Plan as Bernard Baruch insisted that the veto not be allowed for fear of its being used by the Soviet Union to evade the inspection and control provision of the plan.

Generally speaking, it has been the United States which has been the most preoccupied with the effectiveness of inspection and verification procedures. In the 1950s this concern was often phrased in terms of the need to establish foolproof inspection systems to guarantee that the other side not cheat. The Soviet Union, on the other hand, has been highly sensitive to the possibility that verification procedures would interfere with its closed system by allowing alien ideas to penetrate Soviet society. Soviet leaders believed that Western disarmament plans amounted to little more than an effort to penetrate Soviet territorial sovereignty, having minimal effect upon reducing armament levels. Such concern may well have been justified in the midfifties when the United States proposed its "open skies" scheme, which the Soviet Union regarded as intrusive inspection without corresponding arms reduction.

The Soviet Union, having earlier presented proposals that precluded any inspection, accepted the notion of establishing ground control posts on Soviet and American territory in May 1955 and four months later agreed to aerial inspection in the final stage of disarmament. Soviet officials were reported in 1974 to have been willing to consider on-site inspection for monitoring a proposed chemical weapons treaty, allowing inspectors to visit predetermined locations to ascertain treaty compliance.[24] The first U.S.-Soviet arms treaty providing on-site inspection is the 1976 Peaceful Nuclear Explosions Treaty. This treaty, along with its companion Threshold Test Ban Treaty, has yet to be ratified by the

United States, and the Reagan administration has indicated that it will not support ratification until verification procedures are strengthened in the two treaties. The Soviet Union, on the whole, has been more willing to accept elaborate verification procedures whenever more extensive reductions have been involved. Soviet general and complete disarmament proposals generally included provisions for on-site inspection, ground control posts, and aerial inspection.

At the same time that a rapidly changing technological environment has complicated the control of strategic weapons, that same technology has begun to provide instruments capable of detecting possible arms control violations from outside the country. Photography from satellites is now able to identify something as small as a basketball from hundreds of miles in the air. Satellite electronic devices can detect huge metallic objects like missiles that are placed underground. Supplemented with other sophisticated monitoring devices utilizing ground radar posts and aerial flights near the border, a state is able not only to identify every missile launcher that the other side possesses but to go a long way in ascertaining many of the missile's qualitative characteristics as well.

The techniques used to monitor an arms control agreement that do not intrude upon the territory of another state have come to be referred to as national technical means (NTM). A critical turning point in SALT I occurred when the CIA certified the ability of national technical means to verify the arms control restrictions under negotiation. In June 1973, the United States went a step further by accepting the notion that even the qualitative limits under consideration in SALT II would be verified only by national technical means. For its part, the Soviet Union in both SALT I and II agreed not to interfere with NTM, which in effect has established the concept of "open skies" to a degree that could not have been envisioned when these proposals were first advanced in the midfifties.

The most difficult stage in the weapons cycle to inspect is that of research and development; and, for this reason, few arms control agreements explicitly limit activities in this area. Nowhere in any of the SALT agreements was there an explicit ban on weapons research although the ABM Treaty prohibits the *development* of sea-based, air-based, space-based, and mobile land-based ABM missiles as well as MIRVed ABMs. Article I of the SALT II Treaty provides that the parties "exercise restraint in the development of new types of strategic offensive arms." Weapons explicitly mentioned in the treaty as being prohibited in terms of development include rapid reload launchers, missiles fired from surface ships, and fractional orbital missiles. The testing and deployment of sea and ground-based cruise missiles were to be prohibited only during the protocol phase.

Despite the verification problems involved, detection of a weapons system prior to testing is still possible. Dr. William J. Perry, former undersecretary of defense for research and engineering, indicated on July 18, 1979, that "we monitor the activities of the [Soviet missile] design bureaus and production plants well enough that we have been able to predict every ICBM before it ever began its tests."[25]

As indicated above, detection of testing is one of the easier inspection problems, for ascertaining whether or not a given delivery system was tested apparently can be determined with a high degree of accuracy by national technical means. More difficult are efforts to determine the qualitative capabilities of a given weapons system by observing testing programs. The range of a delivery system, for example, can be purposefully restrained in a test so as not to communicate a weapon's true potential. A particular problem was posed in connection with the SALT II requirement that only air-launched cruise missiles with a range over 600 kilometers are to be counted in the ALCM ceilings. The Soviet decision not to place any limit on the maximum range of the air-launched cruise missile eliminated an equally difficult verification problem but at the cost of doing nothing to restrain a powerful weapons system that is easy to conceal. Additional verification problems may arise with respect to determining whether a cruise missile is ground-, sea-, or air-launched. Also, how does one determine whether the cruise missile is conventionally armed or nuclear armed? The latter would not present such a problem but for the fact that because of the relatively low cost of the cruise missile it would not be an economic absurdity to arm them with conventional weapons. The same cannot be said for most other long-range missiles.

The number of reentry vehicles involved in a given MIRV test may be difficult to determine since feints can be used without releasing a separate missile. What is observable may not be an accurate reflection of the degree of fractionism actually achieved. In order to alleviate U.S. concern on this issue, the Soviet Union agreed in May 1979 to place restrictions on such missile release simulations.

To facilitate the monitoring of testing activities, the ABM Treaty provided that all missile testing be conducted at pre-designated sites, easily observable from outside national boundaries. This principle was carried over into the SALT II Treaty for offensive missile testing. The SALT II Treaty in article XVI also requires that the other side be notified well in advance whenever an ICBM test is to be conducted, except for single ICBM test launches confined to the national territory of the state.

Ground radar stations located outside the country provide the major means for United States' monitoring of Soviet missile tests. Questions were raised about the ability of NTM to do an adequate job of verification following the loss of two U.S. radar monitoring sites as a result of the 1979 Iranian revolution. Although aerial flights close to Soviet borders could provide some of the necessary information, the United States was not reassured on this issue until a similar radar installation was established to monitor Soviet missile-testing programs from Chinese territory. For its part, the Soviet Union relies heavily upon monitoring equipment located on Soviet ships a short distance from the major U.S. testing sites of Cape Canaveral and Vandenberg Air Force Base.

During the SALT II negotiations the United States raised questions concerning the encoding or encrypting of the telemetry in the Soviet missile testing program. Such encoding consisted of efforts to conceal or disguise the electronic signals that were transmitted from the missile to ground stations. But in disguising such signals, which are necessary to determine a missile's performance, the Soviet Union was interfering with the ability of the United States to monitor Soviet missile developments. As long as concern is focused on the quantity of missiles as in SALT I, interference in the telemetry process presented no problem, but since SALT II provides for qualitative limits as well, the United States argued that such a practice interferes with national technical means of inspection. After considerable debate on the issue, the Soviet Union finally agreed to accept a ban on telemetry encryption whenever such encoding would impede verification.

Verifying that states are living up to the quantitative limits of an agreement presents special problems. To deal with one of those problems, the SALT agreements have limited numbers of launchers but not missiles, which are more difficult to verify. The silos in which ICBM launchers are emplaced take some two years to construct, providing ample time to monitor efforts to increase launcher capability. Counting numbers of missiles is more difficult since they may be placed underground or hidden in large buildings located close to existing silos. Because of their huge metallic size, ICBMs are detectable in many, but not all, instances by electronic devices on satellites. Despite possible verification problems, the SALT II Treaty provided that extra missiles may not be stored near launchers since such a practice would introduce the possibility of rapid reload—a particular problem in view of the cold-launch capability of the Soviet Union. This process enables the Soviets to raise the ICBM out of its silo, fire it with minimal damage to the silo, and therefore to use the silo for another launch. The ABM Treaty provided a similar proscription against developing rapid reload capabilities for ABM launchers.

If a launcher is allowed to become mobile, additional verification problems may arise. A conflict is created between the deterrent objective of developing an invulnerable retaliatory capability in which mobility would be a major asset and the arms control objective of adequate verification. This conflict in part explains the meandering position of the United States on the issue of mobile ICBMs. In the SALT I agreements, the United States appended a unilateral statement prohibiting the development of mobile ICBMs, largely because of concern about verifiability. The increasing vulnerability of the ICBM caused the United States subsequently to express more concern about protecting its ICBM capability, making missile mobility a more attractive option.

Verification considerations continued to plague U.S. decisions about a mobile ICBM basing-plan as more than thirty plans have been examined and found wanting for one reason or another. President Carter rejected the proposed multiple aim point (MAP), which would have involved a large shell game. Under this plan MX missiles would be moved from one silo to another so as to keep the Soviet Union uncertain about the exact location. Since silos provide the basis for counting launcher capability, the plan created serious verification problems.

The Carter administration finally decided in favor of a racetrack system making use of 200 MX missiles and 4,600 shelters located in Utah and Nevada. Each missile would move around a track containing 23 shelters, and presumably the Soviet Union would not know exactly in which shelter the MX was located. Verification would be possible since the missiles would be shown in open trenches from time to time.

For its part, the Soviet Union minimized verification problems related to mobile ICBMs when it agreed in SALT II to dispense with its SS-16 mobile ICBM. The West was concerned not only with the problems involved in counting the number of SS-16s in Soviet arsenals but also with the prospect that the Soviet Union might convert the intermediate-range mobile SS-20 into an intercontinental-range SS-16. The conversion requires only an addition of a third stage rocket since the SS-20 already provides the necessary first two stages.

Since the great strength of submarines is that they are highly mobile, it might seem that these weapons systems would create the most serious verification problems, but submarines must come to port from time to time. If the invulnerable retaliatory capability necessary for an effective deterrent is to be guaranteed, it is important that verification techniques not be so refined that they can spot all nuclear submarines at a given time. Capabilities for counting numbers of submarines and SLBMs positioned on them have generally been viewed as adequate without improving current technology.

A more serious verification problem related to both ICBMs and SLBMs is that of identifying the number of MIRVs positioned on each missile once it is deployed. Since inspection is restricted to national technical means, the main procedure used for verification is that of monitoring MIRV tests. Although the procedure allows a state utilizing national technical means to ascertain the potential MIRV capability of a missile, it does little to distinguish between a missile that is actually deployed in a MIRV mode and one which is not. An important breakthrough was made when the Soviet Union agreed to count any missile that has been tested with multiple independently targeted warheads against the 1,200 MIRV limit in SALT II even if the missile is deployed with a single warhead missile as was planned by the Soviets.

Although the Nixon administration linked on-site inspection to any acceptance of a MIRV ban, it is by no means clear that such inspection would solve the verification problem once the missiles are deployed. In a press briefing on December 3, 1974, Secretary of State Henry A. Kissinger noted that "you couldn't inspect every missile every day. With the time delays that would be involved until you get to the site, they could easily take off the MIRV warhead and put on a single warhead, have a MIRV storage, and when you leave put the MIRV back on the missile."[26]

As an aid to identifying SLBMs and ICBMs that have been MIRVed, SALT II required that externally observable design features be provided. A similar requirement was made with respect to the heavy bombers that will be carrying cruise missiles. In the parlance of arms control such efforts have been referred to as providing functionally related observable differences or FRODs.

As part of the verification procedure, SALT I established a bilateral Standing Consultive Commission (SCC) to deal with alleged treaty violations. The SCC has considered a number of allegations from both the Soviet Union and the United States, all of which until recently were satisfactorily resolved. According to a 1982 estimate, thirty-four complaints on the SALT I regime were made by both sides and all were settled "by the cessation of the objectionable activity or a satisfactory explanation of it."[27] For example, in the summer of 1973 the United States accused the Soviet Union of illegally constructing new silos which the Soviets argued were designed for command and control functions, not missile launchers. After discussion in the SCC, the United

States accepted the Soviet explanation. Subsequent accusations of Soviet testing of anti-aircraft radars in what might be considered an ABM mode in violation of the ABM Treaty led the Soviet Union to desist from the practice. The Soviet Union in March 1976 acknowledged a technical violation in its schedule for dismantling some fifty-one obsolete missiles as new weapons came on line. It was indicated that the delay was related to inclement weather, and the Soviet Union soon corrected the problem.

For its part, the Soviet Union accused the United States of interfering with NTM when the latter placed covers over missile silos under construction to protect workers from severe winter weather in Montana. After hearings before the SCC, the United States changed the practice. Other allegations were made with respect to U.S. radar programs and the status of Atlas and Titan ICBM launchers. Satisfactory explanations were provided in each instance.

The necessity for reliable verification increases with more extensive arms reductions. When armaments are reduced to a low level, the ability of a state to evade the provisions of a treaty can be more critical in upsetting the arms balance. Since the SALT agreements have been little more than cosmetic, the inability to detect minor violations will have little impact upon national security; remaining arsenals will continue to provide a sufficient deterrent.

Evaluating verification requirements should be related to the probabilities that a state will attempt to violate a disarmament agreement. Presumably the state favored the agreement or it would not have ratified it. Rather than take risks that would provide a legal justification for the other side to abrogate a treaty, a state will be interested in demonstrating compliance. A 100 percent guarantee of detection is unnecessary since a state may well be sufficiently deterred with a 50 percent probability of being caught. When placed in this perspective, the estimated 80 percent reliability in detecting mobile missiles, one of the more difficult inspection problems, becomes much more acceptable.[28]

WAS SALT WORTH ITS SALT?

Considerable optimism greeted the successful conclusion of SALT I in May 1972, as U.S. government officials suggested savings in strategic defense spending of $5 to $15 billion over the next five years. On July 9, 1979, Secretary of Defense Harold Brown told the Senate Committee on Foreign Relations that the just signed SALT II Treaty would save as much as $30 billion over the next decade.[29] Despite such optimistic assessments, the strategic arms budgets in the United States and the Soviet Union have risen considerably above levels established before the opening of the SALT Talks with the number of strategic nuclear weapons more than quadrupling since 1969. Even had SALT II been ratified, Secretary Brown's assessment may have been overly optimistic, for defense spending was beginning to rise even before the treaty was signed.

In reviewing what has been achieved in a decade of Strategic Arms Limitation Talks, there is reason to be pessimistic. Agreements reached both within and outside SALT have had little, if any, impact on the reduction of armaments. For example, the SALT I agreements contained no provisions for reducing existing weapon systems. Nor was there much constraint upon qualitative improvements as both sides were allowed to modernize and MIRV their missiles. Admittedly, the Anti-Ballistic Missile Treaty nipped in the bud what might have become a very costly ABM race, but whether such a race would have occurred, given the increasing skepticism about the effectiveness of such a system, is highly debatable. American scientific opinion was overwhelmingly united during the seventies in opposition to anti-ballistic missile systems, recognizing that there were just too many ways of countering any ABM system through such devices as MIRVs, decoy missiles, and penetration aids.

In order to evaluate the utility of partial measures such as those reached at SALT, one needs to examine the cost of reaching such agreements. These costs have included the concessions that have been necessary to placate domestic interests, the price paid for ''bargaining chips'' that have not been cashed, and the suspicion and distrust that have arisen owing to concern over treaty evasions.

Because it has sometimes been more difficult to work out a compromise with various interests within the United States and the Soviet Union than between the two governments, certain agreements have, in fact, accelerated the arms race. This was true in the case of the Limited Test Ban Treaty of 1963 and the Threshold Nuclear Test Ban Treaty signed in 1974 by the United States and the Soviet Union. In both instances, military interests asked for and received an accelerated nuclear-testing program compatible with the respective treaties.

Similar trade-offs to domestic forces have been apparent at several stages during the SALT talks. According to one reporter, the Joint Chiefs of Staff were reticent about even approving the negotiations as such unless the Nixon administration would support the deployment of MIRV.[30] John Newhouse, in his comprehensive chronicle of the SALT I negotiations, has indicated that the acceleration of the Trident program was Kissinger's quid pro quo to the Joint Chiefs for supporting the Soviet edge in missile capability provided in SALT I.[31]

The political cost to future agreements inherent in efforts to sell the SALT agreements to the U.S. Congress should also not be overlooked. Interest in obtaining Senate support for SALT I led the Nixon administration to support the Jackson amendment, which called for equality of arms levels in any future agreements. On the surface, such expectations would appear to be well taken; but, in the case of negotiations for strategic arms limitation, the amendment has made negotiation difficult because of disagreement on what constitutes essential equivalence, as noted above.

It would seem that the SALT agreements have actually worked to the advantage of certain groups involved in weapons procurement. The Interim Offensive Arms Agreement in particular may have benefited military interests. It gave the appearance of inequality, allowing those in favor of increased spending to exploit the issue. Since the public often does not understand the advantages that a state has in a number of other military areas to offset such inequalities, it tends to be susceptible to arguments for increasing armaments in areas not limited by treaty.

Concessions to generate support for the SALT II Treaty can also be found during the Carter period. The *New York Times* reported, for example, that the White House agreed to press for improved air defenses and a new medium-range bomber in an effort to induce the Joint Chiefs of Staff to accept the exclusion of the Soviet Backfire bomber from the treaty.[32] President Carter, perhaps motivated by the uphill battle to get Senate approval for the SALT II Treaty, made numerous concessions in 1979 to those favoring a stronger military establishment. These included agreement to increase the defense budget by $13 billion, the decision to go ahead both with MX and a longer-range Trident missile, the acceptance of a mobile basing system for MX, a stepped up civil defense program, and a draft registration. In addition, Carter decided to position intermediate-range ballistic and cruise missiles in Europe and to fire Paul Warnke as SALT negotiator and head of the Arms Control and Disarmament Agency, replacing him with the more conservative Lt. General George M. Seignious. It is important to remember that all of these moves were taken prior to the Soviet incursion into Afghanistan in December, leading President Carter to declare that he had misjudged Soviet intentions. It was after the Soviet invasion that the president asked that the SALT II Treaty be shelved although it was not clear at the time whether the treaty would have achieved the required two-thirds Senate vote approving ratification.

If these arguments for supporting arms control negotiations are not sufficiently persuasive to influence the military conservative, one need only look at yet another advantage provided by such negotiations—they can be, and have been, used to justify the production of "bargaining chips," in the form of new weapon systems. The production of such chips creates pressures for the other side to develop its own bargaining chips, and the stimulation of an arms race rather than arms reduction is the inevitable outcome.

Throughout the SALT talks there was a constant search for a bargaining chip to enable one side or the other to prevail. The ABM became the first of many such chips as the Johnson administration, in its waning days, proposed to make the Sentinel ABM system a bargaining chip for the upcoming SALT negotiations. Earlier arguments for the system as a protection against a possible nuclear strike from China, as a device for countering an accidental missile launching, and as a protection against a first strike, had all been found wanting. The Nixon administration also used the bargaining chip argument in trying to sell its Safeguard ABM system. The U.S. SALT negotiator, Gerard Smith, went so far as to send an urgent telegram to members of the Senate in August 1970 suggesting that a vote in favor of limiting the Safeguard system to two sites, instead of the twelve proposed, would be detrimental to the outcome of SALT.[33] Without such an intervention, the restriction on Safeguard quite likely would have passed. As it was, the proposal failed by five votes.

The Nixon administration also sought to justify the MIRV system as a hedge against the Soviet ABM. MIRV was to have made it clear to the Soviet Union that it would never be able to provide an effective defense against a United States retaliatory strike. There was no discussion of stopping MIRV developments once agreement on the ABM was reached and, as indicated above, MIRVing continued at a rapid pace.

Perhaps the best illustration of how a military bargaining chip can force the development of unneeded weapons and, in turn, impede the prospects of arms control, is found in the development of the cruise missile. According to John W. Finney, it was Secretary of State Henry Kissinger who proposed that the Pentagon undertake development of long-range cruise missiles as a bargaining chip for the SALT II negotiations. Kissinger reportedly lamented in private conversations that he "didn't realize the Pentagon would fall in love with cruise missiles."[34] Similar second thoughts had been expressed by Secretary Kissinger about the MIRV system, which had earlier been sold as a bargaining chip but after production became a serious obstacle to reaching agreement because of the inspection problems it created. Kissinger is reported to have said that he wished he "had thought through the implications of the MIRVed world more fully in 1968–70."[35] The best time to stop an arms race involving any weapon system is before work begins on the weapon—at a time before vested interests become committed and before deployment complicates inspection.

Despite the recurring failure to derive any arms control benefits from bargaining chips, both sides have continued to use the bargaining chip argument in support of a number of weapons systems. Such arguments have been made by Pentagon and administration officials with respect to proposals for Trident, the B-1 bomber, NCA defense, the development of an advanced airborne command post, the maneuvering reentry vehicle, MX, the cruise missile, and Pershing II missile.

According to some authorities, the SS-9 represented an effort by the USSR to create its own bargaining chip. Also the rapidity with which the Soviet Union rushed into development of the SS-16 through SS–20 series was suggestive of a desire to increase its bargaining position during SALT II. The same can be said of the scheduling of a series of ICBM tests at the end of May 1972, just as SALT I was signed, and further tests conducted on the eve of the resumption of the SALT talks on February 20, 1974. The Soviet resumption of hunter-killer satellite tests in 1978, following a two-year moratorium, was also reported to have been scheduled to coincide with the SALT talks.

Bargaining chips tend to increase fear on the part of the adversary, and the traditional reaction is one of responding in kind. Soviet leader Yuri V. Andropov warned that if the United States went ahead with the MX, the Soviet Union would be forced to counter it with an analogous missile. He also noted that long-range cruise missiles would be built to meet the threat of U.S. cruise missiles.[36] If either side emphasizes bargaining chips it becomes all the more difficult for the moderates in the other country to plead for realistic arms restraint. Ammunition is merely provided for the more hawkish elements to press for higher defense budgets and to sabotage any effort towards arms reduction.

On the whole, bargaining chips have been costly, but if it could be shown that partial agreements such as those reached in SALT had stimulated more extensive reductions of armaments, they would be worth the price. Unfortunately, this does not seem to have been the case. Instead, the agreements to date have tended to generate increased suspicion and have actually slowed down the momentum toward more significant agreements.

Suspicion about possible evasions of an arms control agreement is likely to be pervasive in a world that is high in threat-perception and heavily armed. Indeed, a state may be trapped by public pressures into retaliating against an adversary's violation (or assumed violation) even if it is not in that state's interest to do so. There is something more compelling about the need to react to perceived increments of weapons controlled by a treaty than to buildups not so regulated. Such suspicion is likely to set back the cause of disarmament further, and even to accelerate the arms race. A number of accusations of alleged Soviet violations of the SALT I agreements have been noted, including assertions that the Soviet Union had tested a type of radar system that could be utilized in an ABM system, that it had replaced smaller ICBMs with missiles above the size-limitations agreed on, and that it had used decoys and camouflage to interfere with United States national technical means of verification. The Soviet Union in turn accused the United States of camouflaging some of its missiles. Ambiguities of this sort, as well as those arising over the unilateral interpretations that were publicized by the United States and the Soviet Union at the time of signing the SALT agreements, are likely to pose further difficulties in the future. Rather than serving as confidence-building measures as some have suggested, verification procedures are just as likely to increase mutual suspicion and distrust. This is certainly the direction that verification issues have taken during the Reagan period as will be pointed out in the next chapter.

WHO GAVE UP WHAT?

The evidence seems clear that during the SALT negotiations both sides made numerous concessions—a prerequisite for successful negotiation. These moves can be evaluated from yet another perspective by examining which side was able to negotiate an agreement more to its liking. Such an assessment requires the comparing of preferences with final outcomes as has been done for the SALT II Treaty in table 4.1.

Since the positions of the United States and the Soviet Union changed over time, the preference shown reflects the position most vigorously pressed by each state before resolution. The preferred position might be viewed as the most favorable one considered realistically possible among a range of alternatives; obviously, in the strict sense, the preferred position would restrict only the weapons of the other side while leaving one's own options open.

In addition to setting forth the preferred positions of the two sides on the various provisions of the SALT II Treaty, the table indicates whose

Table 4.1 Results of SALT II Compared to Preferred Positions

SALT II Provisions	U.S. Preference	Soviet Preference
Equal aggregates (missiles-bombers)	*Equal aggregates (missiles-bombers)	Extend interim levels (bombers excluded)
Ceiling 2,250 (1982)	Ceiling 2,000 or less	Ceiling (2,400–2,500)
1,320 MIRV sublimit (cruise on bomber = one MIRV)	More MIRVs to compensate for Soviet throw-weight	*Proposed as low as 1,100. U.S. basically set 1,320 level
1,200 sublimit on MIRVed missiles	*Low number to allow at least 100 bombers with cruise missiles	Preferred 50 more to limit number of bombers with cruise
820 MIRV sublimit on ICBMs	*U.S. concern to limit MIRVed ICBMs although a lower number would have been preferred	A larger sublimit would be to Soviet advantage
300+ limit on Soviet heavy missiles; U.S. to have none	Limit Soviets to 150 heavy ICBMs; U.S. not interested, in heavy missiles for itself	*Not to reduce 300+ level achieved at SALT I
Limit fractionism of MIRV (10-ICBM; 14-SLBM)	*Limit fractionism to level Soviets already capable of according to U.S.	Claimed fractionism had not proceeded as far as U.S. claimed
If missile tested with MIRV all will be considered MIRVed	*Count if tested with MIRV	Wanted to deploy same ICBM in both single and MIRV mode
Test and deploy one new ICBM	Varied over time. Restrict after own tests and deployment and before those of other	Varied over time. Restrict after own tests and deployment and before those of other
Notify in advance of certain ICBM launches	Limit number of ICBM tests	*No limit to tests proposed
Allow mobile land- and air-launched ICBMs (light variety only)	Unilateral statement opposing in 1972. Reversed 1974–75	Refused to accept ban in 1972; later began to favor ban to stop MX

SALT II Provisions	U.S. Preference	Soviet Preference
Complete ban on SS-16 mobile missile	*Concerned about verification problems and mobile ICBM potential when combined with intermediate range SS-20	Wanted SS-16 for its ICBM potential when combined with SS-20 launchers
Extra missiles not to be stored near launchers	*Concerned about Soviet reload capabilities using same launcher	Appeared not to have raised the issue
Ceiling on throw-weight and launch weight of both heavy and light missiles	*Concerned about qualitative improvements of existing missiles; will impede somewhat	Appeared to be interested in keeping options open
Ban on ballistic missiles (600 + Km) not yet employed (e.g., FOBs and surface ships)	Interested in prohibiting FOBs, which Soviets have developed	Less interested than U.S. in emplacing missiles on ships
Forward-based systems not included in treaty	*Exclude; consider only at SALT II or MBFR	Want included, particularly if low ceilings on delivery systems are established
Statement agreeing not to increase production or capability of Backfire Bomber	Would have liked to have included in ceilings; settled for Soviet statement	*Backfire should be excluded entirely from ceilings
Not to circumvent treaty by providing technology and weapons to allies	No inclusion or compensation to USSR for NATO allies' strategic forces	Include allied strategic weapons in ceilings or compensate USSR
Air-launched cruise missile range not limited	*2,500 + kilometer range desired	ALCM to be limited to 600 kilometers in range

SALT II Provisions	U.S. Preference	Soviet Preference
Average of 28 cruise missiles per bomber	*Variable number: 35 + on some, less on others	Wanted a limit of 20 per bomber
ALCMs of 600 + Km range may be positioned only on heavy bombers	Had been interested in deploying ALCMs on FB-111s (Provision will prevent deployment on Backfire)	Didn't want to see ALCMs positioned on FB-111s
Exchange data regularly on own arsenals	*Wanted Soviets to be more forthcoming on force levels	Tradition of secrecy on military strength force levels
National means of verification	Would have liked to have seen on-site inspection	*Limit to national means of verification
Not to interfere with national means of inspection	*Concerned with evasion issue far more than Soviets	Tends not to admit such action as a possibility
Ban on any telemetry encryption impeding verification	*Highly concerned on this issue; Soviets accept U.S. draft language	Not concerned about establishing controls to prohibit the masking of missile tests
Protocol limits: testing and deployment of mobile ICBMs and ASBMs; ban on deployment of sea and ground based cruise	*Wants to keep option open on all noted systems; since none of activities are scheduled before 1982 restrictions are moot	Less interested in systems than U.S. Will want to extend restrictions if possible
Protocol to expire December 31, 1981	*Wanted specific expiration date (Ranged from Octber 1980-June 1981)	Protocol to expire three years after ratification
Treaty to expire in 1985	*Favored 10-year treaty to expire in 1985	Wanted permanent treaty

*Preference appears to be more compatible with final outcome.

position seemed to prevail in the final outcome. Asterisks indicate whose position was best reflected in the treaty's actual provisions.

Of the twenty-eight provisions, twenty-two are more consonant with the position of one side or the other. In most cases—seventeen of the twenty-two—the provision seems closer to the position of the United States. In six cases, both sides apparently compromised in roughly equal measure or varied their positions so substantially over time that their preferences were not clear.

Obviously, the provisions of the treaty are not equally important; no quantitative measure can provide a definitive picture of which side's concessions were more critical. The structure of the treaty appears to be more in keeping with the positions taken by the United States, despite the fact it refused to ratify SALT II. One objective not achieved was a lower ceiling on Soviet ICBMs to reduce the vulnerability of United States land-based missiles, and the final U.S. decision to accept only national means of verification represented a significant retreat from its original position.

It might be noted that the United States is viewed by some analysts as taking less extreme positions during negotiations than the Soviet Union. As a result, the Soviet Union may only appear to have made more concessions, while in truth it merely gravitated to the more equitable and realistic positions that the United States assumed from the beginning.[37] Such an interpretation is undoubtedly affected by one's own values, and Soviet leaders are likely to see the United States negotiating positions as extreme.

Of course, detractors might well argue that the give-and-take in the SALT negotiations has been largely irrelevant, because the agreements have been little more than cosmetic in their effect, allowing both sides to produce whatever weapons they seriously wanted. No weapons system that the United States has been highly interested in building was prohibited by the SALT II Treaty. Restrictions on land- and sea-based cruise missiles and the mobile MX missile were to be limited to the duration of the protocol, which was scheduled to expire at the end of 1981, thus leaving these options fully open. Although there were restrictions placed on the Soviet Union, including the requirement to dismantle some 250 missiles by 1982, the proscriptions were not severe. Since the Soviet Union has not been as prone to dismantle its missiles when more modern versions come on line, it has a number of relatively obsolete liquid-fueled missiles in its arsenal that it could easily afford to dismantle.

A similar analysis could be made for the SALT I agreements in which perhaps the payoffs to each side were more balanced in terms of preferences. During the talks on the anti-ballistic missile, the Soviet Union achieved its basic objective of limiting the development of the Safeguard ABM system. The United States could rest assured that it would not be forced to enter into a costly ABM race with the Soviet Union—a race that would threaten the stability of the nuclear deterrent system. At the same time options for research and development on the anti-ballistic missile remained open for both parties.

With respect to the Interim Offensive Arms Agreement, the United States was able to obtain a five-year freeze on the number of SLBMs and ICBMs. This freeze was especially important for the United States, which had no plans to add to its number of offensive missile systems during the five-year period. Both sides perhaps lost in the failure to freeze the qualitative arms race. This was particularly unfortunate since it allowed the development of MIRVed weapons, thereby increasing the number of strategically deliverable nuclear warheads severalfold during the course of the SALT negotiations. The period since the signing of SALT I has also witnessed the development of cruise missile technology, which complicates efforts to achieve verifiable arms control.

CONCLUSION

Little progress was made on controlling strategic nuclear weapons during the early postwar disarmament negotiations. As long as the United States had nuclear weapons and the Soviet Union had none, successful negotiation on nuclear arms control was impossible. It was only after the Soviet Union began to approach the United States in terms of strategic capability that serious strategic arms control negotiations became a reality.

The decade of the seventies proved to be the most productive of any in terms of reaching agreements on strategic arms. Among the agreements signed during the decade were the Anti-Ballistic Missile Treaty and the Interim Offensive Arms Agreement during SALT I, the SALT II Treaty, and a number of other agreements dealing with such issues as accidental war, the stationing of weapons on the seabed, and restrictions on biological and environmental warfare.

Despite the achievements, a number of complicating factors interfered with efforts to negotiate more significant limitations on strategic arms. Among these was the problem of what to do about forward-based systems in Europe. These systems were viewed, perhaps justifiably, as strategic weapons by the Soviets, given the ability of such weapons to reach targets within the Soviet Union. Determining which weapons systems were equivalent and how strategic power should be compared between the superpowers also presented difficulties as did concern about whether to establish qualitative and/or quantitative limits on strategic nuclear weapons. Finally, verification has presented a number of problems for arms control as the United States has traditionally been highly concerned about having adequate verification and the Soviet Union, with its more closed society, has feared too much intrusion. By the 1970s the development of verification procedures using satellite technology had progressed to the point that the United States found it possible to accept national technical means of inspection as an adequate verification system. For its part, the Soviet Union agreed not to interfere with national technical means.

Despite the seeming progress made on arms control during the decade, a number of questions remained as to whether the SALT agreements were in fact worth their salt. Rather than slowing the nuclear arms race, strategic arms increased substantially during the decade of SALT. At the same time, the costs of reaching what were essentially cosmetic agreements were exceedingly high as the SALT process added to U.S.-Soviet strategic arsenals as a result of the success achieved in arguing for the creation of military bargaining chips and the tendency to reward conservative domestic groups for their support for arms control by building additional weapons not covered by treaty restrictions. The suspicions aroused over the verification procedures also did little to improve the strategic or political relationship between the United States and the Soviet Union.

The SALT decade ended on an ominous note as the SALT II Treaty was withdrawn from Senate consideration, never to be ratified. In evaluating the SALT II Treaty, the evidence suggests that the United States, for the most part, obtained its generally preferred position more often than did the Soviet Union as seventeen of twenty-two provisions of the treaty were found to be more compatible with the position taken by the Carter administration than those assumed by the Soviet Union.

Among the many lessons about negotiating behavior that can be derived from the SALT experience is, first and foremost, the importance of rough military parity before agreement can be reached. Even then, it is often difficult to agree to anything other than a freeze upon weapons at the point of relative parity. If, as in the case of the United States, no ongoing strategic weapons are being built, expecting to gain anything beyond a freeze is quite unrealistic.

The international climate appears to have affected progress in SALT, showing that progress can be made on arms control when states are willing to make arms control agreements the centerpiece of a policy of détente. Tensions in distant areas can be used as a pretext for slowing progress on arms control as in the case of events taking place in Angola in 1975, in the horn of Africa in 1978, and the Soviet invasion of Afghanistan in 1979.

The negotiations of the seventies proved to be among the most businesslike of the entire postwar period. Part of this was undoubtedly due to the fact that the negotiations were conducted bilaterally and often informally. This reduced the temptation of turning the negotiations into propaganda forums.

Domestically, the decade of the seventies showed a more activist Congress in the field of arms control than previously. On the whole, Congress proved to be more of a restraint on arms control than a facilitator as illustrated by the 1972 Jackson amendment and the opposition to strategic arms control voiced by a strong minority during the Carter era. The decision to withdraw the treaty from Senate consideration probably had as much to do with concern as to whether the necessary two-thirds vote could be achieved as it did with the Soviet invasion of Afghanistan in 1979.

The fact that President Nixon was able to obtain overwhelming congressional support for the SALT I agreements underscores again the advantages that a more conservative president with proven anti-communist credentials has in selling agreements to Congress and the American public. Such credentials, however, may be less suited to the reaching of agreements with the Soviet Union as the case of President Ronald Reagan demonstrates—an issue to which we now turn our attention as we explore arms control negotiations in the 1980s.

5

Arms Control in the Eighties

As suggested in the preceding chapter, the 1970s proved to be one of the most successful decades in the postwar period in terms of the negotiation of a number of arms control agreements. Among these were the SALT I and SALT II treaties as well as agreements dealing with nuclear testing, biological weapons, the emplacement of nuclear weapons on the seabed, and measures designed to reduce the dangers of nuclear war. But the 1980s began on an ominous note with the decision of President Jimmy Carter to shelve the SALT II Treaty on the pretext of the Soviet invasion of Afghanistan in December 1979. The first year of the decade and Carter's last year as president was consequently a bleak year for arms control as several on-going bilateral negotiations on such topics as chemical arms, a comprehensive test ban, conventional arms transfers, and the militarization of the Indian Ocean were disrupted.

With the defeat of President Carter in the November election, a new administration came into power in which not a few of its members, beginning with President Ronald Reagan himself, were extremely hostile to the arms control effort. The general consensus among the president and his close advisors was that the Soviet Union had taken advantage of the arms control process during the seventies to engage in an unprecedented arms buildup. As a result, a "window of vulnerability" had been created as the Soviet Union neared a first strike capability that made the U.S. ICBM retaliatory capability vulnerable. Past arms control efforts were viewed by the new administration as fatally flawed, restricting primarily the U.S. arms efforts but not that of the Soviet Union. Furthermore, the Soviet Union was seen as having violated a number of the arms control agreements previously negotiated.

Believing as it did that the Soviet Union was in a militarily superior position, the Reagan administration felt it was necessary for the United

States to engage in a massive arms buildup before participating in any further arms control negotiations. Failure to do so would place the United States in an inferior bargaining position. As a result, priority was given to a planned $1.6 trillion arms buildup over a five-year period—a target that would more than double U.S. defense spending.

The emphasis upon a substantial arms buildup began to generate concern about the dangers of a revitalized arms race, resulting in a public outcry in favor of arms control. The movement, stimulated as it was by new studies pointing to the dangers of a "nuclear winter" that would destroy much of life as we know it on planet earth, led to demonstrations in favor of arms control throughout the United States. Resolutions in support of a freeze on nuclear weapons obtained considerable support not only on Capitol Hill but also in several state and local referenda on the subject.

Similar pressures favoring arms control negotiations were also mounting in Western Europe, primarily in reaction to the 1979 NATO decision to place U.S. cruise and Pershing II missiles on the territory of several European states. In fact, the ground swell in Europe was so extensive that it threatened to destroy the deployment effort entirely as European parliaments began to have second thoughts about the decision.

About the same time, the Soviet Union undertook a massive propaganda campaign in Western Europe designed to exploit the divisions over the issue among European allies. Several offers were made by the Soviets to freeze further emplacement of intermediate-range nuclear forces in return for restraint on the Western side.

As a result of these various pressures, the United States on November 30, 1981, reluctantly entered into bilateral negotiations with the Soviet Union on the issue of intermediate-range nuclear forces (INF). Progress has been slow with respect to negotiating controls on intermediate-range delivery systems, but the consensus is that prospects for controlling these weapons is brighter than it is for obtaining agreement on strategic arms or strategic defensive systems—subjects that will be discussed after the problems and tortuous course of the INF negotiations are examined.

INTERMEDIATE-RANGE NUCLEAR FORCE LIMITATIONS

Although the United States had been successful in keeping restrictions on intermediate- and short-range delivery systems out of the SALT agreements, the Joint Statement of Principles and Basic Guidelines for Subsequent Negotiations on the Limitation of Strategic Arms, which was signed along with the SALT II Treaty in 1979, provided that in subsequent SALT rounds either state may raise any issue relative to the further limitation of strategic arms. For the Soviet Union this meant the issue of U.S. forward-based systems, which the Soviets argued had strategic potential since such weapons were capable of hitting targets in the Soviet homeland. European states, given their concern about the extensive Soviet INF modernization program, were also placing increasing pressure upon the United States to begin negotiations. In fact, the December 1979 NATO decision to deploy 572 U.S. intermediate-range nuclear missiles on European soil required that a dual-track approach be used in which arms control negotiations would be undertaken in an effort to obtain reciprocal reductions in Soviet INF forces in return for agreement not to deploy the full contingent of 464 cruise and 108 Pershing II missiles. According to the plan, deployment would begin in December 1983 if agreement on restrictions were not reached before then.

Soviet efforts from the beginning have been designed to thwart the 1979 decision to place U.S. intermediate-range nuclear weapons on European soil. Before the two-track decision was even finalized, President Brezhnev in March and again in October and November 1979 warned NATO against deploying such weapons, promising to undertake immediate negotiations on the subject if NATO would refrain from deployment. Threats were made suggesting that deployment would ruin any chance of arms control for intermediate-range nuclear forces. After the NATO Council approved the decision in December, the Soviet Union rebuffed efforts to implement the second track calling for negotiations, saying that it would not negotiate as long as the deployment decision was upheld or the United States had not ratified the SALT II Treaty. By the summer of 1980, the Soviet Union had reconsidered its stance and agreed to enter negotiations without condition. Preliminary discussions were held with the Carter administration in the fall, but these were disrupted by the November elections in the United States that brought a new administration into power. It was over a year later before the Intermediate-range Nuclear Force Talks were begun.

The INF Negotiations

A major reason for the delay was the considerable bureaucratic in-fighting on the issue that occurred within the new Reagan administration. After several months of internal debate, agreement was finally reached on the so-called zero option, which required that both the United States and the Soviet Union eliminate all land-based, intermediate-range nuclear missiles. The obvious problem with such a proposal is that it was totally nonnegotiable. The United States at that time was asking the Soviet Union to destroy about 225 European-based SS-20s, and in return the United States would simply promise not to deploy comparable systems. The zero-option proposal would also have required that the Soviet Union dismantle 75 SS-20s in Asia that were targeted primarily against the Peoples Republic of China.

Adding to the inequity of the proposal from the Soviet perspective was the fact that no restrictions were imposed upon the deployment of cruise missiles on ships and submarines (SLCMs). Even if the United States were to forego its planned 464 ground-launched cruise missiles (GLCMs), unlimited cruise deployment could still proceed, albeit at sea, but potentially within sufficient range of the same Soviet targets. The acceleration of the U.S. production of these weapons during the early eighties did little to reassure the Soviet Union even though the United States was planning to arm a high proportion of the SLCMs with conventional rather than nuclear warheads.

Many military strategists within the United States government wanted not only to include the SS-20 in the proscribed weapons, but to extend the ban to cover Soviet SS-22s on the grounds that forward deployment of these systems, which have a range of less than 1,000 kilometers, threatens West European targets. Pressure from some within the U.S. government, as well as from European governments, resulted in the decision to exclude such systems in the proposed ban, for demanding the destruction of both SS-20s and SS-22s would appear far too one-sided. The inclusion of SS-22s in the ban might also lead the Soviet Union to make similar demands with respect to comparable shorter-range American nuclear systems stationed in Western Europe.[1]

The proposed zero option had the advantage of simplicity and appeared attractive on the surface, giving it considerable propaganda value. At the same time, it had been a proposal advanced earlier by German Chancellor Helmut Schmidt, albeit at a time before the Soviet Union had deployed so many of its SS-20s. By canceling an entire class of weapons, verification would also be considerably simplified. The discovery of a single vehicle would suffice to demonstrate evasion, whereas counting numbers is far more difficult, particularly when mobile systems like the SS-20 are involved.

Despite these advantages, dissatisfaction over the proposal within Western quarters began to increase as a result of the U.S. government's refusal to budge from what some regarded as only an initial bargaining ploy. The State Department, prior to the official tabling of the proposal, had actually favored what was called a zero-plus option in which the United States in its opening move would assert its preferences for zero but also indicate at the outset a willingness to consider a negotiated compromise higher than zero. The State Department was overruled on this issue as the negotiators were instructed to hold firm on the zero-only option. Indeed, the United States officially continued to do just that until President Reagan in March 1983 announced his willingness to accept an interim agreement establishing equal global levels of intermediate-range nuclear forces at the lowest mutually acceptable number.

The opening position taken by the Soviet Union in the INF talks proved to be just as nonnegotiable as that taken by the United States. The Soviet plan called for a 300 ceiling on intermediate-range nuclear missiles and aircraft for each side. The proposed reduction to 300 delivery systems was to be reached by 1990 with an interim stage of 600 in 1985. The problem with this proposal from the United States perspective was that it included not only aircraft and missiles but it would also count British and French nuclear forces in the ceiling. The United States would be allowed to retain less than 40 aircraft since French and British intermediate-range nuclear launchers stood at around 262 at the time. Under the plan the Soviet Union would be able to retain 300 triple-headed SS-20s in Europe as well as an unrestricted number of shorter-range nuclear-armed missiles and aircraft capable of striking targets in Western Europe from sites in Eastern Europe. Comparable shorter-range delivery systems located in Western Europe would be ineffective against the Soviet homeland.

As an alternative to the above proposal, the Soviet Union in the early stages of the negotiations suggested that all intermediate-range and tactical nuclear weapons be eliminated in Europe. This proposal would force all U.S. forward-based nuclear systems out of Europe as well as require the total elimination of French and British nuclear force capabilities. Although the Soviet Union would have to withdraw all of its intermediate-range nuclear missiles from the European part of the Soviet Union, Soviet strategic nuclear systems would remain as the only nuclear forces in Europe. Perhaps recognizing the total nonnegotiability of this proposal, the Soviet Union gave scant attention to the idea in subsequent rounds.

The United States and the Soviet Union disagreed intensely over what the actual European balance of forces was between East and West and exactly which forces should be affected. According to figures provided by the Soviet Union early in the negotiations, the two sides were about equally balanced in terms of intermediate-range nuclear forces with about 1,000 delivery systems on each side even prior to the introduction of the planned 572 Pershing II and cruise missiles. In its count, the Soviet Union included some 250 British and French systems, primarily composed of SLBMs, along with a number of U.S. tactical aircraft unable to reach Soviet territory from Western Europe. Since Soviet calculations sought to include all Western weapons systems capable of delivering nuclear weapons to Soviet territory, American aircraft on all six aircraft carriers in the U.S. Atlantic fleet were counted, despite the fact that only one or two were on patrol in European waters at any point in time. More extreme was the Soviet insistence upon including aircraft located in the United States simply because such aircraft could be transferred to the European theater. At the same time, the Soviet Backfire bombers located in Europe and elsewhere as well as Soviet SS-20s stationed in Asia were not counted. Soviet calculations included the Pershing I missile while exempting their own SS-12s and SS-22s which had comparable ranges. Prior to mid-1981, the Soviet Union was even counting Poseidon ballistic missiles aboard submarines that were assigned to NATO even though these weapons had already been covered by the SALT agreements.

For its part the United States objected strenuously to the inclusion of British and French forces, arguing that none of the latter's forces were committed to NATO. Although some British nuclear capabilities were designated for NATO's use, their primary function was to defend the United Kingdom. The United States also argued that it could not negotiate away the arms of another state. After all, the INF talks were bilateral, just as the Soviet Union had desired. The Soviet Union already enjoyed compensation for British and French nuclear forces, for, under the SALT agreements, it had been allowed to retain its heavy missiles as well as a considerably higher throw-weight capability. In return, the United States was allowed to keep its forward-based systems.

In the autumn of 1981, the United States presented quite a different picture with respect to the balance of intermediate-range nuclear forces between the two superpowers. Instead of equality, administration officials argued that the Soviet Union enjoyed a six to one advantage with some 3,825 weapons compared with 560 for the United States. Included in the U.S. numbers were some 2,700 Soviet fighter-bombers which the United States claimed to be slightly above the range of 1,000 kilometers but which the Soviet Union claimed to be below that threshold. The United States exempted both the Pershing I missile and F-4 Phantom fighters from its list on the grounds that they had a range of less than 1,000 kilometers—the range used to distinguish intermediate-range delivery systems from short-range ones. And so the game of numbers goes on, not so much in terms of disagreement over exactly how many weapons of a given variety each state has, but more over the issue of which systems should be counted as intermediate-range nuclear weapons.

Further complications in evaluating the military balance arose from the perspective of the qualitative aspects of weapons. Although the Soviet Union may have had more aircraft than the West, their quality was not as high. Similarly, the Soviet INF arsenal of SS-4s and SS-5s had become essentially obsolete, based as it was upon old liquid-fuelled missiles. It was concern about the obsolescence of these weapons that had led the Soviet Union to press for modernization with its SS-20 program in the first place. In fact, as the Soviet Union modernized, it dismantled some 650 of its SS-4s and SS-5s.

While the issue of equivalence was such a major stumbling block in the Strategic Arms Limitation Talks, it became just as difficult a problem in the Intermediate-range Nuclear Force Talks. In fact, the problems were perhaps even more complex in the latter because of the need to consider allied capabilities in addition to those of the United States and the Soviet Union.

In looking at the issue as to whether French and British forces should be taken into account in evaluating the balance of nuclear forces in Europe, it might be noted that the nuclear capabilities of these two states during the early eighties amounted to only about 4 percent of that of either the United States or the Soviet Union. However, both Britain and France are making rapid strides in a program of modernization that will eventually involve the replacement of all of their remaining single and clustered warheads with MIRVed SLBMs. The British, for example, plan to convert to the Trident II missile system, which represents the latest technological advance of the United States. It is estimated that by the 1990s the British will have an eightfold increase in target coverage.[2]

One complication in the INF talks, which was not a serious problem in the strategic arms talks, was the issue of the dual-capable quality of many aircraft and intermediate- and short-range missiles. Unlike the case for ICBMs, arming shorter-range missiles with conventional explosives can be cost effective. Indeed, Pershing I missiles as well as a number of cruise missiles have been armed both ways. It was the U.S. government's desire to protect the conventionally armed Pershing I missiles from being traded away that precluded a trade-off for Soviet SS-22s—a move that was favored by U.S. negotiator Paul Nitze. Negotiations over the cruise missile have also been difficult given the interest in using these vehicles for both conventional and nuclear missions.

The problem of negotiating controls on intermediate- and short-range missiles was complicated as the United States considered development of delivery systems that could be transformed with the insertion of a "clip-in" warhead, allowing either a nuclear or a conventional warhead to be inserted just prior to launch.[3] The new designs required for this flexibility would have destroyed any remaining distinguishing differences between nuclear and conventional missiles, making the problem of verification difficult at best, particularly for an agreement allowing a conventionally armed but not a nuclear-armed delivery system.

It was largely because of the dual capability of aircraft that the United States, especially its military, was hesitant to include such weapons in the negotiations. By calling the talks the Intermediate-range Nuclear Force Talks rather than using the more traditional term of Theater Nuclear Forces, the United States hoped to exclude short-range aircraft and tactical nuclear weapons from the discussion. According to Strobe Talbott, keeping aircraft out of the INF negotiations was such an obsession with the Joint Chiefs of Staff that the Assistant Secretary of Defense, Richard Perle, exploited that interest in order to obtain military support for the zero-only option.[4] Although the Joint Chiefs were predisposed to the zero-plus option, which would have allowed a limited number of INF missiles on both sides and was favored by the Department of State, Perle made it clear that such a stance would reopen the debate to include aircraft in the opening U.S. position. The threat of raising the issue was sufficient to convince the Chiefs to reconsider their position, and the end result was that aircraft were to be discussed only in some vague second phase of the negotiations, if at all.

In presenting the U.S. position in Geneva, Ambassador Paul Nitze noted several differences between aircraft and missiles that justified their separate treatment. Aircraft are designed to play a dual role, have a slower flight time, are more vulnerable to air defenses, and, unlike missiles, they are manned. Some of these distinctions are blurred when it comes to the cruise missile, which, as pointed out, can be made dual capable at a reasonable cost. The cruise missile, which is essentially a pilotless, jet-fuelled plane, also has a speed more comparable with that of aircraft as it flies about 600 miles per hour. Despite its slow speed, the cruise missile is far less vulnerable to air defenses than are manned aircraft. Its ability to fly low and to follow the terrain with highly sophisticated computer maps, makes the cruise missile relatively invulnerable to air defenses.

Complications also arose over the issue of what to do about intermediate-range nuclear forces deployed in Asia. According to the initial Soviet proposals, there would be no restrictions placed upon the number of INF forces deployed in that region. Therefore, if an agreement required the removal of such forces from Europe, they could simply be redeployed in Asia. Such a possibility created a highly sensitive issue for both U.S. allies in the region and China, as might be expected. Western European countries were also concerned because of the fact that, given the mobility of the SS-20, any such weapons reduced by agreement in Europe could simply be returned at a later date should circumstances merit such a move. For these reasons the United States has always insisted that global rather than regional ceilings on intermediate-range missiles be established.

Just as the Strategic Arms Limitation Talks allowed the SS-20 and the Backfire bomber to slip into the so-called gray area of noncoverage, so too have many INF proposals allowed weapons capable of carrying out the same European missions to escape control. For example, the Soviet short-range SS-21, SS-22, and SS-23 missiles can all strike Western European targets, particularly if deployed in Eastern Europe as was done in response to the U.S. deployment of cruise and Pershing II missiles in Western Europe beginning in November 1983. To the extent that the proposals have focused on intermediate-range missiles only, thousands of aircraft have been left uncovered. The narrow focus on restricting ground-launched cruise missiles overlooked the equally capable sea-launched cruise missile, which can be deployed on ships and submarines. Indeed, the United States has dramatically increased deployment of the latter, illustrating once again the balloon effect of arms control negotiations. Attempts to squeeze off one weapons system simply produces pressure for expansion elsewhere.

Although most attention in the INF talks was given to the Pershing II and cruise missiles on the American side and to the SS-20 for the Soviet Union, many other nuclear systems exist in the European theater and from time to time were discussed in the INF talks. When these talks opened in November 1981, the United States had 6,000 tactical nuclear warheads in Europe. Some 1,000 nuclear warheads had been removed the year before as part of the NATO two-track decision. In 1982 NATO agreed to reduce the number by a further 1,400 warheads, leaving only 4,600 theater nuclear warheads.

The primary reason for these reductions was related to the fact that they were becoming somewhat obsolete. Moreover, it was felt that by withdrawing more short-range battlefield nuclear weapons, the danger of escalating to a nuclear level during a future crisis or war would be reduced. Whatever the motivation, the fact remains that far more nuclear warheads were removed from European soil than were to be introduced under the two-track proposal calling for 572 new warheads. The critical difference in the old warheads and the new ones is that the latter are more threatening to the Soviet homeland, particularly the Pershing II missile, which is capable of striking targets in the Soviet Union in a matter of twelve minutes with a circular error probability (CEP) of less than 100 feet. The majority of the nuclear warheads already in Europe were for tactical use in the battlefield with a range below 100 kilometers.

The Soviet Union was reticent about negotiating limits on short-range delivery systems in Europe, for several of its own systems, such as its SS-12s, SS-22s, and SS-23s as well as various aircraft, would have been affected. The Soviets proposed that these systems be dealt with only after the central issue of intermediate-range nuclear missiles was settled. At the same time, the Soviet Union sought to control U.S. short-range delivery systems such as the Pershing I missile and F-4 fighters by suggesting incorrectly that their range surpassed 1,000 kilometers.

As a result of the many differences between the superpowers, progress during the early months of the INF negotiations was negligible. The United States was asking the Soviet Union to dismantle all of its intermediate-range missiles in return for a United States promise that it would not build any such weapons. The Soviet Union with its 300 ceiling was proposing substantial reductions in U.S. forward-based systems with virtually no constraints upon itself other than having to dismantle a number of obsolete SS-4s and SS-5s, which it had planned to do anyway. The complete nonnegotiability of the positions taken was readily recognized by the negotiators themselves, leading to the so-called walk in the woods proposal in the summer of 1982. Ambassador Paul Nitze suggested to his Soviet counterpart, Yuli Kvitsinsky, that the two meet together informally to try to work out a formula to overcome the negotiating impasse. The tentative agreement reached called for a ceiling on intermediate-range missiles of 75 launchers each. By restricting the count to launchers rather than missiles, the plan would have allowed the United States to deploy some 300 cruise missiles since each launcher was comprised of four cruise missiles. No Pershing II missiles, which seemed to frighten the Soviet Union most, would have been deployed. In turn, the Soviet Union would have been allowed only 225 intermediate-range missile warheads west of the Urals since each SS-20 has three warheads. The Soviets would also be allowed 90 SS-20s in Asia. The plan included some rather high ceilings on intermediate-range bombers as well as some limitations on shorter-range missiles, but no mention was made of French and British forces, and global equality in numbers was not required.

The plan ran into problems in both Washington and Moscow. Many officials in the United States government believed Nitze had exceeded his instructions. Of perhaps greatest concern was the required trade-off involving the nondeployment of the Pershing II missile, which President Reagan referred to as a "fast-flier" in contrast to the slow-flying cruise missile. Many officials were also concerned about backing off the requirement for equal global limits.

A number of commentators have argued that the United States was the first to reject the "walk in the woods" compromise as President Reagan on September 13, 1982, decided to stick with the zero-option proposal.[5] When Ambassador Nitze returned to Geneva at the end of the month, he was informed of the Soviet rejection of the compromise. Whether this rejection came as a response to the earlier U.S. decision cannot be certain. At any rate, Soviet negotiator Yuli Kvitsinsky was rebuked on continuing the informal process unless he could assure Washington's approval in advance of any tentative agreement.

Knowledgeable observers have suggested that it is quite unlikely that Kvitsinsky would have made the sorts of concessions he did in order to reach agreement without instructions from Moscow. Accordingly, it is reasoned that the Soviet Union must have approved of the general thrust and backed off because of Washington's rejection of the proposal. Ambassador Nitze, however, argues that the Soviet Union rejected the agreement first and that aspects of it were quite acceptable to the United States government.[6] Whatever the correct interpretation, the compromise did not work, and the INF negotiations stalled for several months.

During 1982–83, the Soviet Union undertook a number of initiatives in an effort to stop the imminent deployment of U.S. cruise and Pershing II missiles in Europe scheduled for late 1983. On March 16, 1982, President Leonid Brezhnev announced a unilateral quantitative and qualitative freeze on intermediate-range missiles in Europe, offering even to reduce a certain number of missiles if conditions were right. The moratorium was to last as long as negotiations on INF continued or until the United States began to deploy intermediate-range nuclear missiles on European soil. If the Soviet Union could have obtained U.S. compliance with the moratorium, it would have had no incentive to negotiate, for its objective would have been achieved.

There is some dispute as to whether or not the Soviet Union lived up to its announced unilateral moratorium. Of particular concern was whether the Soviet Union intended to include in the moratorium those sites that were under construction at the time of the announcement. According to Soviet arms expert David Holloway, the Soviet Union appears to have abided by its unilateral moratorium, except for completing work on two sites involving some 18 SS-20 missiles.[7] This view has also been supported by Raymond L. Garthoff, who believed that those sites under construction were not included just as similar sites were not included in the Interim Offensive Arms Agreement in SALT I.[8] Richard Perle, in a letter to the *Washington Post*, disputed the Garthoff assessment, arguing that the Soviet Union's own announcement referred to "termination of preparation for the deployment of missiles . . . including an end to the construction of launching positions for such missiles."[9] The latter phrase Mr. Perle took to mean an end to all construction, including that already begun. He was also disturbed that the Soviet moratorium in practice did not seem to apply to SS-20s located in Asia, which he regarded as capable of reaching West European soil. Whatever the correct interpretation, the Soviet moratorium impressed many Europeans and other advocates of restraint, leading to second thoughts about the proposed U.S. deployment.

In addition to promises of restraint on further INF deployments in return for similar U.S. restraint, the Soviet Union threatened military expansion if the United States proceeded with its planned deployment. On March 19, 1982, for example, Soviet leaders indicated that they would develop sea-based cruise missiles to counter the U.S. INF threat. The Soviet Union also began in the summer of 1982 to deploy short-range delivery systems such as SS-21s and Fencer fighter bombers on East German soil to counter the threatened NATO deployment.

Having backed away from the "walk in the woods" compromise and under increasing domestic and allied pressure to do something about the problem of nuclear weapons, President Reagan in a January 1983 letter to the European people offered to meet Yuri Andropov at the summit to sign an agreement encompassing the zero option. In making this proposal, the president knew that it would be rejected just as Gorbachev realized that his 1986 proposal for a quick, one-issue summit to sign a comprehensive test ban would not be received positively by the United States. The promise of a summit, which the adversary appeared to prize more highly in each instance, seemed not to have been a sufficient reward to compel what was perceived as a bad agreement.

Pressure for at least appearing to talk seriously about arms control continued to build, reaching a peak in the United States with the showing of the film *The Day After* in January 1983 and huge peace rallies throughout the United States. Further momentum for the peace movement resulted from President Reagan's March 8 speech before an evangelical conference in which he labeled the Soviet Union the "focus of evil" in the world. Given an increasingly bad press on the peace issue, the Reagan administration on March 29, the last day of the fourth round of the INF talks, tabled its so-called interim INF proposal. This plan represented the first significant official modification in the U.S. position on INF since the zero option was first introduced in 1981, although hints had been made prior to that time that the United States would accept something less than zero. Nevertheless, the United States continued to insist that the proposal was only an interim one and that it still preferred zero INF forces for both superpowers.

In many respects, the interim compromise was more in keeping with the initial December 1979 NATO decision that set the number of missiles higher than was thought necessary for the particular mission that NATO planners had in mind. The primary reason for introducing the missiles in the first place was not so much to match the SS-20 on a warhead per warhead basis but rather to bolster the credibility of extended deterrence. It was assumed that some of the 572 planned missiles would be traded away in negotiations with the Soviet Union. Europeans have always seemed insecure about the willingness of the United States to use its nuclear might to defend Europe against a massive conventional strike. Since it was felt that NATO's conventional forces were inferior to Soviet conventional forces, even with some 300,000 U.S. troops on European soil, European leaders have been concerned to couple the U.S. nuclear deterrent system with the defense of Europe. Given the predictable consequences of nuclear war, it was feared that the United States, in the event of a Soviet strike in Europe, would have a high incentive to remain on the sidelines or at least to limit the war, whether conventional or nuclear, to European soil. Comments made by President Reagan in October 1981 about the possibility of limiting nuclear war to the European region had hardly been reassuring to U.S. NATO allies.[10]

In presenting the interim proposal, Ambassador Nitze suggested that an acceptable range of equal levels of intermediate-range nuclear missiles for the two superpowers might be anywhere from 50 to 420 nuclear warheads each. The Soviet Union rejected all levels that would involve any U.S. deployment. It also objected to the inclusion of Asian INF forces in the global balance and the exclusion of British and French nuclear forces.

Despite Soviet rejection of the interim proposal, a number of formal concessions were made by the Soviet Union during the months leading to the scheduled U.S. deployment of cruise and Pershing II missiles. In the third round of the INF talks in the fall of 1982, the Soviet Union went so far as to suggest that some cooperative verification measures could be added to national technical means—a position it was unwilling to accept during the SALT negotiations. Several more concessions were made in January 1983 as the Soviet Union proposed reducing the level of inter-mediate-range nuclear forces to the number of nuclear weapons found in the French and British arsenals. At the time this was estimated to be 162 delivery systems, comprised largely of submarine-launched ballistic missiles. The Soviet Union for the first time also agreed to negotiate its shorter-range SS-21, SS-22, and SS-23 missiles. As pointed out earlier, these systems were capable of striking West European territory when deployed in Eastern Europe. Both concessions, however, remained contingent upon the United States' foregoing its deployment of intermediate-range missiles on European soil.

In May the Soviet Union indicated a willingness to consider warheads in the count as well as missiles. Counting warheads instead of missiles would be beneficial to the West if one were balancing U.S. and Soviet intermediate-range nuclear forces alone since the United States cruise and Pershing II missiles are single warhead weapons, while the SS-20 has three warheads. As long as French and British forces were not fully MIRVed, such a proposal could still benefit the West. In fact, according to Soviet calculations, 140 rather than 162 SS-20s would be all that would be required to offset French and British nuclear forces. As these two NATO states modernize their forces, particularly as more SLBMs are MIRVed, a count based upon warheads would begin to favor the Soviet Union. A single MIRVed SLBM, armed with 14 warheads as permitted in the SALT II Treaty, would allow the Soviet Union to deploy almost five SS-20s with three warheads each. But even if agreement could be reached on counting warheads rather than missiles, it was obvious that disputes about the count would remain as the United States and the Soviet Union disagreed on how many warheads France and the United Kingdom had at the time. The Soviets claimed the two states had a total of 440 warheads, and the United States argued it was only about 300.

In August the Soviet Union reassured the NATO allies somewhat by making it clear that any reduction of existing SS-20s would result in the destruction of the weapons rather than redeployment in Asia. China and U.S. Asian allies could therefore breathe easier. In a proposal made on October 26, the Soviet Union offered several small concessions to the West. Included among these were less severe restrictions on conventionally armed NATO aircraft and a freeze on the number of SS-20s in Asia, leaving that number at 108 missiles. On the eve of deployment itself, the Soviet Union offered unilaterally to scrap all of its SS-4 intermediate-range nuclear missiles in return for a U.S. deferral decision on the installation of its European missiles. It was probable that the Soviet Union would have dismantled them anyway, but it should be noted that with the reduction of both the SS-4s and SS-5s, the Soviet Union had reduced considerably more deliverable nuclear megatonnage than it had created with its deployment of SS-20s. The latter missile, however, is more accurate, albeit not nearly as accurate as the Pershing II and the cruise missile. It has been estimated, for example, that the Pershing II's kill probability against hardened targets is six times greater than that of the SS-20.[11]

A feeler was floated by Kvitsinsky on November 12 which suggested that British and French INF forces might be compensated for elsewhere, presumably in the START negotiations, thus allowing more U.S. aircraft into the ultimate INF ceilings proposed by the Soviet Union. But this offer was subsequently denied by the Soviet press agency TASS. It was also hinted that the Soviet Union would reduce its SS-20s to 120, but, as usual, the Soviet concessions required that no deployment of U.S. Pershing II and cruise missiles be permitted. Even if the Soviets were willing to go as low as 120 SS-20s, it should be noted that a better deal could have been obtained by the United States prior to the fateful December 1979 decision. At that time the Soviet Union was offering to freeze its buildup of SS-20s, which then stood at around 100 missiles, in return for a U.S. pledge not to deploy intermediate-range missiles in Europe.

In yet another effort to stall the planned deployment, the Soviet Union sought to influence European opinion by making a number of concessions in 1983 that would be particularly appealing to Western Europe. In January, for example, it offered NATO a nonaggression pact that would cover both conventional and nuclear weapons. The Soviet Union also agreed to remove all chemical weapons from Europe and, in another attempt to generate goodwill, it reacted positively to the Swedish proposal for a 300-kilometer nuclear-free zone in Central Europe. In fact, the Soviets did the Swedes one step better by proposing that the size of the zone be increased to 500-600 kilometers.

INF Deployment and Its Aftermath

With the delivery of the first nine Pershing II missiles to the Federal Republic of Germany on November 23, 1983, the Soviet Union, as it had threatened for months, broke off the INF talks, refusing to set a date for their resumption. The Soviet Union also made good on its threat to leave the START talks two weeks later. Thus 1984 became the first year in over fifteen in which bilateral strategic arms control negotiations between the United States and the Soviet Union were not held. Some bilateral negotiations did take place as the two met in June to discuss the verification requirements for a treaty banning chemical weapons. The Standing Consultative Commission established under the SALT I agreements to resolve conflicts over verification in the SALT process also met on two different occasions during the year. But all in all the year was a bleak one for arms control. Progress on arms control in 1984 seemed to be even less than that of the previous year—a year which the Arms Control Association had called the worst year for arms control since 1962.

In response to the U.S. deployment, the Soviet Union began to increase its own intermediate-range nuclear force. In the year following its walkout from the INF talks, the Soviet Union started construction on ten new SS-20 bases, which amounted to the most in any year since the SS-20 was first deployed in 1977.[12] A number of SS-22 missiles were shipped to East Germany, and on October 13, 1984, the Soviet Union announced that it had begun deployment of long-range cruise missiles aboard aircraft and submarines, many of which would be positioned close to U.S. territory.

With the Soviet Union's boycott of the arms control process, it was time for the United States to take the initiative in an effort to gain a reputation as peacemaker. Besides, 1984 was a presidential election year, and public opinion polls continued to show the public to be at odds with the president on arms control policy. Pressure for a more conciliatory position on the part of the Reagan administration was being exerted by several European allies that were having second thoughts about the two-track decision. In early May 1984 Prime Minister Bettino Craxi of Italy proposed suspending the deployment of further intermediate-range missiles if the Soviet Union would resume negotiations, and the following month, the Netherlands government announced that it would cancel deployment plans on Dutch soil if the Soviet Union would freeze further SS-20 development.[13]

On January 16, 1984, President Reagan delivered a highly conciliatory speech in which he noted that "1984 finds the United States in the strongest position in years to establish a constructive and realistic working relationship with the Soviet Union."[14] But it was perhaps Reagan's comments made almost a year earlier calling for a strategic defense system that set in motion the forces that ultimately brought the Soviet Union back to the negotiating table. As U.S. plans for the Strategic Defense

Initiative (SDI) gathered momentum, the Soviet Union began to express increased interest in negotiating controls on space systems. In June 1984 Soviet leader Konstantin Chernenko proposed immediate negotiations on banning anti-satellite and other space weapons. The United States agreed, but only on condition that the talks also encompass offensive weapons. Having recently made a point of walking out of the offensive missile talks, the Soviet Union rejected the condition. It was November before the Soviet Union was willing to swallow its pride and agree to the resumption of arms control negotiations that would cover both offensive and defensive weapons systems.

The Soviet Union, placed in the embarrassing position of returning to the arms control negotiations in January 1985 without obtaining satisfaction on the issue that caused its walkout in the first place, seemed determined to salvage its bargaining reputation by taking a hard stance in the resumed negotiations. Shortly after the first round of the Geneva talks ended, Paul Nitze cited a number of retractions from earlier Soviet positions.[15] In 1983, for example, the Soviet Union was willing to allow some longer-range air-launched cruise missiles, but in 1985 the Soviets were demanding that none exceed 600 kilometers. The Soviet 1985 proposals included no constraints on the deployment of SS-20s in Asia while in 1983 the Soviet Union had agreed to a limit of 108. It also seemed to have shown greater flexibility on the issue of allowable U.S. aircraft in the earlier talks. So much for the argument that building bargaining chips makes an adversary more conciliatory. The Strategic Defense Initiative may have increased Soviet incentive to return to the bargaining table, but it did not necessarily make the Soviet Union more conciliatory.

Having increased its intermediate-range nuclear force capability during 1984, the Soviet Union in April and again in October 1985 proposed a moratorium on further INF buildup. Soviet willingness to accept a moratorium on the deployment of intermediate-range delivery systems at that time was probably related to the fact that it had just begun flight testing the SS-28, which was to be the replacement missile for the eighteen year-old SS-20. The Soviet Union went a step further in November by actually reducing the number of SS-20s deployed in Europe from just under 300 to 243. But in making the reduction, it did so in a way that would permit quick reactivation.

During the November 1985 summit, President Reagan and Mikhail Gorbachev called for accelerated progress toward an "interim" INF agreement. Gorbachev for the first time also hinted that some American INF systems might remain in Europe and that a treaty restricting intermediate-range delivery systems might even be possible without agreement on strategic nuclear weapons and space defenses.[16]

As part of a renewed arms control offensive, Gorbachev visited Paris in the fall of 1985 during which he made proposals with particular appeal for West Europeans, perhaps in hopes of dividing the alliance. He promised President Francois Mitterand that the Soviet Union would accept an agreement on European missiles "outside of direct connection with the problem of space and strategic arms."[17] He also called for direct talks with France and Britain on the topic of nuclear weapons.

Continuing the conciliatory position assumed in the fall of 1985, Gorbachev on January 15, 1986, officially announced that he was no longer demanding that the Soviet Union be compensated for French and British nuclear forces. Instead, he proposed that only the United States and the Soviet Union be required to eliminate their European-based INF missiles over a 5- to 8-year period and that France and Britain pledge to freeze their respective nuclear systems. In effect, the Soviet Union was accepting the proposed U.S. zero option except for the failure to include Asian-based INF missiles in the ban. Under the plan, the United States would also have to agree not to transfer intermediate-range nuclear missiles or Trident II SLBMs to either Britain or France. Even this requirement may have been relaxed somewhat when Soviet Foreign Minister Eduard Shevardnadze, in a visit to London in July 1986, informed his hosts that the freeze does not affect French and British plans to "modernize their nuclear arsenals."[18] Important concessions were also made regarding verification as Gorbachev agreed to the on-site monitoring of the destruction of missiles.

The United States response to the various Soviet initiatives came in its February 24, 1986, proposal, which spelled out in detailed stages what the United States had suggested in more general terms in its 1983 interim proposal. According to the U.S. plan, intermediate-range missiles would be reduced during the first stage to 140 in Europe for each side along with a proportionate reduction in Asia. In the second stage those levels were to be reduced by an additional 50 percent, and in the third stage, scheduled to end in 1999, there were to be no INF missiles. Collateral limits would be made on short-range missiles, but no constraints were to be placed upon French and British nuclear forces.

As a result of the conciliatory behavior shown by the Soviet Union on the subject of intermediate-range nuclear forces during 1985–86, American officials noted that in preparing for the round of Geneva talks, which began in May 1986, they were able to identify 12 to 16 areas where U.S. and Soviet positions had converged.[19] This represented a substantial improvement over Ambassador Paul Nitze's 1982 analysis in which he found the two states to be divided on 33 issues related to controlling intermediate-range delivery systems.[20]

At the Reykjavik Conference in October 1986, agreement was reached that would have allowed each side to retain one hundred intermediate-range nuclear warheads as long as they were deployed out of range of European soil. Disagreement continued on how far to the east the Soviet Union would have to deploy its 33 allowable SS-20s and whether the United States could position its 100 Pershing II missiles in Alaska or would be confined to the continental United States. A possible solution was provided by Gorbachev in May 1987 when he offered to scrap all intermediate-range nuclear missiles on a global basis. The price, however, would be high since he made the offer contingent upon U.S. agreement to withdraw its nuclear arsenals deployed in Japan, South Korea, and the Philippines, and to restrict the movement of aircraft carriers in the region.

Also complicating the issue of controlling intermediate-range nuclear forces was the problem of what to do about short-range nuclear missiles. After the United States raised this issue, demanding that it be able to match Soviet short-range nuclear capabilities which stood at about 1,000 missiles, Gorbachev agreed to include the issue in the INF talks. During Secretary of State George Shultz's visit to Moscow in April 1987 Gorbachev offered to eliminate all shorter-range missiles with a range of 500 to 1,000 kilometers which the Soviets had deployed in Europe. The proposal was essentially a unilateral offer since the United States did not deploy any such weapons at the time.

The Soviet proposal to eliminate this category of weapons created a furor in both the United States and Europe as the Europeans feared that it would mean the beginning of the decoupling of the U.S. nuclear deterrent. But such a concern would appear not to be valid if one recalls that the United States would still retain some 4,500 nuclear devices on European soil capable of delivery by the remaining bombers and missiles stationed in Europe. The Federal Republic of Germany objected to the plan since it might force Germany to dismantle the 72 Pershing IA missiles under its control and only reluctantly agreed after the United States exerted considerable political pressure. Military interests in the United States opposed the idea since it would prevent them from deploying a shorter-range version of the Pershing II missile which would be achieved by eliminating one stage of the Pershing.

With the Soviet Union's removal of the linkage between an INF agreement and SDI in February 1987 and its decision to allow on-site inspection of factories and launch sites, considerable progress has been made—so much so that the two sides were able to agree upon a joint-working treaty proposal in early June. If agreement is reached on this issue as now seems quite likely, President Reagan will have achieved the zero option which he advocated in 1981—a proposal which was non-negotiable at the time, but with changed circumstances and a different Soviet leadership now appears achievable.

Although the United States and the Soviet Union may be successful in negotiating a ban on intermediate and short-range nuclear missiles, the meaningfulness of the agreement remains in doubt as a result of the probable exclusion of sea-based cruise missiles from the agreements. The United States is in the process of producing several thousand such weapons that can be armed with either conventional or nuclear warheads. Since the Reagan administration, unlike its predecessor, made no effort to establish functionally related observational differences between conventional and nuclear armed SLCMs, the verification problem is a virtual nightmare. Without reasonable prospects of verification, the United States, as is perhaps appropriate, will continue to reject any effort to control the weapon system. The Soviet Union, having successfully tested its own sea-launched cruise missile, proposed in July 1987 to limit the number to 400 nuclear-tipped SLCMs on each side.

The utility of any agreement on intermediate-range nuclear forces is likely to be undermined if similar constraints are not placed upon strategic weapons. With separate proposals being made in strategic and intermediate-range arms talks, it was possible for the United States and the Soviet Union to make a concession in one set of negotiations and take it away in the other. For example, the Soviet 1986 concession on allowing SLCMs to be deployed on submarines was undermined by the Soviet inclusion of SLCMs in their overall strategic ceiling levels. Even with agreement on limiting INF weapons, the Soviet Union can still use strategic weapons against Europe as indeed a number of SS-11s and SS-19s have been so targeted, and retargeting them against the United States would be difficult.

The existence of two sets of negotiations has allowed considerable gamesmanship on the part of both sides. The Soviet Union excluded the Backfire bomber from its classification of intermediate-range systems, but continued to deny that the Backfire had intercontinental-range capability. The United States has also been involved in a shell game in which it has argued that British and French forces should not be considered in START, for they are intermediate-range delivery systems and must not be considered in INF because they are strategic.[21] What all of this underscores is that any student of European regional arms control must also be aware of what is happening in concurrent strategic arms control, and it is to this topic that we now turn our attention.

STRATEGIC ARMS REDUCTION

In attempting to develop a position on the issue of strategic arms control, the Reagan administration first had to decide how to handle the issue of the unratified SALT II Treaty. While campaigning for the presidency, Reagan had declared the SALT II Treaty to be fatally flawed, particularly because of problems of verification and the failure of the treaty to do much about the huge Soviet military machine. Amending the treaty to meet the many objections appeared impossible, leading to recommendations for a fresh beginning. In an effort to separate his administration from past arms control policies, President Reagan insisted upon renaming the strategic arms talks, which finally got underway on June 29, 1982, the Strategic Arms Reduction Talks (START). This did not, however, resolve the issue of what to do about the SALT II Treaty, which the Soviet Union wanted to see ratified.

Complying with SALT

Despite the fact that a large number of senators from both parties favored the submission of the SALT II Treaty for a vote on ratification, several administration spokespersons argued that SALT II was no longer viable. Secretary of the Navy John Lehman declared in March 1981 that the United States should no longer consider itself bound by the treaty, and in testimony before the Senate Foreign Relations Committee on May 11, 1982, Secretary of State Alexander Haig declared that "we consider SALT II to be dead. We have so informed the Soviet Union."[22]

It was not long before new life was given to a treaty that had been pronounced dead as a number of bureaucratic forces pressed hard for continued U.S. adherence to the SALT agreements. Among these were the influential Joint Chiefs of Staff who felt that the SALT I and SALT II agreements placed important restrictions on further Soviet military buildup. At the same time, the SALT ceilings did not currently restrict any U.S. force modernization that had been planned under the ambitious military buildup of the Reagan administration. As a result, President Reagan on May 19, 1982, declared that the United States would not undercut the Interim Offensive Arms Agreement of SALT I or the SALT II Treaty so long as the Soviet Union did likewise. As part of this promise, the administration rescinded the planned deployment of fifty MIRVed Minuteman III missiles that would have surpassed the SALT II nuclear warhead limits and would have required an increase in silo size beyond the 5 percent allowed. The administration also agreed in accordance with the SALT II Treaty to place functionally related observation devices (FRODs) on the B-52 bombers that were to be used to carry cruise missiles.

As weapons modernization continued during subsequent years, a decision had to be made on whether or not to remain in compliance with the SALT obligations. Although debate was intense on the subject within the U.S. administration, the forces favoring support for the SALT limits prevailed for several years. Additional Poseidons were dismantled as new Trident submarines came on line. The Soviet Union likewise met its obligation to stay within the SALT limits by destroying some 540 missiles and a number of Yankee-class submarines.

Continued adherence to the treaty was threatened in 1982 when the Reagan administration chose a new basing-system for the MX missile. The plan, referred to as Dense Pack, would have involved the placement of a hundred MX missiles in close proximity to each other so that in-coming Soviet missiles, forced to concentrate on a compact target, would destroy each other in a process called "fratricide." It was believed that a sufficient number of MXs would survive, allowing the United States to strike a retaliatory blow. Former SALT negotiator Paul Warnke has argued that Dense Pack would have violated obligations in both the Interim Offensive Arms Agreement and the SALT II Treaty "not to start construction of additional fixed ICBM launchers."[23] Ultimately the administration backed off from the plan, not so much over any concern about violating the SALT agreements but rather as a result of scientific, public, and congressional objections to Dense Pack.

As December 31, 1985, approached—the date on which the SALT II Treaty would have terminated had it been ratified—a number of voices within the U.S. military urged that the administration seek an extension of some of the provisions of the unratified treaty.[24] On June 10, 1985, President Reagan surprised many people by announcing that despite charges of Soviet noncompliance, he would "go the extra mile" for arms control by dismantling yet another Poseidon nuclear submarine to accommodate deployment of a planned Trident submarine and thus remain within the SALT ceilings.[25] The policy of not undercutting SALT was reaffirmed by Reagan just a week before the scheduled 1985 expiration date, but the president was unwilling to commit the United

States to a full-year extension as had been proposed by General Secretary Mikhail Gorbachev.

The policy of compliance with SALT continued for several months thereafter, despite vigorous campaigning by Caspar Weinberger and others who argued that because of continuing Soviet violations of SALT and other arms control agreements, the United States should take compensatory action by exceeding the SALT limits. The campaign was not initially successful, for on April 21, 1986, it was reported that the United States had decided to dismantle yet two more Poseidon submarines and thus remain in compliance with SALT as the seventh Trident submarine was brought on line.[26] Given this decision, it was quite unexpected when the president announced on May 27, 1986, that the United States would no longer make its strategic planning decisions on the basis of the SALT restrictions and that the United States would in all probability exceed those limits when it deployed its 131st bomber loaded with air-launched cruise missiles later in the year. It was also indicated that the administration would continue with its planned Poseidon dismantlement, not because of concern about complying with SALT, but rather because it made economic sense to do so. Six years into the Reagan administration it appeared that conservative forces had finally destroyed a hated symbol of U.S.-Soviet détente. The SALT II Treaty, which had been declared dead several years earlier, seemed to have finally met that fate on November 28, 1986, with the threatened cruise missile deployment. The Soviet Union, while noting that the U.S. action freed it from its SALT commitments, indicated that it would continue to adhere to the SALT II Treaty for the time being.

Perhaps the major factor leading to the decision to scuttle SALT in 1986 was the fact that the Joint Chiefs of Staff had taken a neutral stance on the subject, declaring continued compliance to be a political question not a military one. As long as it would restrain Soviet military programs without appreciably affecting the U.S. strategic buildup, as the Chiefs continued to believe it might, SALT adherence was beneficial to U.S. military interests.

A number of arguments have been made over the years by opponents of the SALT agreements to justify their opposition to continued compliance. In the first place it was argued that the Soviet Union had violated the SALT agreements on numerous occasions and that the United States should therefore take action to assure that it is not placed at a disadvantage. The two most serious violations, according to the administration as it sought to justify the May 1986 decision, were the Soviet construction of the mobile SS-25 intercontinental-range ballistic missile and the continued efforts by the Soviet Union to encrypt the telemetry of its missile tests in violation of the prohibition on interference with the national technical means of verification used by the other side.

As will be recalled, the SALT II Treaty allowed only one new intercontinental-range ballistic missile, and this the Soviet Union declared to be the SS-24, which was first tested in the fall of 1982. In December 1982 the Soviet Union tested the SS-25, which it began to deploy three years later. The Soviet Union claimed that the latter missile was only a modernized version of the SS-13 while the United States declared that the new missile went beyond the 5 percent SALT II allowance on the size of a new missile as measured by its length, largest diameter, launchweight, and throw-weight. ACDA Director Kenneth L. Adelman has argued that the SS-25 is not just "slightly" larger than the SS-13 but is roughly twice its size.[27] According to another analysis, intelligence community experts believe that the SS-25 exceeded the 5 percent limit only with respect to throw-weight, and even that is ambiguous since estimates have been so inconsistent that the variation might still be within the 5 percent range.[28] The Soviet Union has asserted that assessments of the throw-weight of the SS-25 have been overestimated by the United States because of the inclusion of a heavy package of test instruments.

Second, in declaring itself no longer bound by SALT, the United States argued that it was necessary to negotiate a new treaty that would provide substantial reductions in strategic arsenals. According to U.S. officials, SALT did little to cap Soviet strategic growth as the Soviet Union was able to increase the number of its strategic nuclear warheads from 5,000 to 9,200 while adhering to the SALT II limits.[29] Of course, in doing so it was only catching up to the United States, which had an appreciable lead in warheads over the Soviet Union when SALT II was signed.

Third, it was suggested that even if the SALT agreement had some restraining effects on Soviet strategic growth, it was unlikely that the Soviet Union would markedly increase its strategic power even if U.S. rejection of the treaty would allow it to do so. Economic restrictions and security interests would probably dictate little change in Soviet strategic spending whether the United States continued to comply with SALT or not. It is interesting to note in this regard that some of the very same people in the administration who were saying earlier that SALT II should not be ratified since it would allow the Soviet Union to "break out" of the arms constraints by developing a first-strike capability were arguing in 1986 that even without SALT constraints the Soviet Union was unlikely to add appreciably to its missile capability.

Fourth, it was noted that since the SALT II Treaty had expired several months before, there was little need to continue to adhere to its restrictions. The treaty limits could have been followed until a replacement treaty was negotiated, and there was precedence for such an approach. Both sides continued to honor the Interim Offensive Arms Agreement long beyond its 1977 expiration date. It could be argued that had the expiration date of the SALT II Treaty been a major consideration for the administration, it would have ended its involvement with SALT on December 31, 1985, rather than almost five months later.

Fifth, some administration officials perhaps saw rejection of the SALT II Treaty as the first step toward a possible renegotiation or even a U.S. abrogation of the 1972 ABM Treaty that was a part of the SALT I agreements. The ABM Treaty had become a particular target for those favoring the Strategic Defense Initiative, popularly referred to as "Star Wars," since SDI would probably violate portions of the ABM Treaty.

Finally, some administration advisors favored strong presidential action on the SALT II Treaty as a way of enhancing the president's bargaining strength in arms control negotiations. By no longer adhering to the SALT limitations, the United States was implicitly communicating that it might engage in an unlimited arms race that by all accounts the Soviet Union cannot afford at this time as Mikhail Gorbachev has been attempting to change Soviet priorities by paying more attention to domestic economic development.

In making the decision to end adherence to the SALT II Treaty, the administration considerably misjudged the reaction of both the United States Congress and its NATO allies. On June 19, 1986, the House of Representatives overwhelmingly approved a nonbinding resolution by a vote of 256 to 145, urging the president to remain in compliance with SALT. Threats were also made by Congress to restrict spending on any weapons system that would exceed the SALT limits.

During a NATO meeting held in Nova Scotia within days of the U.S. announcement, the foreign ministers present unanimously criticized the decision.[30] Even Prime Minister Margaret Thatcher of Britain, Reagan's closest NATO ally on strategic matters, was highly critical of the president's move. The fact of the matter is that Europe has become more interested in arms control while the United States has become less interested. The pattern was essentially the opposite of that of the seventies.

Even though the United States was clearly justified from the standpoint of international law in making the decision to consider itself no longer bound by the SALT II Treaty, the question remains as to whether or not it was a wise decision politically and militarily. By rejecting the continuance of the SALT obligations, the United States lost the opportunity to call attention to alleged Soviet violations of the treaty. No longer would it be able to raise such issues and perhaps be able to resolve some of them as it had during various meetings of the Standing Consultative Commission in the past.

Second, since the Soviet Union was in a better position than the United States to increase its offensive arsenal rapidly, taking away the SALT ceilings would be to the American disadvantage. The Soviet SS-18, which had so preoccupied U.S. military planners in the past, could easily be MIRVed to 20 or 30 warheads rather than limited to the ten allowed under SALT II. The Soviet Union also has an advantage over the United States in the number of existing plants for constructing additional missiles. Congressman Les Aspin has estimated that because of production-line disparity alone, Soviet forces could grow 65 percent by 1989 compared to 45 percent growth for the United States.[31] A June 1985 CIA study estimated that the Soviet Union could rapidly expand its strategic forces to nineteen thousand warheads from the current ten thousand if released from SALT II restrictions.[32] Congressional and budgetary restraints within the United States would make it difficult for the U.S. to follow suit.

Third, removal of the limitations on numbers of strategic weapons would allow the Soviet Union to modernize further without destroying existing weapons. Although Assistant Secretary of Defense Richard Perle has argued that it makes little difference whether the Soviets dismantle their SS-11s and SS-13s in view of the relative obsolescence of these missiles,[33] the fact of the matter is that the additional numbers of missiles would increase pressures to add to the U.S. strategic forces to guarantee ICBM survivability. Concern about the huge Soviet military offensive capability, which would only grow larger without the SALT dismantling requirements, was the major reason that the Reagan administration rejected the SALT II Treaty in the first place.

Fourth, the rejection of the SALT II Treaty would allow the Soviet Union to engage in unrestricted missile testing. Under the treaty all multiple ICBM tests and individual tests directed outwardly from the country were to be announced well in advance. This provision was designed to lessen the danger of misconstruing a test with an actual attack, but it has the additional advantage of allowing the adversary to monitor a testing program more closely. This is important, particularly if one wants to ascertain if the other side is testing multiple missile launchings. Such tests would be essential for any state planning a first strike since, to be successful, such a strike would require the coordinated launching of hundreds of missiles.

Finally, the verification opportunities provided by the treaty would be lost if SALT were overthrown without a replacement. Under such conditions, the Soviet Union would have little difficulty concealing its strategic weapons tests and deployments. Without the SALT verification requirements, silos could be covered and mobile missiles hidden. It would also no longer be illegal to interfere with the national technical means of verification of the other side. Although the Soviet Union may not have adhered fully to the restrictions on the encryption of its missile tests, it has still allowed the United States to collect considerable information about Soviet missile capability—information that may well be lost without SALT.

Regardless of one's views about continued compliance with SALT, one might legitimately ask why the administration chose to make the announcement in May 1986 that it would no longer adhere to the SALT limits after having lived up to them for several years. After all, the decision had already been made in April to dismantle two Poseidon submarines, thus keeping the United States under the SALT limit for several more months. The proposed deployment of cruise missiles on the 131st B-52 bomber that threatened to exceed the SALT ceiling was more than six months off, and the United States even then could have stayed within the SALT II limits by destroying a few additional delivery systems. In fact, the Navy itself had planned to dismantle the *Alexander Hamilton*, but the *Hamilton* was given a reprieve at the last minute as the United States substituted another Poseidon submarine that had been damaged by running aground. With minimal destruction of existing systems, the United States could have remained under the SALT II ceiling until 1988 when the seventh Trident was scheduled to be commissioned.

There are both economic and military reasons justifying the dismantlement of Poseidon submarines, and these were used by the administration in arguing for the spring 1986 destruction of the two Poseidons. The nuclear reactors in both had reached their useful life, and the submarines were in desperate need of refurbishing. It was estimated that keeping them in commission would have cost $300 million each, diverting scarce military resources from areas that were viewed as more important.[34]

The reason for the decision no longer to adhere to the SALT limitations was probably due largely to bureaucratic compromise. With a divided administration, the decision allowed those who opposed arms control agreements and the entire SALT process to claim a victory. At the same time, those elements within the administration favoring continued adherence to the SALT limitations had some breathing space since the anticipated violation of the SALT agreements regarding the size of missile forces was still some months away. Supporting the position of the arms controllers, the decision provided that the two submarines would be dismantled rather than merely mothballed as the Pentagon had preferred.

Confusion surrounded the decision to back away from the no-undercut policy because of the varying interpretations presented by President Reagan. But when the conflicting statements were sorted out, it was clear that the United States regarded the SALT agreements dead and would no longer make its strategic planning contingent upon SALT restrictions. The final nail was driven into the SALT coffin during a special July 1986 meeting of the Standing Consultative Commission (SCC) called to review the U.S. decision rejecting continued compliance with SALT. At this time, the United States informed the Soviet Union that the 1972 Interim Offensive Arms Agreement and the SALT II Treaty would no longer be "fitting subjects in the SCC."[35]

In some respects the decision was very similar to President Eisenhower's announcement on December 29, 1959, that the United States no longer felt itself bound by the unilateral moratorium on nuclear testing, despite the fact that it had no immediate intention to resume testing. The Eisenhower statement may have unfortunately helped minimize the world outrage against the Soviet Union when the latter eventually broke the moratorium in September 1961 and began engaging in the most extensive series of nuclear tests in history. After all, it was the United States which had first declared itself to be free to resume nuclear testing. The Soviet Union may likewise use this latest United States announcement regarding SALT as an excuse for engaging in even more blatant and excessive violations of the SALT agreements. Unless there is an immediate military need and willingness to reverse an arms control restraint, a nation might do well to think about the implications of making premature announcements of this sort.

A New Start with START?

As has been indicated, the Reagan administration came into power with a number of reservations about arms control, and only after considerable domestic and international pressure did it agree to participate in negotiations on the subject. Since so much energy had been spent criticizing SALT, it was necessary to present proposals that diverged from past U.S. positions. A major consideration in opposing SALT had been that the agreements failed to reduce strategic arms to any appreciable degree. It was therefore to be expected that the United States would present more sweeping proposals calling for substantial cuts in existing strategic arms.

The opening proposals for strategic arms reduction presented by the Reagan administration were doomed to failure from the beginning, focused as they were upon deep reductions in Soviet ICBM capability, which represents the major part of the Soviet nuclear deterrent. Under the American plan, introduced by President Reagan in his May 1982 Eureka College speech, both sides would have been required during the first phase to reduce the total number of individual missile warheads by about a third to a level of 5,000 each, positioned on no more than 850 land or sea-based missiles. Only half of the 5,000 warheads could be placed on land-based missiles, which are the most accurate and threatening to the United States. What the administration seemed to have in mind in making the proposal was a complete restructuring of the Soviet strategic arsenal so that less reliance would be placed on Soviet ICBM capability and more on its SLBM forces.

From the standpoint of a credible deterrent posture it might appear highly desirable to force the Soviet Union to place a higher percentage of its strategic power into SLBM capability, but the proposal was a threat to Soviet strategic interests. The Soviet Union was being asked to install half of its strategic capability on SLBMs, thus placing it at a distinct disadvantage since the bulk of Soviet SLBMs are of the older liquid-fueled variety. Furthermore, the Soviet Union is forced to operate from far fewer overseas naval bases than the United States, making it impossible for the Soviets to have as high a percentage of submarines on active duty as the United States. Equal numbers under these conditions would mean unequal capabilities.

Since the Soviet Union has about 75 percent of its strategic nuclear power on land-based missiles compared to 25 percent for the United States, the proposal would have required that the Soviet Union reduce its ICBM force by 1,500 missiles compared to 850 for the United States. The "collateral constraints" also included in the U.S. proposals would have forced the Soviet Union to reduce substantial numbers of its medium and heavy ICBMs that form the bulwark of Soviet nuclear capability. Only 210 such missiles would be allowed, down from the existing 788. Within these limits the Soviet Union would have been required to reduce its largest and best missile, the SS-18, by two-thirds from its current number of 308 to 110. At the same time, the United States would have been allowed to build both the highly accurate and destructive MX and Trident II missile systems.

While concentrating upon reducing the most powerful of the Soviet strategic forces during the first phase, the initial U.S. START proposal would have deferred action aimed at controlling those weapons in which the United States had a considerable advantage—the cruise missile and the heavy bomber—until the second phase. Further restrictions upon Soviet nuclear capability would also have been required in the latter phase as the Soviet Union would have to reduce its total nuclear throw-weight to levels compatible with those of the United States. Some objective observers believed, however, that the USSR was justified in maintaining the extra throw-weight given its less accurate missiles and inability to have as many submarines on station at any given time.

The extremity of the United States position in its initial START proposals was recognized by Alexander Haig, who was secretary of state at the time the proposals were made. Haig writes in his memoirs that the proposed limits on ICBM warheads "would require such drastic reductions in the Soviet inventory as to suggest they were unnegotiable."[36] Although a case can be made for beginning a round of negotiations with extreme positions, negotiation requires at least the promise of some benefits for the other side.

The Soviet response to the Reagan strategic arms control proposal was presented initially in July 1982 and confirmed publicly in December by Yuri V. Andropov shortly after he had succeeded Leonid Brezhnev as head of the Communist party. The Soviet plan provided for a reduction in strategic delivery vehicles, including both missiles and bombers, to 1800. To meet such levels, the Soviet Union would have to reduce the number of its strategic delivery systems more than 25 percent compared to about 10 percent for the United States. These reductions were close to those proposed by President Carter in March 1977 but fell far short of the 850 missile limit in the Reagan plan. In contrast to American proposals, the Soviet plan did not specify a sublimit on the number of ICBM warheads, and the number of bombers would be restricted from the beginning instead of waiting until the second phase.

Although one can argue that the initial U.S. START proposal was nonnegotiable, the Soviet plan included various provisions that made it totally unacceptable to the United States. Chief among these was the requirement that the United States dismantle its forward-based systems. The pattern had become well established as virtually all new strategic arms negotiations have begun with similar demands. The Soviet argument for insisting upon a ban on forward-based systems is that such weapons can strike Soviet territory and thus must be regarded as strategic. After it is clear that no progress can be made so long as such a proposal is on the table, the Soviet Union has usually dropped the requirement, asking the United States to respond to the Soviet gesture with concessions of its own. In the case of the START talks, the appropriateness of including forward-based systems in the Soviet proposals was questionable since such systems were more relevant to the ongoing INF talks.

Just as the United States attempted to limit Soviet areas of strength, the Soviet Union in its proposals sought to reduce U.S. advantages, particularly with respect to intercontinental-range bombers and air-launched cruise missiles. Limits on bombers were made an integral part of the Soviet ceilings on delivery systems, albeit with the Soviet Backfire bomber exempted as before. More serious was the seeming Soviet retraction on air-launched cruise missiles that were limited to a range of 600 kilometers. Previously the Soviet Union had agreed to an unlimited range for such missiles as long as they were not deployed on more than 120 bombers with an average limit of 28 missiles per bomber. It was not until July 1983 that the Soviet Union returned to its SALT II position by dropping the 600 kilometer restriction.

In July 1983 the Soviet Union added explicit sublimits to its overall proposed ceiling of 1,800 delivery systems. Under the modified plan each side would be restricted to a sublimit of 1,200 MIRVed delivery systems, consisting of ICBMs, SLBMs, and bombers loaded with cruise missiles. Such a sublimit represents a reduction of 120 delivery systems from the SALT II levels. MIRVed ICBMs and SLBMs would be limited to 1,080 of which 680 could be ICBMs. Of particular concern to the United States was the fact that the Soviet plan would allow the Soviet Union to retain all of its SS-18 and SS-19 missiles.

Both the United States and the Soviet Union held rigidly to these proposals for a number of months as little progress was made in the START negotiations. When the United States finally modified its START position in 1983, the change was primarily due to domestic pressures rather than a reaction to any moves made by the Soviet Union. For example, its June 1983 plan calling for a relaxation in the 850 ceiling for land- and sea-based missiles was proposed in an effort to accommodate the development and deployment of the Midgetman missile as proposed by the President's Commission on Strategic Forces. This blue-ribbon commission, commonly referred to as the Scowcroft Commission, had been appointed by President Reagan to develop an acceptable plan for basing the MX missile. Over thirty previous basing-modes had been proposed—all of which failed for various political, economic, or strategic reasons. In recommending that some 100 MX missiles be placed in existing silos on an interim basis, the Scowcroft Commission recognized that the problem of ICBM vulnerability would not be solved. Consequently, it went on to recommend that the United States should in the future attempt to place less reliance on stationary MIRVed ICBMs and instead develop a smaller mobile ICBM, which was dubbed the Midgetman. It was believed that the Midgetman missile would help stabilize the nuclear deterrent system, because it would be less threatening and a less inviting target than current multiple-warhead missiles. Since each Midgetman would have only one warhead, the 850 limit on ICBMs and SLBMs would be unduly restrictive, leading the United States to suggest that 1,100–1,200 missiles would be a more appropriate ceiling. Although the U.S. willingness to increase the number of allowable missiles represented movement toward the Soviet position, the limit of 2,500 warheads on land-based missiles would remain, making the proposal just as objectionable from the Soviet perspective. At that time a 2,500 warhead ceiling would have meant a cut of more than half in the Soviet warheads on intercontinental missiles while permitting a slight increase in comparable American warheads.[37]

Similarly, the administration's decision in October to incorporate the idea of build-down into the U.S. START proposal was not a direct reaction to any Soviet initiative but was rather a response to congressional pressure. Forty-five senators had cosponsored a resolution supporting the build-down proposal, making it clear that their support of the MX missile would be dependent upon the administration's accepting the idea of build-down. In its simplest terms build-down required that each superpower remove more than one nuclear warhead for each new one deployed. The plan, as incorporated into the United States proposal, would attempt to encourage the Soviet Union to place more of its strategic capability into less vulnerable mobile systems by requiring that more warheads be destroyed if a nation deploys fixed, land-based missiles than if it deploys sea-based or mobile land-based missiles. Accordingly, two old warheads would have to be destroyed for every new fixed ICBM warhead; three warheads, for every two new SLBM warheads. Only mobile land-based missile warheads could be replaced on a one-to-one basis. In order to assure that reductions would actually occur, the American plan also required an annual build-down of at least 5 percent, regardless of whether or not modernization occurred.

As might be expected, U.S. governmental interests were hardly unanimous in their support for the plan. The Arms Control and Disarmament Agency strongly opposed build-down until overruled by the president.[38] The Joint Chiefs of Staff were unenthusiastic, but ultimately acquiesced, surmising correctly that the Soviet Union would reject the plan anyway. The civilian chiefs in the Defense Department opposed the build-down plan; the National Security Council was cool to the idea; and the State Department remained neutral. The primary support came from the president's political advisors, who were concerned primarily about congressional and public criticism of the president's record on arms control.

In the short term, the build-down proposal could be quite destabilizing, particularly as long as the United States and the Soviet Union continued to rely upon fixed multiple-warhead ICBMs. U.S. plans for deploying 100 MX missiles with ten warheads each would require the dismantlement of 2,000 nuclear warheads. As many as 550 Minuteman IIIs with three warheads each and 350 Minuteman IIs and Titans, each armed with one warhead, would have to be reduced. From a relatively secure 1,050 launchers, the United States would have to deter the Soviet Union with only 250 land-based missiles. A very attractive target for a Soviet preemptive attack would consequently be provided. The required reductions would also make the Soviet Union, particularly to the extent that it wanted to continue relying upon its powerful SS-18, far more vulnerable to a U.S. preemptive strike, leading to even greater pressures upon the Soviet leaders to initiate a nuclear attack.[39]

Concessions made by the United States with respect to heavy bombers and ALCMs, areas in which it enjoyed the advantage, were more meaningful, but perhaps not as significant as might appear at first blush. The U.S. spring 1983 proposal to establish a ceiling of 400 heavy bombers was of little interest to the Soviet Union since the Soviet Backfire bomber would be counted in the totals. As pointed out in the last chapter, whether or not to include the Backfire as a strategic weapon was a controversial issue since that bomber does not have intercontinental-range capability to fly to and from the United States without refueling.

The October proposal to collapse the two phases of the U.S. START plan into a single one may have been potentially more important, but since the specific restrictions proposed for the second phase held little interest for the Soviet Union, other than the fact that bombers and air-launched cruise missiles would be regulated, the significance of the move is questionable. The Soviet Union obviously could not be pleased with that part of the plan that moved the ceilings on nuclear throw-weight, where the Soviets enjoyed a considerable superiority, into the first phase. Although the United States showed some flexibility in indicating that the total throw-weight need not be reduced as low as current

American levels, the proposal remained unacceptable to the Soviet Union since it was also made clear that the United States would have the right to increase its own throw-weight to whatever level was agreed upon.

In a similar vein, the meaningfulness of the flexibility shown by the United States on the issue of air-launched cruise missiles may have been more apparent than real. Although the June 1983 American proposal called for limits on ALCMs that would be lower than the 28 average per bomber agreed upon in SALT II, the United States was already adhering to a unilateral pledge, made at the time of signing the SALT II Treaty, not to place more than twenty ALCMs on each B-52 bomber. In fact, it was only installing twelve per bomber. In deploying air-launched cruise missiles on the B-1 bomber, the Reagan administration planned to position only twenty-two per bomber, somewhat below the average allowed. To agree to lower numbers in effect was doing no more than continuing existing U.S. policy.

Prior to Mikhail Gorbachev's rise to power in March 1985 about the only strategic arms concessions offered by the Soviet Union, aside from returning to positions it had already agreed upon in SALT II, were those spelling out sublimits on the number of MIRV missiles that would be allowed to each side. There are several plausible explanations for the rigidity shown by the Soviet Union in the START talks. Perhaps the main reason for its lack of flexibility was related to its belief that a SALT II Treaty had already been negotiated and it was the responsibility of the United States to ratify an agreement that the U.S. had already signed. Second, strategic arms issues did not lend themselves as readily to the Soviet objective of dividing the Western alliance system as did the issue of intermediate-range missiles. As a result, greater Soviet flexibility was shown with respect to the latter negotiations. Third, the Soviet Union had threatened to end all talks on strategic arms control as well as the INF talks if the United States deployed Pershing II and cruise missiles in Europe, and it made good on its threat within two weeks of the initial deployment. Finally, the lack of Soviet initiatives and flexibility on strategic arms was undoubtedly related to the fact that within a period of only three years after the Soviet Union tabled its initial START proposal it had four different leaders—Leonid Brezhnev, Yuri Andropov, Konstantin Chernenko, and Mikhail Gorbachev. Under such conditions a state must necessarily be more preoccupied with internal matters rather than foreign affairs. The rapidity of the changes hardly provided adequate time for a new Soviet administration to develop its own arms control policy.

The Gorbachev Initiatives

With the resumption of arms control negotiations under the rubric of the Geneva umbrella talks, which began in March 1985 and consisted of separate negotiations on strategic arms, intermediate-range nuclear forces, and strategic defensive systems, there was renewed hope for some progress on offensive arms control. Soon after the Geneva talks got underway, Konstantin Chernenko died, leaving the reins of power to his successor, Mikhail S. Gorbachev. Although the succession may have slowed the new government somewhat, by mid-1985 the Soviet Union began offering more arms control initiatives than it had at any time in the postwar period. These included a number of unilateral initiatives that have already been noted, such as a freeze on further deployment of INF forces in April 1985 and extended in October. The Soviet Union also instituted a unilateral ban on nuclear testing on August 6, 1985, extending it several times despite the fact that the United States failed to follow suit.

A number of concessions involving verification measures were also made during the early Gorbachev period. These included agreement to open Soviet space laboratories to outside inspection; acceptance of monitoring posts to verify Soviet and American troop reductions in central Europe; proposals to allow on-site inspection of Soviet nuclear tests (in return for U.S. acceptance of a test ban moratorium); agreement to allow on-site verification of INF missile destruction;[40] procedures for monitoring long-range missiles as they leave the factory; restrictions on mobile missiles that would confine them to specified areas in order to facilitate detection; and agreement to make trains carrying SS-24 mobile ICBMs look different from ordinary rail cars.[41] When these moves are added to the Soviet January 1985 proposal for on-site verification of chemical weapon production centers and its February agreement with the International Atomic Energy Agency to provide inspection of Soviet peaceful nuclear energy facilities, it is clear that the Soviet Union had come a long way in terms of agreeing to more onerous inspection requirements.

In a dramatic reversal of its strategic arms proposals that until that time had called for only minimal reductions below the SALT II levels, the Soviet Union in late September 1985 introduced a plan calling for a 50 percent reduction in offensive delivery systems, contingent on the cessation of U.S. efforts to develop its proposed strategic defense system. In a compromise with the United States position, the Soviet plan also called for sublimits on a given weapons system to be placed at 60 percent of the total. Although this was 10 percent higher than what the

United States wanted, it was a considerable improvement over existing Soviet force structures in which land-based missiles represented 75 percent of the total.

Although on the surface the Soviet Union finally seemed to be accepting the Reagan administration's proposals for extensive cuts in strategic delivery systems, the proposed Soviet reductions would affect both U.S. intermediate-range and intercontinental-range delivery systems while exempting comparable Soviet INF forces. The rationale was that American intermediate-range nuclear forces could reach Soviet territory but Soviet INF forces could not strike American territory. For good measure, the Soviet Union also included all of the U.S. nuclear forward-based delivery systems in the proposed cuts and a ban on modernization that threatened the U.S. Trident II D-5 missile, the Stealth bomber, and the Midgetman missile while allowing the Soviet Union to deploy its new SS-23, SS-24, and SS-25 missiles as well as a new bomber.[42] The result was that the Soviet proposal was a complete nonstarter. What the Soviet Union was asking was an across-the-board 50 percent reduction of all U.S. systems—short-range, intermediate-range, and intercontinental-range—while allowing only its intercontinental-range systems to be included in the reductions. Fifty percent clearly did not mean 50 percent for the Soviet Union. Nevertheless, the Soviet Union was able to capitalize upon world headlines showing it to be in favor of substantial arms reductions. Clearly the Soviet Union had assumed the upper hand in the arms control propaganda war.

During the next several months a virtual blizzard of arms control proposals came from Soviet sources. In almost all cases the proposals were presented publicly in major speeches and were often published in paid advertisements in Western newspapers. While continuing to support its proposal for a 50 percent reduction in those weapons that the Soviet Union labeled as strategic, the Soviet Union in October called for a quick 200–300 reduction in ICBMs on both sides to show good faith. The next month it offered to reduce its heavy ICBMs in return for U.S. limits on the planned Strategic Defense Initiative.

The Soviet Union's most radical disarmament measures were proposed by General Secretary Gorbachev in January 1986 when he presented a fifteen-year plan calling for complete nuclear disarmament in which all nuclear weapon states were expected to participate.[43] The proposal for the first time placed an explicit deadline for the initial 50 percent reduction that was to be reached over the next five to eight years. Also starting in 1990, other countries must freeze their nuclear arms and agree not to deploy them outside their own borders.

Like so many general and complete disarmament proposals of the past, perhaps it is only the first phase that should be taken seriously. As indicated previously, the 50 percent reduction required in this phase was unacceptable to the United States as long as the Soviet Union insisted upon including American forward-based systems in the proposal. An important concession was made in this regard in late May 1986 when the Soviet Union tabled a plan that dropped the demand that U.S. nuclear-capable fighter planes and carrier aircraft within range of the Soviet Union be counted as strategic weapons. The Soviet Union also no longer insisted that submarine-launched long-range cruise missiles be banned. In presenting these important concessions, the Soviet Union at the same time took a step backward when it modified its strategic reduction requirements by calling for a one-third reduction rather than a 50 percent reduction as previously proposed. This change meant a new ceiling for each side of 8,000 strategic nuclear charges (warheads and bombs). With a 60 percent limit on nuclear warheads based on land-based missiles, some 4,800 ICBM warheads would be allowed under the new plan. The earlier ceilings, placed at 6,000 and 3,600 warheads, respectively, were actually somewhat more acceptable to the United States than were the new limits.

United States concessions to the various Gorbachev initiatives were relatively slow in coming, partially as a result of serious divisions within the Reagan administration itself. In early November 1985 Secretary of State George Shultz met Gorbachev in Moscow where he presented the American response to the Soviet September proposal for a 50 percent reduction in strategic arms. The U.S. plan, which represented the first new U.S. strategic arms proposal in two years, accepted the notion of a 50 percent reduction but made explicit recommendations on how those reductions might be applied. According to the proposal, reentry vehicles on ICBMs and SLBMs would be limited to 4,500 warheads, 500 less than provided in President Reagan's Eureka proposal. A subceiling of 3,000 warheads on ICBMs would be allowed, roughly halfway between the earlier U.S. proposal of 2,500 and the proposed Soviet limit of 3,600. The American proposal also called for a 1,500 ceiling on the number of air-launched cruise missiles and a 350 limit on heavy bombers. A 50 percent reduction in ballistic missile throw-weight would be required of the Soviet Union, but Soviet throw-weight would still be left at a figure slightly higher than that of the United States. In essence, these proposals changed previous U.S. strategic arms control proposals very little other than providing adjustments for slightly deeper cuts to match the Soviet-proposed 50 percent reduction. Even the build-down concept was retained as the suggested means for implementing the agreed reductions. Two weeks after Shultz's visit to Moscow Mikhail Gorbachev and Ronald Reagan met at the Geneva summit where they confirmed that one of their primary goals was to obtain a 50 percent reduction in strategic arms.

Perhaps the most controversial aspect of the U.S. November 1985 plan was its proposed ban upon the deployment of mobile, land-based intercontinental ballistic missiles. Not only would adherence to such a provision be strongly resisted by the Soviet Union, which was in the process of deploying the mobile SS-24 and SS-25 ballistic missiles; but many U.S. military strategists, beginning with members of the Scowcroft Commission, felt that American security could be enhanced by producing the mobile Midgetman missile in order to assure an invulnerable ICBM capability.

Some have suggested that the U.S. inclusion of a ban on mobile ICBMs, at that time, was merely a bargaining ploy to be relinquished as soon as the United States perfected the Midgetman, which was not expected to be operational until the early 1990s. Others would have been just as pleased if such a missile did not enter the U.S. arsenal, and for them the proposal was supported as a way of obtaining their procurement preferences. Although mobile missiles can help stabilize nuclear deterrence by making land-based missiles less vulnerable, their effect on arms control can be devastating since verifying such weapons, particularly in the absence of a complete ban upon them, is difficult at best.

A number of military experts opposed production of the Midgetman because it would compete with other preferred weapons systems for funds. Despite its relatively small size, the Midgetman was not an inexpensive weapons system. In fact, according to a 1985 Air Force estimate, each warhead on the Midgetman, in view of the missile's mobility and need for an operating team, would cost four times as much as each one on the MX.[44] To make the missile cost-effective, some Pentagon officials began suggesting that the Midgetman be increased in size and carry additional warheads, defeating the purpose of the missile in the first place. Indicative of the general lack of support for the Midgetman in the Pentagon was Secretary of Defense Caspar Weinberger's blunt acknowledgement in the fall of 1985 that ''the Midgetman is a missile that is designed by Congress . . . and we are working on it because that's our direction.''[45]

Apparently the administration has not been serious about its proposed ban on mobile missiles, for in its FY-1988 budget it asked for an additional 50 MX missiles that would be placed on railroad cars to make them less vulnerable to enemy attack. Although requests were also made at the same time for continued development of the Midgetman, many in the Pentagon believed that budgetary pressures would dictate against the latter, allowing further concentration upon the preferred MX mobile missle system.[46]

At the Reykjavik summit in October 1986, Gorbachev and Reagan apparently agreed to the ultimate destruction of all ICBMs, which would have made the issue of mobile missiles moot. As the meetings have now been reconstructed, it appears that the two reaffirmed the 1985 Geneva Summit goal for a 50 percent reduction in strategic arms to be achieved over a five-year period.[47] In the final sessions at Reykjavik, President Reagan proposed the elimination of all ballistic missiles over a period of ten years. Such a plan would have deprived the Soviets of their most formidable weapons while allowing the United States to capitalize on cruise missiles and bombers where it had a decided advantage. Consequently, Gorbachev countered by proposing the elimination of all nuclear weapons as he had been suggesting since January. Unexpectedly, the president's response was one of agreement.

Subsequently, controversy has raged over the issue both as to whether President Reagan agreed to the elimination of all nuclear arms in ten years as Gorbachev claims or just ballistic missiles as the president now says. Regardless of which position was taken, it is clear that the issue of the follow-on to the first-phase 50 percent reduction had not been settled in Washington or with the NATO allies prior to Reykjavik. A barrage of criticism erupted on both sides of the Atlantic as many defense analysts expressed concern about the need for continued Western reliance upon nuclear weapons, including ballistic missiles, to deter superior Soviet conventional forces. Many military experts within and outside the administration breathed a collective sigh of relief that the wide-ranging tentative agreement on the abolition of strategic nuclear arms ultimately failed as a result of President Reagan's rejection of the Soviet insistence that agreement on strategic weapons be linked to the restrictive Soviet interpretation of the ABM Treaty that would have limited testing of the strategic defense system to the laboratory.

The United States has retreated somewhat from the strategic arms position it assumed at Reykjavik. In April 1987 the Reagan administration decided to extend the time required for the 50 percent reduction in strategic forces from five years to seven years. Moreover, the countdown for this reduction was not to begin until the treaty is signed. The delay apparently was motivated by the Joint Chiefs of Staff's desire to deploy additional weapons, particularly sea- and air-launched cruise missiles. In effect, the proposed 50 percent reduction would represent somewhat less than 50 percent of strategic offensive capability if measured by stockpiles now existing. The administration plan presented in Geneva in May also included no provision for further negotiations aimed at the eventual elimination of all strategic offensive weapons as proposed at Reykjavik.

It is interesting to note that for all of the rhetoric expended by the Reagan administration accusing the Soviet Union of noncompliance with past arms control agreements, little attention has been given to issues of verification in the U.S. START proposals. As a result, numbers rather than specific debate on verification requirements have been the most frequently raised issues in the strategic arms talks. Nevertheless, it is clear that the Reagan administration's proposals will demand far more onerous verification requirements than those introduced by the United States during the SALT era. For example, the insistence upon counting missiles rather than launchers and upon measuring comparable throw-weight will require considerable on-site inspection. This, coupled with the administration's insistence that something more than adequate verification be required, does not augur well for the prospects of reaching agreement on strategic arms reduction.

THE STRATEGIC DEFENSE INITIATIVE

On March 23, 1983, President Ronald Reagan presented a vision to the American people in which the world would no longer need to live under the threat of nuclear retaliation but rather could rely on a system capable of defending against a nuclear attack. Few experts took the plan seriously at the time, particularly as it might apply to population defense. Nevertheless, some saw the proposal as a way to build a limited system to reduce the vulnerability of ICBMs in order to provide a more credible deterrent—in effect a return to an anti-ballistic missile system which had been strictly limited by the ABM Treaty in 1972. Yet the image of a shield against nuclear weapons gradually captured the popular imagination. The stage had been partially set by the anti-nuclear movement, which had painted such a horrible picture of the dangers of nuclear war that many Americans had an intense need to believe that there might be a defense against such weapons of mass destruction.

As indicated in the last chapter, during the sixties and seventies military experts had concluded that an ABM system might not be effective and would in fact tend to destabilize the nuclear deterrent system. Scientific developments in the eighties led some to reevaluate this assessment.

Scientists began to see potential in such new technologies as laser and high-energy particle beams as a way of defending against a missile attack. These new assessments caught the attention of the president, resulting in a proposed $26 billion research effort over a period of five years to determine the feasibility of developing such a system.

The proposed system was called the Strategic Defense Initiative or more popularly "Star Wars." The initial concept called for a three-tiered system in which missile interception would focus first upon the missile's boost phase during which satellites would warn of missile launchings within seconds. Response at the boost phase would have to be virtually automatic since there would be less than five minutes to intercept. In the second phase there would be an attempt to intercept the remaining missiles during the twenty-minute flight phase. The terminal phase, lasting about two minutes, would seek to destroy any remaining warheads as they re-entered the atmosphere.

It was believed that if each layer of the three-tiered system could be made 90 percent effective, only eight out of 8,000 RVs would be able to arrive on target, thus providing a nearly perfect defense.[48] Many technical questions were raised about the proposed system, leading many scientists to question its efficacy. There are just too many actions that an adversary can take to counter a system designed to intercept ballistic missiles, even in the case of the latest technological advances using lasers and particle beams. For example, the adversary may develop fast-burn boosters; it may insulate its offensive missile boosters to absorb the beam's energy; it can make the missile spin or shift its trajectory so that a laser beam cannot focus long enough to penetrate the target; a liquid film can be secreted, making penetration of the target difficult; thousands of decoys such as balloons or other chaff can be launched, making it impossible for the defender to determine which objects contain nuclear warheads; space mines may be placed in the path of American space weapons; or an ICBM attack can be concentrated and the number of warheads substantially increased to overwhelm any conceivable strategic defensive system. Additional counter measures might include the use of offensive systems that are less vulnerable than ICBMs to anti-ballistic missile systems, such as cruise missiles and SLBMs that fly at a lower trajectory. Even bombers loaded with stand-off missiles and gravity bombs can be expected to deliver some of their payloads. Finally, an aggressor might attack the communications and computer systems of the defender, neutralizing the defender's ability to detect and respond to a launch.

For a missile defense system to be a desirable option, the cost of building that system ought to be less than the cost of countering the system offensively. Esimates of the cost of SDI have been placed at $500 billion to $1 trillion (or 20-50 percent of what the United States spent on strategic nuclear weapons between 1945 and 1985).[49] The engineering requirements of building such a system are likewise enormous as it has been noted that anywhere from 2,750 to 5,000 launchings of shuttle or shuttle-sized rockets would be required to place all of the needed hardware into space.[50] In view of the delay and problems encountered as a result of the Challenger space shuttle explosion, the prospects for such a feat appear difficult at best.

Given the many ways of countering a strategic defense system and the numerous technological complexities involved, it is little wonder that an overwhelming number of the 451 members of the prestigious National Academy of Sciences responding to a written questionnaire believed that it was most unlikely that a survivable and cost-effective system could be built within the next twenty-five years. This survey, which was limited to those scientists from relevant fields such as physics and mathematics, revealed that 78 percent of the respondents felt that the prospects were "extremely poor" or "poor." Only 4 percent said the odds of success were better than even.[51]

Another problem confronting the Strategic Defense Initiative has been the generally negative reaction given the proposal by American allies.[52] After so much energy had been expended in attempting to couple the U.S. deterrent system with that of Europe through the deployment of INF forces on European soil, the United States threatened to undo the whole process by pressing the allies to support the Star Wars proposals. SDI, rather than reassuring European leaders, raised doubts about whether the United States would come to the aid of the allies in the case of a Soviet attack, particularly if the U.S. felt secure with its defensive shield. They feared that an effective strategic defense system could lead the United States to ignore Europe, while concentrating upon a strategy of "Fortress America." Others refuted this notion, suggesting that the additional security provided the United States would make the U.S. feel more secure about going to the defense of Europe, recognizing that it would not be decimated in the process. Secretary of Defense Caspar Weinberger sought to reassure European doubts by suggesting that SDI would be "equally effective against SS-20s and other intermediate-range Soviet weapons."[53]

Transferring ABM components to Western Europe would not only violate article 9 of the ABM Treaty, but it is also questionable whether a sufficiently effective nuclear shield could be developed against shorter-range delivery systems with their lower trajectories. At minimum, from the allied perspective, SDI would force the Soviet Union to develop comparable defensive systems—systems that may not be effective against the overwhelming offensive might of the United States but would be sufficient to neutralize the much smaller French and British nuclear deterrent systems.

The United States seemed out of step with much of the rest of the world as well on the issue of space-based weapons. It was the only state to abstain on a 1984 General Assembly resolution calling for peaceful uses of outer space. Some 150 United Nations members voted in favor of the resolution.[54]

The effectiveness of the Strategic Defense Initiative is also dependent upon a restrained Soviet reaction to the U.S.'s building such a system. The danger is that a defensive shield is likely to accelerate an offensive arms race. Although part of the brief of the Reagan administration in support of SDI suggested that the Soviet Union would be more likely to accept an agreement on offensive arms control if it recognizes that such weapons would not be effective against such a shield, it is just as likely that the opposite might occur. Scientists at the Lawrence Livermore National Laboratory, a federal nuclear design lab, suggested that if both superpowers build missile defenses, the United States might have to compensate by building heavier and more powerful nuclear warheads.[55]Caspar Weinberger noted on the eve of the 1985 Reagan-Gorbachev summit that even a probable Soviet defense would require that the United States increase its offensive forces.[56]

An illustration of the fact that the Soviet Union also thinks in offensive terms when trying to cope with the defensive systems of the other side can be found in its June 1986 arms control proposal. According to the proposal, the United States would be able to engage in SDI research, but in return the Soviet Union asked for an increase from 6,000 to 8,000 in the number of strategic offensive warheads that would be allowed each side. The dilemma is that without meaningful restraints on offensive arms, which a state is reluctant to accept since it needs a hedge against defensive systems, no missile defense system can be totally effective. According to Richard D. DeLauer, the undersecretary of defense for research and development during Reagan's first term and a strong supporter of SDI, "this is why we need arms control."[57]

Rather than simply accelerating an offensive arms race, efforts to build a defensive shield against nuclear weapons may induce a preemptive strike on the part of the adversary. If the Soviet Union, for example, believes that the United States is nearing a highly effective defensive shield against a nuclear strike, incentives will be high to initiate a strike before the system is completely in place. With the installation of what is perceived as an effective U.S. defensive shield, the Soviet Union would realize that it would no longer have a deterrent against the United States.

Perhaps in partial recognition of the provocative aspects of building SDI, the Reagan administration sought to reassure the Soviet Union by offering in November 1985 to sell missile defenses to the Soviet Union at cost. Given the high level of distrust between the two superpowers, it is hardly likely that the Soviet Union would accept such an offer, much less that the American public would allow it to be put into effect. Considerable dismay arose among the American public when President Reagan first broached the topic of sharing defensive systems with the Soviet Union during a 1984 campaign debate with Walter Mondale.

Criticism was also leveled against the Strategic Defense Initiative since its full development would violate a number of arms control agreements. These include first and foremost the 1972 Anti-Ballistic Missile Treaty. Among provisions of the ABM Treaty which would be violated if the Strategic Defense Initiative were developed are article I, which says in part that each party "undertakes not to deploy ABM systems for a defense of the territory of its country" and article V, which requires that the parties undertake "not to develop, test, or deploy ABM systems or components which are sea-based, air-based, space-based, or mobile land-based." Agreed Statement D requires the parties to discuss ABM systems and components that might be created in the future and demands that such systems be in accord with other articles of the treaty.

The debate on the compatibility of SDI with the ABM Treaty revolved largely around the question of whether or not research on ABM systems would be allowed and what constituted research. The ABM Treaty did not ban research, recognizing that it would be difficult, if not impossible, to verify such a ban. That the Soviet Union also accepted such an interpretation when the ABM Treaty was signed is suggested by a statement made in support of ratification of the treaty by A. A. Grechko before the Presidium of the Supreme Soviet on September 29, 1972. In this speech Grechko indicated that the treaty "places no limitations whatsoever on the conducting of research and experimental work directed toward solving the problem of defending the country from nuclear missile strikes."[58]

The Reagan administration has gone to great lengths in an attempt to justify tests that many experts, including those who were involved in the negotiations themselves, believe would violate the ABM Treaty. In April 1985, the Defense Department released a report listing fifteen SDI experiments to be conducted in the next five to ten years that it asserted would not violate the treaty.[59] In making such a claim, it appeared to be engaging in considerable subterfuge. For example, the Department of Defense argued that since the proposed target was a satellite rather than a missile, two of the tests would not violate the treaty. Yet it was clear what the ultimate target for these systems would be, particularly since the United States was in the process of developing the F-15 anti-satellite killer system, which had already proven itself effective. By testing the SDI laser "below the power level and beam quality required for a ground-based laser ABM weapon," the Pentagon rationalized that its proposed laser tests would remain in compliance with the ABM Treaty. Missile boost-phase and midcourse tracking surveillance systems would be tested, according to the report, but these tests would not violate the treaty since the experimental system involved "would not be provided with the capability necessary to achieve ABM performance levels."

In the fall of 1985 lawyers for the Defense Department and the legal advisor for the Department of State, following a quick review of the negotiating record, concluded that the ABM Treaty prohibited only the military deployment of new space-based systems. Their argument was that the record revealed that the United States had failed to convince the Soviet Union that "exotic" ABM systems should be banned. The United States should therefore take a similar position, treaty language notwithstanding. The Defense Department study concluded that the negotiating record justified both testing and deployment of exotic ABM systems such as lasers and directed energy beams, whereas the legal advisor to the State Department indicated that it allowed only testing.[60] The fact that virtually all of the principal negotiators of the ABM Treaty disagreed with both of these views did not seem to bother the advocates of these revisionist interpretations.

The United States has also used alleged Soviet violations of the ABM Treaty as a potential justification for no longer adhering to the treaty. The primary Soviet violation cited in this connection is the Soviet construction of the Krasnoyarsk radar system, which the United States claims, given the geographical location of the system in Siberia, is designed for tracking ballistic missiles rather than providing early warning of a nuclear attack. According to former SALT negotiator Paul C. Warnke, if one used the reasoning of the Pentagon's 1985 report noted above, the Soviet Union would not be in violation of the ABM Treaty until some time in 1988, when the Krasnoyarsk facility is expected to be activated.[61]

The criticism directed against the Soviet's Krasnoyarsk and other radar installations would seem to have less legal and moral standing since the United States itself is pressing ahead with plans to construct two new large phased-array radars in Greenland and Britain. The compatibility of these radars with article VI of the ABM Treaty and Agreed Statement F has been raised by a number of authorities. Agreed Statement F holds that large phased array radars may be deployed only at ABM sites or on the periphery of each side's territory. Article VI prohibits future radars "except at locations along the periphery of its national territory and oriented outward." The Reagan administration claims that it is not building any new radars but merely modernizing existing ones. According to some authorities, an earlier classified U.S. statement made it clear that the United States would not be allowed to replace such radars with large phased array radars.[62]

Despite laying the groundwork for justifying a possible U.S. abrogation of the ABM Treaty, the Reagan administration, largely in response to an outcry against such a move on the part of Congress and several NATO allies, initially announced that it would continue to live within the more restrictive definition of what is allowed with respect to research on the Strategic Defense Initiative. In an effort to bargain with Congress, rather than the Soviet Union, the administration threatened in the spring of 1986 to reconsider its decision to abide by the ABM Treaty if Congress went ahead with its plans to reduce the budget of the SDI program.[63]

In addition to violating the ABM Treaty, the Strategic Defense Initiative would be incompatible with the 1967 Outer Space Treaty, which prohibits the deployment of nuclear weapons in space. Those parts of the program that utilize only conventional explosives, such as the F-15 anti-satellite system, would not be affected since the Outer Space Treaty applies only to nuclear weapons and weapons of mass destruction. Space-based weapons such as the X-ray laser, which uses large mirrors positioned in space to reflect beams capable of destroying missiles, would constitute a violation since nuclear explosions are used to produce the laser beam. This particular weapon would also violate the Limited Test Ban Treaty, which disallows nuclear explosions in all environments except underground.

In 1981 the Soviet Union sought to close the gap in the coverage of the Outer Space Treaty by proposing that all weapons, not just nuclear ones, be banned from deployment in outer space. The Soviet Union's August 1983 proposal went a step further by proposing a ban upon the testing and use of all weapons in outer space. The latter proposal also included a ban on manned spacecraft used for military purposes, which many U.S. officials thought the Soviet Union would attempt to apply to the U.S.

shuttle program. A ban on the testing of anti-satellite systems was also included in the draft treaty as well as the requirement that all existing systems be destroyed.

Regardless of the desirability or the legality of the Strategic Defense Initiative, there is no question but that the plan caught the attention of the Soviet Union. SDI was clearly responsible for inducing the Soviet Union to return to the negotiating table, which it had left in November 1983 as a result of the U.S. deployment of the Pershing II and cruise missiles in Europe. The Soviet Union's arms control position since that time has been largely directed toward restricting the development of the Strategic Defense Initiative, probably due in large measure to a recognition that it could not compete effectively with the United States in a technological space race of the magnitude envisioned in the Reagan plan. The Soviet position has been that no research, testing, development, or deployment of such systems should be allowed. A hint of greater flexibility on the issue was suggested by a September 1985 *Time* magazine interview with Mikhail Gorbachev in which Gorbachev suggested that some research on SDI would be allowed.[64] Subsequent discussion, however, had made it clear that the Soviet Union is unwilling to accept anything more than basic laboratory testing of space-based systems.

The Soviet Union, in an effort to get the United States to agree to its proposed ban on space-based weapons, offered to link such a ban to substantial reductions of offensive missiles. After getting nowhere with this proposal, because of President Reagan's insistence that the strategic defense initiative was nonnegotiable, the Soviet Union initiated a new approach in which it sought to at least delay American deployment of its proposed space-based defensive system. The Soviets proposed that the two superpowers agree not to withdraw from the ABM Treaty for a period of fifteen to twenty years and that they work to tighten the language on allowable research, development, and testing of new missile defense systems. The Soviet Union seemed particularly interested in closing the loophole in the ABM Treaty that allows a state to withdraw with six months notice.

Prospects for a renegotiated ABM Treaty improved somewhat in July 1986 when President Reagan sent a letter to Gorbachev in which he indicated a willingness to discuss the disputed issues related to the ABM Treaty. The letter was viewed by some within the administration as a way of signaling that the United States was willing to bargain with the Soviet Union on space-based defenses.[65] In this way the president could save face on his position on SDI, which he had continued to argue was not negotiable.

Although the United States was unwilling to commit itself to the Soviet's proposed 15-20 year guarantee of the ABM Treaty, the president indicated that a seven-and-a-half year delay in the deployment of space-based defense systems would be acceptable if the Soviet Union would agree to accept U.S. proposals for an expanded definition of research to include the development and testing of ABM components rather than just laboratory research.[66] In agreeing to such a delay the United States would not be conceding much since the director of the Strategic Defense Initiative, Lieutenant General James A. Abrahamson, announced about the same time that deployment could not begin for another decade even if the research proved SDI to be a desirable option.[67] The administration in effect gave Moscow a choice: either adhere to the ABM Treaty with its right of withdrawal after six months or agree to a new treaty that would allow actual deployment of SDI weapons after 1993.

At the 1986 Reykjavik summit both sides apparently agreed to the notion of a ten-year guaranteed adherence to the ABM Treaty. At the same time, the United States made it clear that it disagreed with the Soviet insistence that the treaty permitted only laboratory research. The U.S. position was that the ABM Treaty allowed not only research but the right to develop and test certain ABM components. It was basically over this issue that the summit failed as the Soviets continued to insist that its interpretation was proper and, more importantly, that agreement on INF and strategic force reductions was contingent upon that interpretation.

In February 1987, in a move led largely by Secretary of Defense Caspar Weinberger, the Reagan administration declared that it would follow the broad interpretation of the ABM Treaty that would allow testing of exotic ABM systems. Because of concern that the SDI might not continue as a viable program beyond the Reagan era, there was great interest in conservative circles for beginning deployment of a first-stage space defense system, utilizing kinetic heat-seeking missiles to intercept Soviet ICBMs. Even though such weapons would be obsolete by the midnineties when lasers and high particle beam weapons are expected to be ready for possible deployment, it was believed by some that the beginnings of a space system would be necessary in order to keep the SDI program alive beyond the current administration. It has already been shown on many occasions that if a substantial investment can be made in a given weapons system many groups will have a vested interest in keeping the system alive. Besides, continuing a system will be the only way to justify the billions already spent. But according to former Secretary of Defense Harold Brown, the kinetic-kill missile proposed by the administration for early deployment would clearly violate the ABM Treaty even when using the broad interpretation of the treaty since such technologies were clearly available when the treaty was negotiated.[68] There is some reason to believe that the primary objective of the Reagan administration for advocating accelerated testing and partial deployment of ABM components was more related to the desire to scuttle the ABM Treaty itself. Such a move would obviously be an open invitation to the Soviet Union to ignore its obligations under the treaty.

Additional evidence of the administration's hostility to the ABM Treaty is provided by President Reagan's April 1987 decision to reduce the time-span for adhering to the treaty from the ten years agreed at Reykjavik to five years. In contrast with earlier U.S. policy, the U.S. arms control negotiators in Geneva have also been ordered not to discuss the issue of treaty interpretation in the negotiations.

The prospects for an agreement on limiting the Star Wars program remains relatively remote, particularly as long as the Reagan administration continues to believe so strongly in the potential of the system. Even though some within and outside the administration might favor a temporary agreement prohibiting the testing and deployment of various SDI weapons systems while allowing research to continue, there is concern that any such restrictions might lead Congress to reject funding for the research program. After all, if eventual testing and deployment cannot be guaranteed, why waste billions of dollars for research on a system that may never be deployed?

ANTI-SATELLITE WEAPONS

Efforts to guarantee the peaceful uses of space have also been complicated by the development of anti-satellite weapons. With the successful test of Sputnik in 1957, the United States became increasingly concerned about the dangers of the use of space for military purposes and the possibility that the Soviet Union would attempt to build anti-satellite weapons of its own. As a result, research was begun on the development of an anti-satellite system (ASAT) under the so-called Satellite Inspection Technique or SAINT program. Under this plan the United States in 1963–64 developed two operational ASAT systems—one deployed at Kwajalein Atoll and the other at Johnston Island. The Kwajalein Atoll ASAT system remained operational until 1967, and the Johnston Island system until 1975.

The Soviet Union tested its first ASAT system five years after the United States. Between 1968 and 1982, U.S. officials detected some 20 tests of a Soviet ground-launched anti-satellite weapons system. Only 45 percent of the tests were believed to have been successful though.[69] The Soviet tests were based primarily upon a technology that the United States had developed in the sixties and subsequently abandoned. The United States ASAT system now utilizes an F-15 airplane that is capable of launching an eighteen-foot missile with such deadly accuracy that only a conventional homing-device is needed rather than an nuclear warhead.

Little attempt was made in formal disarmament negotiations to control ASAT weapons during the sixties and early seventies. Instead, what evolved were tacit understandings on space systems and ASAT weapons.[70] The Soviet Union informally accepted the launching of U.S. Reconnaissance satellites beginning in 1960, despite dire predictions that the Soviet Union would attempt to destroy them. Over time, with the United States tacitly accepting the launching of Soviet space systems, it became established that neither would interfere with the reconnaissance satellites of the other. By 1963 the Soviet Union had dropped its demand for a ban on reconnaissance satellites from its formal arms control proposals. This approach was ultimtely formalized in the SALT I agreements in which the United States and the Soviet Union agreed not to interfere with the national technical means of the other side—means that relied heavily upon satellite surveillance.

The importance of unilateral constraint for arms control can also be seen in the American decision to cancel the SAINT program in 1963. General Bernard Schriever and Eugene Zuckert, the secretary of the Air Force at the time, have noted that the primary reason for the cancellation of the program was fear of escalating the arms race.[71] In addition to cancelling the SAINT program, Secretary of Defense Robert McNamara tacitly communicated a U.S. downgrading of space weapons by using annual military posture statements and testimony before Congress to communicate that the United States believed that there was no military requirement for such systems. The fact that the United States and the Soviet Union agreed in 1963 to renounce the orbiting of weapons of mass destruction weakened one of the prime reasons for developing ASAT weapons. This renunciation was formalized in the 1967 Outer Space Treaty. The Soviet Union also showed restraint when it suspended all ASAT tests from December 1971 to February 1976.

The resumption of Soviet ASAT testing in 1976 placed pressure upon the United States to resume its own tests. Some felt it important tht the United States remain active in the ASAT race in order to deter the Soviet use of such weapons by being able to threathen a comparable retaliatory response. In 1977 the Carter administration proposed bilateral talks on the subject of anti-satellite systems, and these were begun the following year. Little was accomplished during the two years of these negotiations because of the Soviet insistence that the U.S. space shuttle be included among the prohibited systems.

In an effort to provide some inducement to the Soviet Union to engage in serious negotiation, the Carter administration budgeted funds for ASAT testing and development. Under the original plan the system was to be operational by 1985. The first ASAT test in the program, however, did not occur until 1985, delaying the program until at least 1987.

The Reagan administration refused to resume the ASAT talks, largely on the grounds that it felt that such an agreement could not be verified. The administration demanded that a verification system would have to be virtually foolproof, particularly since the United States had relatively few military satellites and their loss could be disabling. Verification of ASAT weapons is exceedingly difficult since one is dealing with easily concealable weapons as well as weapons that are used for conventional and other purposes. Even satellites can be employed as anti-satellite weapons by maneuvering them into the path of another satellite. Effective verification would require at minimum on-site inspection of numerous launches.

Another factor in the Reagan administration's rejection of engaging in talks on the subject of anti-satellite weapons related to the administration's commitment to the Strategic Defense Initiative. To the extent that the United States was determined to develop a comprehensive anti-ballistic missile system, it was impossible to support an ASAT ban. After all, the very same weapons, whether based upon more traditional BMD systems or upon more exotic laser and directed particle beams, can be used in attacking satellites. The technical problems of overwhelming satellite systems are much simpler than attacking incoming missiles since satellites are fewer in number, are more detectable, and move in more predictable ways. By the same reasoning, it might be argued that the continued existence of ASAT testing and deployment makes a ban on satellite missile defense systems an impossible task, for ASAT weapons, with some upgrading, could threaten ballistic missiles as well. According to a Pentagon official involved in space policy, the overlap between anti-satellite technology and "Star Wars" is so great that if the United States is forced to stop testing ASAT weapons, "it would slow down certain parts of S.D.I. today and probably prevent the completion of the research program."[72]

Recognizing this problem, Kenneth Adelman on the eve of the resumption of U.S. ASAT testing in September 1985 virtually ruled out any agreement on such weapons even if some of the troublesome verification problems could be solved. In issuing his blanket condemnation of a ban on ASAT, Adelman noted that the administration had concluded that "it could not foresee any possible agreement to limit anti-satellite weapons that would be in the national interest."[73]

Congress did not share such a view as the House of Representatives amended the FY 1985 defense authorization bill by banning U.S. tests against objects in space unless the Soviets resume their own tests of anti-satellite weapons. The Soviet Union had unilaterally suspended such tests in 1983. The following year the Republican-controlled Senate voted 61 to 28 to allow full-scale testing of anti-satellite weapons only if the president certifies that he is willing to negotiate limits on such weapons with the Soviet Union.

Part of the congressional opposition to the U.S. ASAT program has to do with weaknesses in the program itself. Congressman George Brown, citing a General Accounting Office study, concluded that the study "shows that the ASAT program is way over budget, way behind schedule and unable to meet its mission requirements. If Congress gives this program the go-ahead, we'll end up with a multi-billion dollar boondoggle that's obsolete the day its employed."[74] Recognizing some of these problems, the Pentagon has cut the number of F-15 ASAT missile bases from two to one and reduced the number of missiles it planned to buy by two-thirds.[75] At the same time, it threatened to escalate the ASAT arms race by focusing on the more promising anti-satellite technology under development in the SDI, such as lasers and particle beams.

A persuasive argument can be made that the United States may actually benefit more from restrictions on ASAT testing and deployment than would the USSR. The United States is far more dependent upon military satellites for communication, command, control and intelligence-gathering (C^3I). Some 70 to 80 percent of all U.S. long-haul military C^3 is transmitted by satellite relay. Satellites are vital to American intelligence operations as well since the United States does not have the information-gathering advantages of dealing with an open society that the Soviet Union does. Consequently, anything that will protect U.S. military satellites will benefit U.S. interests. A ban on the testing of ASAT would also lock in the technological superiority in anti-satellite systems that the United States now enjoys. Finally, a ban at this time would preclude the development of a Soviet ASAT system that could threaten the security of high-orbiting space systems that are now largely immune to existing Soviet ASAT systems. Both states, of course, would stand to benefit economically from restrictions on ASAT testing and deployment, for such systems are not inexpensive. The price of the U.S. ASAT program was pegged at $3.6 billion, which perhaps could be better used to buy a Nimitz-class carrier or 200 F-16 fighter aircraft.[76] Savings could also be gained if the need for building defensive and evasive capabilities into satellites were eliminated.

The time would seem to be ripe for negotiating an ASAT agreement as the Soviet Union continues to adhere to its moratorium on ASAT testing. The price of such an agreement would probably have to include a willingness to forego U.S. plans to test and deploy the Star Wars system. As long as the United States insists upon deploying space-based weapons systems, the Soviet Union will find it necessary to develop a capability to neutralize those weapons. It was perhaps in recognition that the Reagan administration was unlikely to bargain away its planned defensive shield that the Soviet Union dropped its demand for a ban on the testing and deployment of ASAT in 1985. A glimmer of hope for separate negotiations on ASAT weapons arose the following year when the Soviet Union indicated a willingness to negotiate on any one of three space-based systems—ASAT weapons, anti-ballistic missile systems, or weapons able to attack targets on earth and in the earth's atmosphere. At the same time, the Soviets indicated that they would prefer a ban on all three systems.

CONCLUSION

The Reagan administration came into power with a generally hostile attitude toward arms control, believing that past negotiations on the subject and the agreements that had been reached primarily benefitted the Soviet Union. It was also argued by the administration that the Soviets had exploited those agreements by violating a number of their provisions.

The importance of executive leadership for successful arms control negotiations was evident as the Soviet Union was virtually paralyzed on arms control policy during the first Reagan term as it had three different leaders. Similarly, President Reagan failed to exert strong leadership in the arms control area as shown by his inability to generate a consensus on the U.S. negotiating position from the strongly conflicting views shown by various bureaucratic interests. The result was that negotiations often took place without any clear instructions as to what the United States position was.

Given the paralysis within the Reagan administration on arms control, Congress became a more active participant in the process by making specific proposals for negotiating positions, sending representatives to monitor the negotiations, and threatening various administration defense programs that might undercut the interests of arms control.

Both internal and external public opinion also became a greater force to contend with than in previous decades. Considerable pressure was exerted by the nuclear freeze movement in the United States as well as European publics concerned about the emplacement of intermediate-range nuclear weapons on European soil. It was partially because of such activities that a reluctant American administration finally agreed to negotiate.

Public pressure, as well as a recognition that the SALT agreements had some restraining effects upon the arms policies of the Soviet Union, led the administration to announce a no-undercut policy with respect to the SALT agreements as long as the Soviet Union did likewise. It adhered to this policy until May 1986 and then continued to remain in technical compliance with SALT for some time thereafter.

Both the United States and the Soviet Union legitimately can be accused of presenting nonnegotiable positions with respect to intermediate-range nuclear forces, strategic arms, and space-based systems that formed the three major topics of discussion during the Reagan period. Their behavior raises questions about whether either state was serious about arms control. The rhetoric surrounding the talks during the Reagan era was perhaps the most vituperative since the 1950s. Nevertheless, the strategic arms buildup engaged in by the United States appears to have increased Soviet incentive to negotiate on arms control matters. President Reagan's initiation of an extensive research program on strategic defense systems was similarly instrumental in getting the Soviet Union to return in 1985 to the arms talks that it had broken off almost a year and a half earlier. These pressures, however, were not sufficient for obtaining negotiated agreements, and the eighties so far have to be written off as the least productive for arms control since the early postwar years.

A considerable part of the blame for the lack of progress on arms control during the Reagan years can be placed upon the administration itself. Former SALT negotiator Gerard Smith put the issue very well when he wrote *New York Times* columnist James Reston, asking rhetorically what we Americans would think if the Soviets had:

- Failed to ratify the three latest arms control agreements that their premier had signed;
- Walked away from negotiations for a comprehensive test ban and for limitations on anti-satellite systems;

- Announced that that treaty's correct interpretation permitted the development and testing of systems that the treaty by its very terms prohibited;
- Refrained from starting negotiations about strategic arms for many months, and then made offers that their former minister of foreign affairs had acknowledged to be nonnegotiable and ''absurd'';
- While claiming violations, had refrained from making effective use of the Standing Consultative Commission to resolve disputes or was reported to have denied permission for its delegates to raise the issues;
- Announced that it was breaking out of an agreement setting ceilings on missiles and bombers because of the bad behavior of the other party.[77]

Since these actions accurately describe what the United States had done in its arms control policy in recent years, can there be any question as to why the Soviet Union harbors such suspicion about U.S. negotiating behavior on arms control?

6

Toward a More Secure World

The search for national security through arms control and disarmament has been a disappointing one. Agreements, particularly those involving reductions of armaments, have been few and far between. Whether, on balance, the arms control effort has contributed to increased propects for peace and security in the world is essentially a toss-up. On the one hand, positive outcomes have been achieved, such as the restraints placed upon the spread of nuclear weapons, the adoption of procedures designed to reduce the prospects of nuclear war by accident and miscalculation, and a few agreements imposing ceilings on weapons, all of which have added a certain predictability to military planning. On the negative side, disarmament negotiations may have actually contributed to the heavy burden of arms now seen in the world. The belief that one must negotiate from strength, the need to make payoffs in the form of additional hardware to obtain the support of the military and other conservative groups for a given disarmament policy, and the fear and suspicion evoked by concern that the other party might violate any agreement reached have all tended to accelerate rather than reduce reliance on weapons.

NEGOTIABLE WEAPONS SYSTEMS

An analysis of the postwar disarmament negotiations provides a number of lessons as to which weapons systems are negotiable and why. Such an analysis also underscores why so little has been achieved in some forty years of effort, involving thousands of meetings and hundreds of proposals. Several reasons can be identified that help explain why the United States might prefer to focus negotiations on one weapons system while the Soviet Union prefers to address another. Since the nature of the arms

172

race is always changing as new strategies and weapon refinements are developed, these preferences never remain static. Each party reacts to the strategic situation of the moment. For this reason, arms control negotiations have often had a musical-chairs quality, with one side gravitating to the position of the other just as the latter moves on. This pattern was evident in the decisions on whether to stress limits on defensive arms, offensive arms, or both. When the two sides began exploring the prospects of strategic arms limitations in 1966–67, the United States preferred to address only anti-ballistic missiles while the Soviets wanted to place the emphasis on offensive weapons; by the time SALT I opened, however, the positions were completely reversed.

Several factors influence the kinds of weapons systems that a state would like to see regulated. First, a state is likely to propose testing restrictions on systems that it has already successfully tested in an effort to prevent the adversary from following suit. For example, during the nuclear test ban negotiations, proposals for an immediate test ban usually followed each U.S. or Soviet test series. After its successful round of ICBM tests in 1972, the Soviet Union proposed a freeze on all new strategic programs. The intent was to keep the United States from developing the Trident and the B-1 bomber while allowing the Soviet Union to retain its four new ICBM systems—SS-16 through SS-19. Similarly, the United States sought to prevent the Soviet Union from testing MIRVs by proposing in April 1970 a ban on MIRV testing and deployment. This proposal would have allowed the United States to continue producing MIRVed weapons, first successfully tested in August 1968, some five years before Soviet tests began.

Second, a state will rarely negotiate with regard to a weapons system that it has not yet achieved but which the other side possesses. The Soviet Union rejected the Baruch Plan in 1946 despite the fact that the United States seemed willing to relinquish its monopoly on nuclear weapons to an international control force. Also, the Soviet Union, not yet having tested its first MIRV system, was reluctant even to discuss MIRV controls during SALT I. When a state does not share in a prohibited weapon technology, it may consider itself at the mercy of its adversary, precariously relying on the latter's promises not to produce the prohibited weapons secretly nor to maintain existing but undetected stockpiles ready for use.

Third, proposals to freeze a weapons system at a particular quantitative level will generally be made by the state with a numerical edge. The United States preferred a freeze of strategic delivery systems at existing levels during the late 1960s, and the Soviet Union pushed similar proposals during the 1970s after the numerical balance had tipped in its favor. The Soviet Union deferred the destruction of strategic missiles to the last stage of its general and complete disarmament proposals when it thought it was ahead in 1959, but it moved that matter to the fore a year or so later when it became clear that the United States was in the superior strategic position. President Reagan's opposition to a freeze in the 1980s was related to the perception that the United States was behind in the arms race, whereas the Soviet Union embraced the freeze movement whole-heartedly.

Fourth, given the concern about developing bargaining chips, states will have to be in a position near equality before a given weapons system is negotiable. The fact that there have been no naval arms control negotiations designed to limit the size of U.S. and Soviet surface fleets since 1945 is related to the fact that only recently has the Soviet surface navy become anywhere comparable to that of the United States.[1]

Fifth, a state may choose to negotiate with regard to a particular weapons system if it believes itself falling behind, qualitatively or quantitatively, and sees little chance of reversing its inferior position. The Soviet Union became more willing to negotiate restrictions on the ABM after 1967 when it realized that its Galosh system around Moscow was not likely to be effective. The subsequent U.S. decision to proceed with its own ABM system, which was likely to be a superior system to that of the Sovit Union, probably accounted for the high priority that the Soviets gave to the conclusion of an ABM treaty during SALT I. The Soviet Union, in attempting to negotiate a ban on the testing and deployment of a strategic defense system, recognized that it would have difficulty competing with the United States in the highly sophisticated ''Star Wars'' technology.

Sixth, if the opposition shows no interest in building a given weapons system, a state will have little incentive for introducing controls on that system in its own proposals. The Soviet Union felt little pressure for negotiating an offensive missile agreement during SALT I since the United States was not adding to its offensive capability, at least in terms of numbers of missiles. The recognition of limited Soviet incentives in the SALT talks led the United States to press for funding new weapons systems that could be used for bargaining chips.

Seventh, a state is likely to try to regulate areas of weapons development in which the adversary would probably be a clear winner in an all-out arms race. For example, some authorities have warned of the danger of allowing unlimited production of sea-based cruise missiles, arguing that the Soviet Union has a great advantage in that realm because it has far more conventional submarines with usable torpedo slots and because it enjoys a superior air defense system capable of intercepting cruise missiles.[2]

Eighth, a strategic arms proposal might originate with the desire to destroy obsolete weapons. U.S. proposals for bomber burnings in the 1960s appear to have been so motivated. Soviet plans to dismantle its SS-4s, SS-5s, and SS-11s were related to the fact that these weapons had come to the end of their useful life.

Ninth, a weapons system may also prove to be negotiable simply because a state is not interested in it, views the weapon as technologically infeasible, or considers it not worth the cost. It was cost-effectiveness calculations that induced the United States and the Soviet Union to ban nuclear weapons in outer space and on the seabed floor. Cost and effectiveness considerations also entered into the willingness to limit the ABM in 1972. As exotic ABM systems appear to be more feasible, particularly those based on laser technology, they have again become non-negotiable weapons systems as far as many within the Reagan administration are concerned.

Tenth, even though a state may hesitate to forego a given weapons system completely, it may be willing to accept temporary limitations. For example, since the United States had neither the ability nor the desire to test or develop the mobile MX missile before 1982, accepting the protocol to SALT II did nothing to change U.S. planning with regard to MX. The same can be said of the restrictions on the deployment of ground- and sea-based cruise missiles—both of which could still be tested during the three-year span of the protocol. The Reagan administration's willingness in 1986 to delay deployment of SDI weapons for a period of seven-and-a-half years was related to the fact that the system was not expected to be ready for deployment for at least a decade.

Eleventh, a proposal to regulate a weapons system might be motivated not so much for its inherent arms control value but rather as a political weapon to exploit divisions within the opposition, whether within the adversary's government or within the opposing alliance system. Moscow's decision to move the destruction of missile systems in its early general and complete disarmament schemes from the third stage to the first seemed partially designed to exploit French interests in a ban on missiles. Other issues raised have included forward-based systems, the neutron bomb, and ground- and sea-launched cruise missiles—all involving serious differences of opinion among the NATO allies. Since the prospect of developing almost any new weapon finds both supporters and opponents in Moscow and Washington, opportunities exist for dividing domestic constituencies simply by raising an issue.

Finally, to be negotiable, a weapons system must be verifiable. Although the United States has been more concerned about verifiability than the Soviet Union, both sides were in agreement that laboratory research on strategic defense systems could continue since there was no way to verify compliance with respect to restrictions on such activities. As the perception of the verifiability of MIRV improved, the Joint Chiefs of Staff reversed their position during the SALT negotiations and agreed to make MIRV a negotiable weapons system.

Obstacles to Disarmament

Our examination of the postwar nuclear disarmament negotiations has revealed a number of obstacles confronting disarmament. Perhaps chief among these obstacles is that of verification as the United States has regarded inspection procedures that would be acceptable to the Soviet Union as being insufficient; and the Soviet Union, for its part, has viewed the verification demands of the United States as too intrusive. While the development of space satellites and a number of other verification technologies has made national technical means of inspection an effective and less intrusive procedure for ascertaining compliance with arms control agreements, the Reagan administration issued a litany of charges that the Soviet Union had violated a number of arms control agreements. Such alleged violations, combined with the demands by the Reagan administration for yet more intrusive verification procedures, made significant arms control measures a virtual impossibility.

The Soviet Union over the years has shown an increased willingness to accept more extensive verification techniques, including on-site inspection to monitor nuclear test bans and to observe restrictions on the production and dismantlement of both long and short range missiles. It has agreed to allow inspectors at chemical production plants and at peaceful nuclear facilities as well as inspectors to observe troop movements and conventional arms reductions. Even if these more intrusive verification procedures are implemented, assessments may still vary as to whether the other side is living up to the letter of an agreement, particularly with regard to those agreements that deal with the qualitative aspects of weapons as opposed to numbers of weapons.

A second obstacle to disarmament has been the problem of asymmetry in weapons systems between the United States and the Soviet Union as well as differing geopolitical requirements for security. How does one ascertain equivalence when states, given different geopolitical situations and technologies, emphasize different weapons systems? Further questions arise about the equivalence of allied forces and the implications of unequal threat situations confronting the Soviet Union and the United States as the former is concerned about a threat from China as well as the nuclear capabilities of U.S. NATO allies. Under such conditions, imaginative arms control proposals and trade-offs will be necessary if one expects to obtain mutually satisfactory arms control agreements. Of one thing we can be certain and that is that attempts to use arms control to force the other side to make dramatic changes in its force structures, as in the case of the Reagan administration proposals that would place severe restrictions on the ratio of ICBMs that the Soviet Union would be allowed, are doomed to failure.

In the third place, although technology might benefit the arms control regime by providing improved verification techniques, technological change is often an impediment to successful negotiation. The belief that one might develop the ultimate weapon or the ultimate defensive system leads decision makers to reject restraints upon military research and development. This, coupled with the fear that the opposition may succeed in breaking out of any arms control restraints established, leads to conservatism in arms control policy as decision makers seek to keep their options open. Moreover, that technology that may contribute to both peaceful activities as well as military purposes makes negotiation on arms control exceedingly difficult as experience with attempts to control nuclear energy make abundantly clear.

A fourth major obstacle confronting arms control and disarmament is that of distrust and tension in the world. The United States, in particular, has insisted over the years that disarmament is contingent upon the peaceful resolution of a number of political disputes. Admittedly, a high level of distrust generated by political differences is hardly conducive to creating the sort of environment necessary to reach a consensus on disarmament issues, but low levels of tension reduce the incentives for doing anything about the arms problem. Indeed, it is because there is tension and an imminent danger of war that arms control becomes all the more important. Perhaps what is needed is a recognition that although arms control agreements entail a certain level of risk so does nuclear deterrence. Neither system is foolproof, and it is perhaps foolhardy to ask so much more of disarmament than we ask of deterrence. Nevertheless, the problem of distrust must be addressed, and any disarmament agreement must include adequate verification procedures. This will not guarantee that an arms agreement may not break down, but adequate guarantees must be provided so that neither side will seriously be disadvantaged by such a failure.

Finally, progress on arms control is complicated by the fact that positions taken on disarmament issues are often dictated by the domestic political situation. The observation that the most difficult negotiations on arms control have generally occurred within governments rather than between governments has become commonplace. The Reagan administration, in particular, was confronted with deep divisions between the State Department and the Defense Department on various issues of arms control. According to one authority, "bureaucratic factors and pressures from labor and industry are of such critical importance to weapons development and procurement decisions that little can be done to control the arms race by negotiation at the international level."[3] Additional complicating factors arise because of the role played by Congress—a role that became a limiting force with respect to the SALT II Treaty and a driving force favoring more serious negotiations during the Reagan period. The positions taken by Congress have in turn been influenced by what has often been a fickle American public on the issues of arms control and disarmament.

Although the Soviet leadership is considerably less constrained by parliamentary and public opinion in formulating its arms control policy than is the United States leadership, deep divisions, dating back to the years of Khrushchev, have existed among various bureaucratic interests. Brezhnev was forced to pay considerable attention to the wishes of the military in formulating his arms control policies. Gorbachev also was subjected to considerable criticism from the military for his nineteen month unilateral test ban moratorium in 1985–87, but nevertheless persisted in the policy.

When it comes to disarmament policy, it has generally been the naysayers who have had the last word. It is always easier to persuade others of possible risks in a new approach to peace than to convince them of the utility of pursuing a different strategy. The military, in particular, has had considerable leverage in this regard because of its expertise on national security matters.

TOWARD MORE EFFECTIVE BARGAINING ON ARMS CONTROL

To the extent that one believes that arms control and disarmament offers a useful approach to improved security, what lessons can be learned from the past to increase the prospects for verifiable and effective arms control in the future? The evidence from several sets of arms control negotiations underscores the importance of reciprocity of concessions, as significant correlations were found in U.S.-Soviet scores during the early postwar disarmament negotiations, the test ban negotiations, and the SALT talks. At the same time, there was some evidence of approach-avoidance behavior, especially in the test ban negotiations, as retractive behavior became evident at the point the two sides were nearing agreement. Such findings raise questions about measuring the meaningfulness of concessions, particularly with respect to long-range and more comprehensive disarmament schemes. Were reciprocation strategies followed in such cases because there was little chance for an agreement on significant reductions being reached, thus making the concessions cheap, or do such concessions represent a serious attempt to reach agreement? It may be that the recent Gorbachev initiatives have been taken largely with the expectation that the United States would never reciprocate, enabling the Soviet Union to assume the moral high ground with respect to the issues of disarmament by making concessions that are never expected to become part of an agreement. Perhaps one should not denigrate the seriousness with which the Soviet Union has approached the issue of arms control in recent years. There appears to be a very real concern about the sluggish Soviet economy. Operating as it is with half the gross national product of the United States, the Soviet Union is forced to devote twice the percentage of its GNP to the military effort just to stay even with the United States.

This is not to suggest, as some officials within the Reagan administration appear to believe, that the Soviet Union will make the preponderant number of concessions on arms control for the sake of agreement. Nor does it mean that the United States can engage the Soviets in an arms race that will bleed the Soviet Union into submission or result in the overthrow of its government because of domestic discontent. Given its ability to demand greater sacrifice on the part of its public, the Soviet Union may find itself better able than the United States to compete in an all-out arms race. It has already demonstrated its ability to compete and even to prevail in the quantitative arms race.

Obviously, if differences on disarmament issues are to be narrowed, concessions will have to be made. Care should be taken in the way such concessions are presented. The United States, for example, might attempt to stagger its concessions more effectively than it has in the past, for it has introduced most of its concessions early in the negotiations. Such behavior tends to raise the aspiration level of the Soviet Union, making agreement more difficult to achieve. There is even some evidence that the assumption of a harder line in the previous round of negotiations results in a more forthcoming Soviet response in the subsequent round. Our analysis of evolving U.S.-Soviet positions on arms control during the Reagan period suggests that perhaps the United States has gone too far in the other direction, begrudgingly changing positions only after considerable pressure has been exerted by Congress, the American public, and U.S. allies to be more compromising in its bargaining position.[4]

With time running out on the Reagan presidency and with some administration officials concerned about the president's place in history and interested in diverting attention from the Iran arms sales controversy, pressure for a more conciliatory U.S. position continues to be exerted. This pressure, coupled with Mikhail Gorbachev's interest in diverting scarce resources from the Soviet military buildup in an effort to stimulate the sluggish Soviet economy, may eventually produce the first nuclear arms control agreement of the Reagan presidency. Past experience as well as current discussion, however, suggests that such an agreement is likely to be a limited one, confined at most to an agreement to remove intermediate-range and short-range nuclear missiles from European soil. Prospects for such an agreement rose considerably as a result of Gorbachev's February 1987 decision to separate agreement on INF from U.S. acceptance of the Soviet position on the Strategic Defense Initiative.

It has been largely because of the failure of arms control negotiations to produce anything more than largely cosmetic agreements that a number of authorities, led by Kenneth L. Adelman, the director of the Arms Control and Disarmament Agency, have suggested that unilateral approaches to arms restraint may actually be preferable to negotiated arms control agreements.[5] Abram Chayes has noted a number of reasons why formal negotiations tend to exacerbate rather than alleviate the arms race. These include the belief that one needs to build bargaining chips in order to negotiate effectively; the tendency in formal negotiations to assume a hostile stance for negotiating purposes; and the pressures generated to build to treaty limits or to intensify efforts in areas not covered by the treaty.[6] One might add to this list the suspicions that are generated by the fear that the other side is evading a negotiated agreement. There is something more compelling about taking action against an adversary if there is a real or imagined violation of a formal agreement than if one is dealing with a tacit understanding. The resulting acrimony in many cases is likely to be a more serious problem for continued security interests and good relations than is the alleged violation itself. Since the negotiating process focuses upon asymmetries in weapon systems, the political decision maker may find it difficult to reject a given weapon system even if that system is not in the nation's particular security interest. The fact that the other side has the weapon and that the weapon is publicized as a result of the negotiating process may create pressures to follow suit. One wonders just how many weapons have been built simply because the other side has them rather than for any intrinsic need for the weapon.

It may be more useful to pursue unilateral approaches to arms control during periods of high tension, particularly since such tension tends to turn formal disarmament negotiations into propagandistic and vituperative sessions that do little to improve relations between the superpowers or to improve the prospects of agreement. Informal and tacit understandings on arms control issues might usefully be pursued when bureaucratic divisions are sharp and public opinion is seriously divided on national security issues; otherwise arms control negotiations become only another political football in the domestic political arena. When a state feels unsure of its bargaining position and is highly concerned about changing that position for fear of losing its bargaining reputation or credibility, it might be useful to pursue tacit dealings rather than formal negotiation.

In utilizing unilateral approaches to enchance national security interests, what is perhaps most important is that the state take actions that will not undermine existing or potential arms control agreements. One might think twice about producing weapons that complicate arms control, such as sea-launched cruise missiles with their inherent verification difficulties. In designing weapons systems, it would seem preferable, to the extent possible, to pay attention to functionally related observable differences (FRODs) in order that distinctions can be made between those systems designed to carry conventional warheads rather than nuclear ones. Nuclear weapons can also be designed in such a way as to reduce the need for reliability testing. In short, what is required is to pay more attention to the arms control implications of new weapons systems—something that the congressionally-mandated Arms Impact Statements were supposed to do. Unfortunately, the consensus is that such statements have generally failed in keeping destabilizing weapons systems and those that threaten the prospects for arms control off the production line.

Perhaps more than anything, arms control and disarmament as an approach to peace require political will—a will to take slight risks and to reject the notion that more arms means more security. It requires a belief that deterrence can work just as successfully at lower levels of armament and that there is no need to match the adversary arm for arm in order to be secure. Disarmament as an approach to peace will also require a willingness to stand up to strong political forces in both the United States and the Soviet Union that have vested interests in an ever larger military component.

Notes

Chapter 1

1. Jonathan Schell, *The Fate of the Earth* (New York: Avon Books, 1982).

2. Carl Sagan, ''Nuclear War and Climatic Catastrophe: Some Policy Implications,'' *Foreign Affairs* 62 (Winter 1983/84): 257–92. For a more recent and less pessimistic review of the research on nuclear winter, see Starley L. Thompson and Stephen H. Schneider, ''Nuclear Winter Reappraised,'' *Foreign Affairs* 64 (Summer 1986): 981–1005.

3. Hannes Adomeit, ''Soviet Risk-Taking and Crisis Behavior: From Confrontation to Coexistence,'' *Adelphi Papers*, no. 101 (Fall 1973).

4. Stephen S. Kaplan, *Diplomacy of Power: Soviet Armed Forces as a Political Instrument* (Washington, D.C.: Brookings Institution, 1981), p. 53.

5. Barry M. Blechman and Stephen S. Kaplan, *Force Without War: U.S. Forces as a Political Instrument* (Washington, D.C.: Brookings Institution, 1978), pp. 128-29. A favorable outcome was defined as one in which two-thirds of the American objectives were obtained.

6. Ruth Sivard, *World Military and Social Expenditures, 1983* (Washington: World Priorities, 1983).

7. Tom Wicker, ''War by Accident,'' *New York Times*, November 21, 1982.

8. John Steinbrunner, ''Nuclear Decapitation,'' *Foreign Policy* 45 (Winter 1981–82): 18.

9. George C. Wilson and Walter Pincus, ''Missile Survival Questioned,'' *Washington Post,* May 19, 1983.

10. Lisa D. Shaw, ''Nuclear Arms Limitation Policy,'' in Paul R. Viotti (ed.), *Conflict and Arms Control* (Boulder, Colo.: Westview Press, 1986), p. 51.

11. Lloyd Jensen, *''The Postwar Disarmament Negotiations: A Study in U.S.-Soviet Bargaining Behavior''* (Ann Arbor: University of Michigan, Ph.D. dissertation, 1963, pp. 234–47.

Chapter 2

1. Earl H. Voss, *Nuclear Ambush: The Test Ban Trap* (Chicago: Henry Regnery Co., 1963), p. xvi.

2. Robert A. Devine, *Blowing on the Wind: The Nuclear Test Ban Debate, 1954–1960* (New York: Oxford University Press, 1978), p. 149.

3. Henry A. Kissinger, ''Nuclear Testing and the Problem of Peace,'' *Foreign Affairs*, 37 (October 1958): pp. 1–18.

4. Voss, *Nuclear Ambush*, p. 159.

5. Glenn T. Seaborg, *Kennedy, Khrushchev, and the Test Ban Treaty* (Berkeley: University of California Press, 1981), p. 17.

6. Harold K. Jacobson and Eric Stein, *Diplomats, Scientists, and Politicians: The United States and the Nuclear Test Ban Negotiations* (Ann Arbor: University of Michigan Press, 1966), p. 246.

7. Voss, *Nuclear Ambush*, p. 338.

8. Alva Myrdal, *The Game of Disarmament* (New York: Pantheon Books, 1982), p. 92.

9. Sir Edward Bullard, "The Detection of Underground Explosions," in Herbert F. York (ed.), *Arms Control* (San Francisco: W. H. Freeman and Co., 1973), pp. 140–50.

10. Arthur T. Hadley, *The Nation's Safety and Arms Control* (New York: Viking, 1961), p. 50.

11. Jacobson and Stein, *Diplomats, Scientists, and Politicians*, p. 386.

12. Ibid., p. 497.

13. Department of State, *Documents on Disarmament, 1945–1959,* (Washington: Government Printing Office, 1960), Vol 2, pp, 1427–36.

14. Eighteen Nation Disarmament Committee, *Official Records*, PV 19, p. 38.

15. Robert S. Jastrow, "Politics of the Afrikaner Bomb," Orbis 27 (Winter 1984): 832.

16. Department of State, *Documents on Disarmament, 1945–1959*, Vol. 2 p. 1591.

17. Michael Wright, *Disarm and Verify* (New York: Praeger, 1964), p. 126.

18. Eisenhower letter to Gordon Gray, June 14, 1961. *The Declassified Documents Quarterly Catalog* (Washington: Research Publications, 1980), p. 216.

19. Seaborg, *Kennedy, Khrushchev, and the Test Ban Treaty*, p. 139.

20. United States Arms Control and Disarmament Agency, *Documents on Disarmament, 1962* (Washington: Government Printing Office, 1963), p. 74.

21. Ibid., 1963, p. 220.

22. Joseph G. Whelan, *Soviet Diplomacy and Negotiating Behavior* (Boulder: Westview Press, 1983), p. 374.

23. Center for Defense Information, *The Defense Monitor*, Vol. 14, No. 8 (1985).

24. Jacobson and Stein, *Diplomats, Scientists, and Politicians*, p. 246.

25. Bernard J. Firestone, *The Quest for Nuclear Stability* (Westport, Conn.: Greenwood Press, 1982), pp. 102-3.

26. Devine, *Blowing on the Wind*, p. 273.

27. Seaborg, *Kennedy, Khrushchev, and the Test Ban Treaty*, p. 222.

28. Stephen Hilgartner, Richard C. Bell, and Rory O'Connor, *Nukespeak: The Selling of Nuclear Technology in America* (San Francisco: Sierra Club Books, 1982), p. 166.

29. Henry A. Kissinger, *Years of Upheaval* (Boston: Little, Brown, 1982), p. 1167.

30. Theo Ginsberg, *The Question of Peaceful Explosions for the Benefit of Non-Nuclear Weapon States*, UN Document, A/Conf. 35/Doc. 2 (July 3, 1968).

31. William B. Bader, *The United States and the Spread of Nuclear Weapons* (New York: Pegasus, 1968), p. 54.

32. Kennedy letter to Senators Mansfield and Dirksen dated September 11, 1963. ACDA, *Documents on Disarmament, 1963*, pp. 490–91.

33. Geneva Conference on the Discontinuance of Nuclear Weapon Tests, GEN/DNT/PV 141, December 1, 1959.

34. Swedish Delegation, "Nuclear Explosives, 1945-83," *Conference on Disarmament*, CD/430, February 7, 1984.

35. Thomas O'Toole, "Talks by U.S.-Soviets on A-Test Curbs Falter," *Washington Post*, January 18, 1975.

36. Zbigniew Brzezinski, *Power and Principle* (New York: Farrar, Straus, Giroux, 1983), p. 172.

37. Seaborg, *Kennedy, Khrushchev, and the Test Ban Treaty*, pp. 296–97.

38. "Soviet Noncompliance with Arms Control Agreements," reprint of President Reagan's Message to Congress in Paul R. Viotti (ed.), *Conflict and Arms Control* (Boulder, Colo.: Westview Press, 1986), p. 170.

39. Walter Pincus, "U.S. Secretly Protested Radiation Leaks from Soviet Arms Tests, Perle Says," *Washington Post*, May 9, 1986.

40. Walter Pincus, "U.S. Seeks A-Test Talks with Soviets," *Washington Post*, March 13, 1983.

41. Walter Pincus, "U.S. Drops Soviet Talks to Continue A-Arms Testing," *Washington Post*, September 8, 1983.

42. Garcia Robles, Conference on Disarmament (CD/PV 297, March 7, 1985), p. 21.

43. Leslie Gelb, "U.S.-Summit Stance: Nuclear Testing Will Go On," *New York Times*, October 4, 1985.

44. Lynn R. Sykes and Jack F. Evernden, "The Verification of a Comprehensive Nuclear Test Ban," *Scientific American* 247 (October 1982): 54.

45. Don Oberdorfer, "Six Nonaligned Countries Offer to Monitor a Nuclear Test Ban," *Washington Post*, October 29, 1985, p. A14.

46. Michael R. Gordon, "New Measures Seen for Soviet A-Test," *New York Times*, November 4, 1985.

47. Don Oberdorfer, "New CIA Calculations Cast Doubt on Test Ban Violations by Soviets," *Washington Post*, April 4, 1986.

48. Gelb, "U.S.-Soviet Stance: Nuclear Testing Will Go On."

49. Dan Caldwell, "Comprehensive Test Ban: An Effective SALT Substitute," *Bulletin of Atomic Scientists* 36 (December 1980): 32.

50. Walter Pincus, "U.S. Reveals Nuclear Arms Suffer Reliability Problems," *Washington Post*, March 12, 1986.

51. See Hugh E. Dewitt and Gerald E. Marsh, "Stockpile Reliability and Nuclear Testing," *Bulletin of Atomic Scientists* 40 (April 1984), pp. 40–41.

52. Donald Kerr, "Nuclear Weapon Test Bans," in Warren Heckrotte and George C. Smith (eds), *Arms Control in Transition* (Boulder, Colo.: Westview Press, 1983), pp. 81–82.

53. Cited in Flora Lewis, "Chicken or Egg?" *New York Times*, February 23, 1986.

54. Bruce Russett and Fred Chernoff, *Arms Control and the Arms Race* (New York: W. H. Freeman and Company, 1985), p. 95.

55. Flora Lewis, "Chicken or Egg."

56. Cristine Russell, "Underground Test Called Crucial for SDI," *Washington Post*, February 15, 1987.

57. R. Jeffrey Smith, "Soviets Agree to Broad Seismic Test," *Science* 233 (August 1, 1986): 511.

Chapter 3

1. William Sweet, *The Nuclear Age* (Washington: *Congressional Quarterly*, 1984), p. 97.

2. Joseph S. Nye, "Prospects for Nonproliferation," in Rodney W. Jones (ed.), *The Nuclear Suppliers and Nonproliferation* (Lexington, Mass.: D. C. Heath, 1983), p. 219.

3. Anthony C. Ross and Peter King, *Australia and Nuclear Weapons* (Sydney, Australia: Sydney University Press, 1966), p. 15.

4. See Kenneth N. Waltz, "Toward Nuclear Peace," in Dagobert L. Brito, et al., *Strategies for Managing Nuclear Proliferation* (Lexington, Mass.: D. C. Heath, 1983), pp. 118-33.

5. Arnold Kramish, *The Peaceful Atom* (New York: Harper and Row, 1963), p. 18.

6. Duncan L. Clarke, *Politics and Arms Control* (New York: Free Press, 1979), pp. 15–16.

7. Cited by Ellen Collier in U.S. Senate Foreign Relations Committee, *Nonproliferation Treaty* (Hearings, February 18 and 19, 1969), p. 463.

8. Bernard J. Firestone, *The Quest for Nuclear Stability* (Westport, Conn.: Greenwood Press, 1982), p. 110.

9. UN Document, A/5976 (September 24, 1965).

10. Eighteen Nation Disarmament Committee (ENDC), PV 268 (June 28, 1966).

11. U.S. Arms Control and Disarmament Agency, *Documents on Disarmament, 1965* (Washington: Government Printing Office, 1966), pp. 347–49.

12. Lloyd Jensen, *Return from the Nuclear Brink: National Interest and the Nuclear Nonproliferation Treaty* (Lexington, Mass.: D. C. Heath, 1974), p. 2.

13. John Simpson, "Diagnosis and Treatment," in John Simpson and Anthony McGraw (eds.), *The International Nonproliferation System* (London: Macmillan, 1984), p. 169.

14. Roger Richter, "Testimony," *Bulletin of Atomic Scientists,* 37 (October 1981): 29–31.

15. "International Atomic Energy Agency Says it Had Inspection Problems in '81," *New York Times*, July 6, 1981.

16. Sweet, *The Nuclear Age*, p. 151.

17. Cited in Robert L. Beckman, *Nuclear Non-Proliferation: Congress and the Control of Peaceful Nuclear Activities* (Boulder, Colo.: Westview Press, 1985), pp. 290–91.

18, ENDC/PV 223 (August 12, 1965), p. 19.

19. For a discussion of the IAEA safeguards system, see Lawrence Scheinman, *The Nonproliferation Role of the International Atomic Energy Agency* (Washington: Resources for the Future, 1985) and International Atomic Energy Agency, *IAEA Safeguards: An Introduction* (Vienna: IAEA, 1981).

20. U.S. Arms Control and Disarmament Agency, *Documents on Disarmament, 1982,* p. 350.

21. *Louisville Courier-Journal*, March 12, 1969.

22. Robert Scheer, *With Enough Shovels: Reagan, Bush and Nuclear War* (New York: Random House, 1982), p. 6.

23. UN Document, A/C.1/PV 1570 (May 17, 1968), p. 2.

24. Jensen, *Return from the Nuclear Brink* p. 79.

25. Ibid., p. 52.

26. Glenn T. Seaborg, *Kennedy, Khrushchev, and the Test Ban Treaty* (Berkeley: University of California Press, 1981), p. 248.

27. Thomas O'Toole, "Talks by U.S.-Soviets on A-Test Curbs Falter," *Washington Post,* January 1, 1975.

28. John Simpson, "Diagnosis and Treatment," p. 172.

29. Michel Eyraud, "La France face a un eventuel traite de non-dissemination des armes nucleaires," *Politique Etrangere*, no. 4–5 (1967): 477.

30. "Reflections on the Quarter," *Orbis* 11 (Spring 1967): 8.

31. *Facts on File,* July 16-22, 1970, p. 509.

32. George W. Ball, "We Are Playing a Dangerous Game with Japan," *New York Times Magazine,* June 25, 1972, pp. 35–36.

33. Lewis A. Dunn, *Controlling the Bomb: Nuclear Proliferation in the 1980s* (New Haven: Yale University Press, 1982), p. 44.

34. *Washington Post*, July 16, 1980.

35. Sweet, *The Nuclear Age,* p. 116.

36. George H. Quester, "Nuclear Proliferation," in Bernard Brodie, et al., *National Security and International Stability* (Cambridge, Mass.: Oelgeshlager, Gunn and Hain, 1983), p. 232.

37. Walter C. Clemens, Jr., "National Security and U.S.-Soviet Relations," in Burns H. Weston (ed.), *Toward Nuclear Disarmament and Global Security* (Boulder, Colo.: Westview Press, 1984), p. 353.

38. William C. Potter, "U.S.-Soviet Cooperative Measures for Nonproliferation," in Jones et al., *The Nuclear Suppliers and Nonproliferation*, (Lexington, Mass.: D. C. Heath, 1985), p. 11.

39. Raymond L. Garthoff, *Detente and Confrontation* (Washington: Brookings Institution, 1985), p. 763.

40. J. B. Devine, "The USA's Nuclear Non-Proliferation Policy," in Simpson and McGraw, (eds.), *The International Nuclear Non-Proliferation System,* p. 112.

41. M. J. Wilmhurst, "The Development of Current Non-Proliferation Policies," in Ibid., p. 44.

42. Richard Kennedy, "Nuclear Trade: Reliable Supply and Mutual Obligation" in Jones et al., *The Nuclear Suppliers and Nonproliferation,* p. 30.

43. Dunn, *Controlling the Bomb,* p. 105.

44. Institute for Defense and Disarmament Studies, *Arms Control Reporter,* April 8, 1985.

45. David Ignautius, "U.S. Pressuring Pakistan to Abandon Controversial Nuclear Arms Program," *Wall Street Journal,* October 25, 1985.

46. Bob Woodward, "Pakistan Reported Near Atom Arms Production," *Washington Post*, November, 1986.

Chapter 4

1. J. David Singer, *Deterrence, Arms Control, and Disarmament* (Columbus: Ohio State University Press, 1962), p. 216.

2. Richard J. Barnet, *Who Wants Disarmament?* (Boston: Beacon Press, 1960), p. 86.

3. Lewis A. Dunn, *Controlling the Bomb* (New Haven: Yale University Press, 1976), p. 28.

4. Edmund Beard, *Developing the ICBM* (New York: Columbia University Press, 1976), p. 121.

5. Ibid., p. 218.

6. U.S. Department of State, *Documents on Disarmament, 1945–59* (Washington: Government Printing Office, 1960), p. 687.

7. "Bulganin Letter to Eisenhower," *New York Times,* February 4, 1958.

8. U.S. Department of State, *Documents on Disarmament, 1945-59*, pp. 973–77.

9. Ibid., pp. 1460–74.

10. U.S. Arms Control and Disarmament Agency, *Documents on Disarmament, 1961,* pp. 439–42.

11. Ibid., 1965, pp. 75–76.

12. *Washington Post,* May 21, 1965.

13. Duncan L. Clarke, "Nixon Installs a 'Peace Cabinet'—But Where Is the Peace Agency?" *War/Peace Report* (January–February, 1973), p. 28.

14. Ted Greenwood, *Making the MIRV: A Study of Defense Decisionmaking* (Cambridge: Ballinger, 1975), p. 116.

15. Raymond L. Garthoff, "SALT and the Soviet Military," *Problems of Communism* 24 (January-February 1975): 29.

16. John Newhouse, *Cold Dawn: The Story of SALT* (New York: Holt, Rinehart and Winston, 1973), p. 107.

17. Gerard Smith, *Doubletalk: The Story of SALT I* (Garden City, N.Y.: Doubleday, 1980), p. 360.

18. Thomas Wolfe, *The SALT Experience* (Cambridge: Ballinger 1979), p. 124.

19. Mark M. Lowenthal, "The START Proposal: Verification Issues" (Washington: Congressional Research Service, June 25, 1982), p. 1.

20. U.S. Department of Defense, *Annual Report of the Secretary of Defense* (Washington: Government Printing Office, 1980).

21. *Defense Monitor*, August 1974, p. 3.

22. U.S. Senate, Committee on Foreign Relations, *The SALT II Treaty, Hearings,* 96th Cong., 1st Sess., Part II, July 16–19, 1979, pp. 242–43 and 258.

23. Roger P. Labrie, *SALT Handbook: Key Documents and Issues, 1972–1979* (Washington: American Enterprise Institute, 1979), p. 291.

24. *New York Times*, May 3, 1974, p. 3.

25. *Defense Monitor*, XI, No. 7 (1982).

26. Labrie, *SALT Handbook*, p. 303.

27. William H. Kincade, "Challenges to Verification: Old and New," *Arms Control* 3 (December 1982): 23.

28. Clarence A. Robinson "SALT Proposals Facing Hurdles," *Aviation Week and Space Technology*, December 9, 1974, p. 13.

29. U.S. Senate, Committee on Foreign Relations, *The SALT II Treaty, Hearings,* Pt. 1, p. 110.

30. Cited by Milton Leitenberg in Committee on Foreign Relations, U.S. Senate, *Detente Hearings*, 93rd Congress, second session, 1974, p. 475.

31. Newhouse, *Cold Dawn*, p. 246.

32. *New York Times*, July 14, 1978.

33. "ABM: Boondoggle or Bargaining Chip," *Nature* 227 (August 22, 1970): 770.

34. John W. Finney, "Cruise Missiles Provoke Conflict with the Military as Well as with Soviets," *New York Times*, January 21, 1976.

35. Roger P. Labrie, *SALT Handbook* (Washington: American Enterprise Institute, 1979), p. 298.

36. "Excerpts from Speech by Andropov on Medium-Range Nuclear Missiles," *New York Times*, December 22, 1982, p. A14.

37. For a discussion of this tendency in United States negotiating tactics and Soviet efforts to exploit it, see Roy O. Kohler, *SALT II: How not to Negotiate with the Russians* (Coral Gables: Advanced International Studies Institute, University of Miami, 1979).

Chapter 5

1. Lawrence Freedman, "Negotiations on Nuclear Forces in Europe, 1969-83," in Hans-Henrick Holm and Nikolaj Petersen (eds.), *The European Missile Crises* (London: Francis Pinter, 1983), p. 136.

2. Eric J. Grove, "Allied Nuclear Forces Complicate Negotiations," *Bulletin of the Atomic Scientists* 42 (June/July 1986): 21.

3. Fred Hiatt and Rick Atkinson, "Insertable Nuclear Warheads Could Convert Arms," *Washington Post*, June 15, 1986.

4. Strobe Talbott, *Deadly Gambits*, (New York: Alfred A. Knopf, 1984), pp. 66–68.

5. Talbott, *Deadly Gambits*, pp. 144–47 and Ir Faurby, Hans-Henrick Holm, and Nikolaj Petersen, "Introduction," in Holm and Petersen (eds.), *The European Missile Crisis*, p. 21.

6. Paul Nitze, Speech delivered to the American Association for the Advancement of Science Convention, New York City, May 26, 1984.

7. David Holloway, "The INF Policy of the Soviet Union," in Holm and Petersen (eds.), *The European Missile Crisis*, p. 106.

8. Raymond L. Garthoff, "The SS-20 Moratorium: Who Is Telling the Truth," *Washington Post*, April 26, 1983.

9. Richard Perle, "Letters to the Editor," *Washington Post*, May 12, 1983.

10. Robert Scheer, *With Enough Shovels: Reagan, Bush and Nuclear War* (New York: Random House, 1982), p. 6.

11. Carl G. Jacobsen, *The President's Arms Posture: Sins of Omission* (Miami: University of Miami Center for Advanced International Studies, n.d.), p. 2.

12. U.S. Arms Control and Disarmament Agency, *1984 Annual Report* (Washington: Government Printing Office, 1985), p. 20.

13. John Borawski, "The Future of INF," *Parameters* 15 (Summer 1985), p. 39.

14. "Transcript of Reagan's Speech on Soviet-American Relations," *New York Times*, January 17, 1984, p. A8.

15. Institute for Defense and Disarmament Studies, *Arms Control Reporter*, May 1, 1985.

16. Walter Pincus, "Soviets Offer INF Draft Pact," *Washington Post*, May 16, 1986.

17. Richard Bernsten, "Gorbachev Urges Arms Agreement with Europeans," *New York Times*, October 5, 1985.

18. Karen De Young, "Soviets Modify Stance on British, French Arms," *Washington Post*, July 17, 1986.

19. Walter Pincus, "Soviets Offer INF Draft Pact."

20. Paul Nitze, Speech delivered to the American Association for the Advancement of Science Convention, New York City, May 26, 1984.

21. Raymond L. Garthoff, "Postmortem on INF Talks," *Bulletin of the Atomic Scientists* 40 (December 1984): 9.

22. Cited in Leo Sartori, "Will SALT II Survive?" *International Security* 10 (Winter 1985–86): 151, and A. A. Tinajero, *President Reagan's START Proposal* (Washington: Congressional Research Service, Library of Congress, June 9, 1982).

23. Judith Miller, "Anti-Arms Groups Relent Plan for MX," *New York Times*, November 24, 1982.

24. Walter Pincus, "Administration Urged to Seek Extension of Some SALT II Curbs," *Washington Post*, March 5, 1985.

25. "Reagan Statement on Arms Accord," *New York Times*, June 11, 1985, p. A10.

26. Walter Pincus and Don Oberdorfer, "Two Subs to be Dismantled," *Washington Post*, April 22, 1986.

27. Kenneth L. Adelman, "Why Mr. Reagan Is Right about SALT," *New York Times*, June 15, 1986.

28. Institute for Defense and Disarmament Studies, *Arms Control Reporter*, 1985.

29. Adelman, "Why Mr. Reagan Is Right about SALT."

30. Bernard Gwertzman, "NATO Faults U.S. on Intent to Drop 1979 Arms Treaty," *New York Times*, May 30, 1986.

31. David Ignautius, "Without SALT the Race is On," *Washington Post*, June 8, 1986.

32. Cited in Don Oberdorfer, "Last Minute Conservative Pleas Influenced Reagan's Decision," *Washington Post*, June 1, 1986.

33. David Hoffman, "Reagan Calls SALT II Dead," *Washington Post*, June 6, 1986.

34. Michael R. Gordon, "Administration Split on Arms Treaty Compliance," *New York Times*, March 27, 1986.

35. Walter Pincus, "U.S. to End SALT II Discussions with Soviet Union Later this Year," *Washington Post*, July 25, 1986.

36. Alexander Haig, *Caveat: Realism, Reagan, and Foreign Policy* (New York: Macmillan and Co., 1984), p. 223.

37. Raymond L. Garthoff, "An Arms Nonoffer," *Washington Post*, June 12, 1983.

38. Gerard Smith, "The Arms Control and Disarmament Agency: An Unfinished History," *Bulletin of the Atomic Scientist* 40 (April 1984): 13.

39. Herbert Scoville, "Build-Down (-Doom?), *New York Times*, October 11, 1983.

40. Stephen S. Rosenfeld, "Signal from Gorbachev," *Washington Post*, January 31, 1986.

41. Michael R. Gordon, "Moscow Said to Signal Willingness to Work on Arms Pact Verification," *New York Times*, June 22, 1986.

42. Paul H. Nitze, "Arms Control," in Joseph Kruzel (ed.), *American Defense Annual, 1986-1987* (Lexington, Mass.: D. C. Heath, 1986), p. 180.

43. "Nuclear Disarmament by the Year 2000," *New York Times*, February 5, 1986, p. A13.

44. Bill Keller, "Doubts Increase over Future of U.S. Land-Based Missiles," *New York Times*, June 17, 1985.

45. R. Jeffrey Smith, "Midgetman Missile Plans Generate Political Debate," *Science* 232 (June 6, 1986): 1186.

46. Richard Halloran, "White House Seeks Funds for Basing MX on Train Car," *New York Times*, December 20, 1986.

47. Michael Mandelbaum and Strobe Talbott, *Reagan and Gorbachev* (New York: Vintage Books, 1987), pp. 171–81.

48. Sidney D. Drell, Philip J. Farley, and David Holloway, "Preserving the ABM Treaty," *International Security* 9 (Fall 1984): 68.

49. Colin S. Gray, "Strategic Forces," in Kruzel (ed.), *American Defense Annual, 1986–1987*, p. 82.

50. Thomas Karas, *The New High Ground: Systems and Weapons of Space Age War* (New York: Simon and Schuster, 1983), p. 181 and William J. Broad, "Reverberations of the Space Crisis," *New York Times*, June 15, 1986.

51. "Doubt Cast on Missile Shield," *New York Times*, October 31, 1986.

52. Peter Osnos, "ABM Plan Spurs European Concern Over Timing, Defense Implications," *Washington Post*, March 30, 1983.

53. *The Arms Control Reporter*, February 10, 1985, p. 575 B. 9.

54. United Nations General Assembly, Resolution 39/59 (1984).

55. Fred Hiatt and Rich Atkinson, "SDI Seen Spurring Warhead Growth," *Washington Post*, June 2, 1986.

56. Ralph Earle, Speech delivered to the American Association for the Advancement of Science Convention, Philadelphia, Pa., May 28, 1986.

57. Charles L. Gellner, "The Reagan Administration," in Paul R. Viotti (ed.), *Conflict and Arms Control* (Boulder, Colo.: Westview Publishers, 1986), p. 34.

58. Alan B. Sherr, "The Languages of Arms Control," *Bulletin of Atomic Scientists* 41 (November 1985): 26.

59. Walter Pincus, "Space Defense Tests to Avoid Treaty Breach," *Washington Post*, April 21, 1985.

60. Don Oberdorfer, "ABM Reinterpretation: A Quick Study," *Washington Post*, October 22, 1985.

61. Walter Pincus, "Space Defense Tests to Avoid Treaty Breach," *Washington Post*, April 21, 1985.

62. Michael R. Gordon, "U.S. Pursues Plan for New Radars Despite Fears of Treaty Violation," *New York Times*, December 12, 1986.

63. Michael R. Gordon, "ABM Pact Tied to Fund Pledge for Star Wars," *New York Times*, May 19, 1986.

64. "Moscow's Vigorous Leader," *Time Magazine*, September 9, 1985.

65. Leslie H. Gelb, "Reagan is Termed Ready to Discuss ABM Pact Change," *New York Times*, July 22, 1986.

66. Leslie H. Gelb, "Reagan Reported to Stay Insistent on 'Star War' Test," *New York Times*, July 24, 1986.

67. Walter Pincus, "Star Wars Chief Says Deployment, if Feasible, Would Take at Least Decade," *Washington Post*, July 24, 1986.

68. R. Jeffrey Smith and Joanne Omang, "Forms of ABM Consultation Not Settled, Shultz Says," *Washington Post*, February 12, 1987.

69. Charles Mohr, "Space Arms: Debate Over the Value of a Treaty," *New York Times*, July 10, 1984.

70. For an intriguing analysis of the tacit bargaining involved in the consensus that evolved on satellite reconnaissance and ASAT systems see Gerald Steinberg, *Satellite Reconnaissance: Informal Bargaining* (New York: Praeger Publishers, 1983).

71. Ibid., p. 84.

72. Bill Keller, "Entwined with 'Star Wars', Anti-Satellite Debate Grows," *New York Times*, August 26, 1985.

73. Charles Mohr, "Official Defends Space-Weapon Test," *New York Times*, September 12, 1985.

74. R. Jeffrey Smith, "Pentagon Plans New Antisatellite Tests," *Science* 233 (July 25, 1986): 409.

75. Walter Pincus, "Pentagon May Discard ASAT System," *Washington Post*, July 22, 1986.

76. Donald L. Hafner, "Approaches to the Control of Antisatellite Weapons," in William J. Durch (ed.), *National Interests and the Military Use of Space* (Cambridge, Mass.: Ballinger Publishing Co., 1984), p. 250.

77. James Reston, "Now the Silly Season," *New York Times*, July 6, 1986.

Chapter 6

1. Philip Towle, "Unilateralism or Disarmament by Example," *Arms Control* 2 (May 1981): 116.

2. Henry S. Bradsher, "Soviets Seek Ban on New U.S. Missile," *Washington Star*, June 26, 1975.

3. George W. Rathjens, "Changing Perspectives on Arms Control," *Daedalus* 104 (Summer 1975): 205.

4. For a more complete discussion of the role of concession strategies in enhancing the prospects for agreement on arms control see Lloyd Jensen, *Bargaining for National Security: The Postwar Disarmament Negotiations* (Columbia, S.C.: University of South Carolina Press, 1988), ch. 3.

5. Kenneth L. Adelman, "Arms Control Without Agreements," *Foreign Affairs* 63 (Winter 1984–85): 240–63.

6. Abram Chayes, "Nuclear Arms Control After the Cold War," *Daedalus* 104 (Summer 1975): 16.

Glossary

Air-launched cruise missile (ALCM). Unmanned jet-propelled missile launched from a flying vehicle.

Anti-ballistic missile (ABM) system. Weapon designed to intercept and destroy ballistic missiles.

Anti-satellite (ASAT) system. Weapon system for destroying or damaging artificial earth satellites.

Ballistic missile defense (BMD). Defensive system designed to protect one's own offensive missiles.

Biological weapons (BW). Living organisms or infective material designed to cause death or disease.

CBM. Confidence-building measures designed to reduce anxiety about the other side's intentions.

Chemical weapons (CW). Chemical substances that have direct toxic effects.

Circular error probability. A measure of delivery accuracy based on a 50 percent probability of falling within a given circle.

C^3I. Refers to command, control, communications, and intelligence functions.

Counterforce. Targeting adversary's force capabilities.

Countervalue strategy. Targeting forces against civilian targets.

Encryption. Encoding communications for the purpose of concealing information.

Fission. Process whereby heavy atoms split into lighter nuclei, releasing considerable energy.

Forward-based systems (FBS). Military bases and launching sites close to the territory of the adversary.

Fractional orbital bombardment system (FOBS). A missile that achieves partial orbit, but then is fired back to earth.

Fractionation. The division of the payload of a missile into several warheads.

Functionally related observable differences (FRODs). Requirement that delivery systems with different missions be designed differently.

Fusion. Process in which lighter atoms, especially those of the isotopes of hydrogen, combine to form a heavy atom and in the process release substantial energy.

Ground-launched cruise missiles (GLCM). Unmanned jet-propelled missile launched from the ground.

Intercontinental ballistic missile (ICBM). A ballistic missile with a range in excess of 5,500 kilometers.

Interim Offensive Arms Agreement. Part of SALT I agreements that froze ICBMs and SLBMs at existing levels for five years.

Intermediate-range nuclear forces (INF). Nuclear weapons with a range of less than 5,500 kilometers. Sometimes called medium-range if over 1,000 kilometers.

International Atomic Energy Agency (IAEA). A U.N.-related agency that monitors compliance with NPT and safeguards agreements as well as promotes the peaceful uses of nuclear energy.

JCS. Joint Chiefs of Staff.

Kiloton. Measure of explosive yield of a nuclear weapon equivalent to 1,000 tons of TNT.

Limited Test Ban Treaty (LTBT). Treaty signed in 1963 that prohibits nuclear testing in the atmosphere, in outer space, and underwater.

Maneuverable reentry vehicle (MARV). Reentry vehicle whose flight can be adjusted to evade ballistic missile defenses and gain increased accuracy.

Megaton. Measure of explosive yield of a thermonuclear weapon equivalent to one million tons of TNT.

Multiple independently targetable reentry vehicle (MIRV). Reentry vehicles, carried by one missile, which can be directed toward independent targets.

Multiple reentry vehicles (MRV). Multiple warheads that cannot be independently targeted.

National Command Authority (NCA). Top national security decision makers in Washington and Moscow.

National Technical Means of Verification (NTM). Assets such as reconnaissance satellites and radars that are under national control and are used to monitor the other sides' compliance with arms agreements.

Neutron weapon. Nuclear device designed to maximize radiation effects and reduce blast and thermal effects.

Nuclear fuel cycle. Refers to steps from mining fissionable materials to enriching and fabricating fuel elements, reprocessing spent fuel, and disposing of waste.

Nuclear Nonproliferation Treaty (NPT). Treaty negotiated in 1968 to prevent the spread of nuclear weapons to additional states.

Payload. Weapons and penetration aids carried by a delivery vehicle.

Peaceful Nuclear Explosives (PNEs). Explosions designed for civilian purposes such as digging canals. United States and Soviets signed a treaty on the subject in 1976.

Plutonium (Pu). A fissionable material that can be used in nuclear weapons.

Rapid reload. Capability of a launcher firing a second missile within a short period of time.

Reentry vehicle (RV). That part of a strategic ballistic missile that carries a nuclear warhead to its target.

Sea-launched cruise missile (SLCM). Unmanned jet-propelled missile launched from a ship or submarine.

Standing Consultative Commission (SCC). A permanent U.S.-Soviet commission established by SALT I to review issues of treaty implementation and verification.

Strategic Arms Limitation Talks (SALT). Talks on strategic weapons involving the United States and the Soviet Union that lasted from 1969 to 1979.

Strategic Arms Reduction Talks (START). U.S.-Soviet strategic arms talks that began in 1982 and were adjourned *sine die* in December 1983.

Strategic Defense Initiative (SDI). The so-called Star Wars system proposed by President Reagan in March 1983 to provide a national defense against nuclear attack.

Strategic nuclear forces. ICBMs, SLBMs, and bombers capable of intercontinental range.

Submarine-launched ballistic missile (SLBM). A ballistic missile carried in and launched from a submarine.

Telemetry. Data transmitted by radio that convey information about a weapons test.

Thermonuclear weapon. Nuclear weapon in which the main explosive is based upon fusion reactions (also referred to as a hydrogen weapon).

Threshold Test Ban Treaty (TTBT). Treaty signed in 1974 placing a 150-kiloton limit on underground nuclear tests.

Throw-weight. The total weight that can be carried by a missile to target.

TRIAD. Refers to the three components of the U.S. strategic force: ICBMs, SLBMs, and intercontintental-range bombers.

Uranium enrichment. The process of increasing the content of uranium 235 above that found in natural uranium for use in reactors and nucleaer explosives.

Weapon-grade material. Enriched uranium or plutonium suitable for a nuclear weapon.

Yield. Released nuclear explosive energy measured in terms of TNT equivalent. See kiloton and megaton.

Index

Abrahamson, James A., 164
Adelman, Kenneth L., 42, 140, 167, 180, 189
Adenauer, Konrad, 57
Adomeit, Hannes, 257
Adriatic denuclearization proposals, 56
Afghanistan invasion, 6, 74, 87, 106
Africa: denuclearization proposals, 56
Air Force, 154
Air Force bases, 101
Aircraft, 131; dual-capability, 123; functional differences from missiles, 124; inclusion by Soviets in INF, 121
Alaska, 135
Algeria, 64
Anderson, Clinton P., 27
Andropov, Yuri, 150, 188; presents first Soviet START proposals, 146; threatens U.S. on MIRV, 108
Anti-ballistic missile (ABM), 32, 85, 87, 89, 91, 99, 105, 107, 114, 141, 155–58, 160–65, 167, 169, 174, 175; Galosh system, 85, 87, 88, 174; Nike-Zeus, 16, 85; North Dakota site mothballed, 87; Safeguard system, 107, 114; Sentinel system, 85; Tallin system, 85; ways to defeat, 105
Anti-Ballistic Missile (ABM) Treaty, 89, 91; restrictions on further development, 89; restrictions on placement of ABM systems, 99; U.S. efforts to reinterpret, 141
Anti-satellite (ASAT) weapons, 108, 165–69; costs, 169; restrictions on testing, 163; testing, 108; and the Strategic Defense Initiative, 167; verification, 167
Arab-Israeli war, 1967, 6
Argentina, 44, 60, 73, 74
Arms Control and Disarmament Agency (ACDA), 42, 82, 140, 148, 180, 184
Arms Control Association, 132

Arms Control Impact Statements, 181
Arms races, 8, 118
Asia, 129; and INF deployment, 130, 133
Aspin, Les, 142
Atkinson, Rick, 189, 190
Atlas missile, 104
Atmospheric tests, 31
Atomic Energy Commission (United States), 17, 19, 27–29, 46, 55, 69
Atoms for Peace proposals, 55, 56, 67, 80
Australia, 57, 66

Bader, William B., 184
Balkans: denuclearization proposals, 56
Ball, George W., 187
Bargaining chips, 7, 107, 108, 133, 154; use of MIRV, 95
Barnet, Richard J., 187
Barnwell reprocessing plant, 72
Baruch Plan, 55, 78, 90, 98, 173
Beard, Edmund, 187
Beckman, Robert L., 186
Bell, Richard C., 184
Berlin crisis, 20
Bermuda talks, 26
Bernsten, Richard, 189
Bikini Atolls nuclear test, 15
Blechman, Barry M., 183
Bolshevik revolution, 79
Bombers, 16, 81; B-1, 150, 173; B-52, 84, 138, 143, 150; Backfire, 97, 106, 122, 125, 136, 147, 149; burnings, 175; F-4, 126; F-15, 166; F-16, 169; Fencer, 128; heavy bombers, 93, 149; nuclear capable, 153; Phantom, 69, 122; Stealth, 152
Borawski, John, 189
Brazil, 60, 64, 70, 74
Breeder reactors, 75
Brezhnev, Leonid, 4, 35, 39, 41, 87, 97, 119, 127, 146, 150, 178; risk-taking behavior, 4; will not be first to use nuclear weapons, 65; proposal for a

196

threshold test ban, 35; signing of SALT
I, 87; and a comprehensive test ban,
40–41; proposed unilateral INF freeze,
127; reaction to NATO INF decision,
119
Brito, Dagobert L., 186
Broad, William J., 191
Brookings Institution, 4
Brown, George, 168
Brown, Harold, 95, 164; estimate of
savings as a result of SALT II, 104
Brzezinski, Zbigniew, 40, 185
Build-down proposal, 148
Bulganin, N. A., 15, 81, 187
Bullard, Sir Edward, 184
Bureaucratic politics, 137, 143

Caldwell, Dan, 185
Canada, 65, 69
Cape Canaveral, 101
Carter, Jimmy, 39–41, 49–51, 67, 70–76,
87, 106, 117, 119, 146, 166, 167
Carter administration: arms control efforts
in the last year of administration, 117;
and breeder reactors, 67; concessions to
conservative groups to obtain support
for SALT II, 106; discussions with
Soviet Union on INF, 119; nuclear fuel
shipments to India, 74; nuclear
nonproliferation, 70, 71; position on
test ban, 39; proposes ASAT talks, 166;
SALT II Treaty withdrawal, 87
Central Europe: denuclearization, 56
Central Intelligence Agency (CIA), 30,
99; downward estimates of nuclear
explosions, 45
Centrifuge process, 67
Challenger space shuttle, 158
Chayes, Abram, 180
Chemical weapons production ban, 132;
verification, 151, 176
Chernenko, Konstantin, 150, 151;
proposed ban on space weapons, 133
Chernobyl nuclear disaster, 47, 67
Chernoff, Fred, 47, 185
China, Peoples Republic of, 18, 31, 32,
35, 52, 57, 86, 107, 120; and IAEA,
62; monitoring sites, 101;
nonproliferation, 58; nuclear assistance
pact with U.S., 74; position on nuclear
testing, 40; sensitivity to INF
deployment in region, 125
Circular error probability (CEP), 126

Civil defense, 9
Clarke, Duncan L., 186, 188
Clemens, Walter C., 187
Clinch River breeder reactor, 67, 72
Cold-launch capability, 101
Cole, Sterling, 56
Collateral damage, 16
Collier, Ellen, 186
Commission on Strategic Forces. *See*
Scowcroft Commission
Communication, command, control and
intelligence-gathering (C^3I), 5, 6, 168
Comprehensive test ban, 14, 21, 23, 32,
34–36, 39–50, 117, 170; offer of six
nonaligned states to verify, 44;
verification 45
Congress (United States), 17, 178; and
ABM, 86, 88; and arms control, 178;
and ASAT testing, 168; build-down
proposal, 148; consideration of PNET
and TTBT treaties, 38; House
Appropriations Committee, 42; efforts
to generate support for arms control,
107; and the Limited Test Ban Treaty,
37; Midgetman support, 154; nuclear
exports to Argentina, 73; nuclear
assistance pact with China, 74; nuclear
freeze, 118; and nuclear
nonproliferation, 74; opposition to
reinterpretation of ABM treaty, 162;
ratification of SALT II, 137; resolution
demanding continued adherence to
SALT, 141
Congressional Research Service, 93
Conventional troop reductions in Central
Europe, 151
Counterforce strategy, 9
Cowboy test series, 23
Craxi, Bettino, 132
Crises control centers (U.S.-Soviet), 9
Cruise missiles, 43, 123–25, 131, 136,
146; air-launched cruise missiles, 147;
and SALT II limits, 94; characteristics,
124; sea-launched cruise missiles, 125,
136
Cuba: Soviet nuclear aid, 70
Cuban missile crisis, 4
Czechoslovakian invasion, 56, 65, 86

De Young, Karen, 189
Defense Intelligence Agency, 27
DeGaulle, Charles, 53
DeLauer, Richard D., 159

Department of Defense, 19, 36, 45, 88, 144, 149, 160, 161, 178; concern about Midgetman, 154; position on ABM, 88; position on build-down, 149; proposed SDI tests, 160
Department of Energy, 61
Department of State, 10, 19, 120, 121, 149, 161, 178; and the build-down proposal, 149; preference for zero-plus in INF, 120, 124
Détente, 39
Devine, J. B., 187
Devine, Robert A., 183
Dewitt, Hugh E., 185
Directed energy beams, 157, 161
Disarmament: effect of distrust, 177; impact of public opinion, 178; obstacles to, 176–78; qualitative vs. quantitative, 94; relation to deterrence, 8; technological constraints, 95
Disarmament negotiations: use for propaganda purposes, 10; ways to improve, 178–82
Dove's dilemma, 73
Drell, Sidney D., 190
Dulles, Allen, 30
Dulles, John Foster, 17, 55
Dunn, Lewis A., 187
Durch, William J., 191

Earle, Ralph, 190
East Europe: nuclear activities, 70
East Germany, 56, 132; IAEA safeguards, 70
Eighteen Nation Disarmament Committee, 24, 30, 58, 59
Einstein, Albert, 15
Eisenhower, Dwight, 15–19, 21, 26–28, 50, 80, 144, 184; position on test ban moratorium, 27, 28
Encryption of telemetry, 101, 140, 143
Enhanced radiation warhead, 16
Erwin amendment, 65
Euratom, 69
Europe: concern about coupling U.S. nuclear deterrent, 129
European balance of forces, 121
Evernden, Jack F., 44, 185
Eyraud, Michel, 186

Farley, Phillip J., 190
Fast breeder reactor, 62. See also Clinch River breeder reactor

Federal Republic of Germany, 18, 56–58, 64, 65, 69, 135; INF deployment, 131; Multilateral Force proposal, 58; nuclear exports, 70
Finney, John W., 107, 188
Firestone, Bernard J., 184, 186
Ford, Gerald, 39
Forward-based systems, 90, 91, 122, 126, 146
Foster, William C., 58, 85
Fractional-orbital ballistic missiles, 96
France, 32, 35, 52, 57, 58, 64, 69, 70, 83, 175; first nuclear explosion, 27; and IAEA inspection, 63; nuclear capabilities, 91, 121, 123; nuclear exports, 70, 71; position on test ban, 16, 40
"Fratricide," 138
Freedman, Lawrence, 188
Functionally related observable differences (FRODs), 103, 136, 138, 181

Gaffney, Frank, Jr., 47
Gallup polls: opinion on nuclear test ban, 17, 28
Garthoff, Raymond L., 128, 187–90
Gelb, Leslie H., 185, 191
Gellner, Charles L., 191
General Accounting Office, 168
General and complete disarmament, 82, 83, 153, 174, 175
Geneva Conference of Experts, 18, 19, 22
Geneva Conference on the Discontinuance of Nuclear Weapon Tests, 23
Geneva Experts' Report, 26
Germany. See Federal Republic of Germany
Gilensky, Victor, 62
Ginsberg, Theo, 184
Glenn-Symington Amendment, 73
Goldstone, 42
Gorbachev, Mikhail S., 47, 48, 128, 133, 134, 139, 141, 150–55, 159, 163, 178–80; arms control initiatives, 151; and complete nuclear disarmament, 152; call for summit to sign a comprehensive test ban, 128; efforts to divide NATO on INF, 134; Geneva summit, 154; Reykjavik Summit, 155; test ban initiatives, 47
Gordon, Michael R., 185, 190, 191
Graham, Billy, 17

Gray, Colin S., 190
Grechko, Marshal Andrei, 160
Greece, 44
Greenland, 162
Greenwood, Ted, 188
Gromyko, Andrei, 79, 86, 97
Grymyko Plan, 55, 79
Ground control posts, 80, 98
Ground radar stations, 101
Grove, Eric J., 180
Gwertzman, Bernard, 190

Hadley, Arthur T., 184
Hafner, Donald L., 191
Haig, Alexander, 190; declares SALT II dead, 137; views U.S. START and INF proposals as nonnegotiable, 146
Holloran, Richard, 190
Hard-kill capability, 46
Hardtack II, 23
Harriman, Averell, 29, 37, 58
Heckrotte, Warren, 185
Helsinki, 86
Hiatt, Fred, 189, 190
High altitude tests: verification problems, 26
Hilgartner, Stephen, 184
Hiroshima bomb, 1, 23, 25, 46, 47
Hitler, Adolph, 81
Holloway, David, 128, 189, 190
Holm, Hans-Henrick, 188
Hot line, 6

Ignautius, David, 187, 190
India, 31, 44, 60, 64, 69–71; nuclear nonproliferation, 63; position on nuclear testing, 15; underground nuclear explosion, 33, 43, 69
Indian Ocean: demilitarization of, 4
Intercontinental ballistic missiles (ICBMs), 81, 83; vulnerability of, 7, 117. *See also* name of each missile
Interim Offensive Arms Agreement, 91, 95, 96, 128, 137, 138, 144; restrictions on missile size, 95; and status of submarines, 91, 96
Intermediate Nuclear Force (INF) talks: Soviet acceptance of on-site inspection, 134; U.S. zero-option proposal, 119, 124, 134; verification, 120, 130; "walk in the woods" proposal, 126
Intermediate-range ballistic missiles, 2, 81; deployment in Asia, 125; dual-track

decision, 119; U.S.-Soviet balance of, 122
International Atomic Development Authority, 55
International Atomic Energy Agency (IAEA), 56, 69, 74, 80, 151; safeguards system, 56, 61, 70
International Conference on the Peaceful Uses of Atomic Energy, 67
International Fuel Cycle Evaluation (INFCE), 72
Invulnerable retaliatory capability, 6, 54
Iran, 74
Iran arms sale, 180
Iranian revolution: effect on monitoring capabilities, 101
Ireland: leadership role on nonproliferation, 57
Israel, 60; pressured to sign NPT, 69
Italy, 132

Jackson Amendment, 92, 106
Jacobsen, Carl G., 189
Jacobson, Harold K., 184
Japan, 66, 69
Jastrow, Robert S., 184
Jensen, Lloyd, 183, 186
Johnson, Lyndon B., 86; and nuclear nonproliferation, 58; threatens India if it proliferates, 69; unilateral closing of nuclear facilities, 84
Johnston Island, 165
Joint Chiefs of Staff, 40, 106, 117, 139, 149, 155; and nuclear testing, 28, 32; objection to restrictions on aircraft, 124; support for SALT treaties, 137
Joint Committee on Atomic Energy, 27
Jones, Rodney W., 186
Jupiter missile, 90

Kaplan, Stephen S., 183
Karas, Thomas, 190
Keller, Bill, 190, 191
Kennedy, John F., 26, 28, 29, 37, 52, 58; American University speech, 29
Kennedy administration, 82; position on nuclear testing, 22
Kennedy, Richard, 187
Kerr, Donald, 46, 185
Khrushchev, Nikita, 3, 4, 15, 18–21, 26, 28–30, 58, 178; nonproliferation policy, 58; nuclear test moratorium, 28; risk-taking behavior, 3
Kincade, William H., 188

Kinetic heat-seeking missiles, 164
King, Peter, 186
Kissinger, Henry A., 17, 35, 88, 94, 95, 103, 106–108, 183; offers Soviets alternatives on ABM, 88; pressing cruise missile on Pentagon, 107; problem of MIRV verification, 103; questioning utility of strategic superiority, 94; quid pro quo to Joint Chiefs for SALT I, 106; second thoughts about MIRV, 108
Kohler, Roy O., 180
Kramish, Arnold, 186
Krasnoyarsk radar system, 161
Kvitsinsky, Yuli, 126, 127, 131
Kwajalein Atoll, 165

Labrie, Roger P., 188
Latin America: denuclearization of, 56
Latter, Albert, 23
Lawrence Livermore National Laboratory, 47, 159
Lehman, John, 137
Leitenberg, Milton, 188
Lewis, Flora, 185
Limited Test Ban Treaty, 2, 14, 18–20, 24, 29, 31–37, 41, 42, 48, 58, 162; advantages and disadvantages, 31; alleged violations, 41
Lodge, Henry Cabot, 188
Logan test, 23
London Disarmament Subcommittee, 81
London Nuclear Supplier Group, 69, 72
Los Alamos National Laboratory, 46
Lowenthal, Mark M., 188
Lucky Dragon, 15

Macmillan, Harold, 24, 26, 28, 30
Mandelbaum, Michael, 190
Maneuvering reentry vehicles (MARV), 108
Markey, Ed, 47
Marsh, Gerald E., 185
Marshall Islanders, 15
Massachusetts Institute of Technology (MIT), 62
Massive retaliation doctrine, 16
McCloy-Zorin talks, 83
McCone, John A., 27
McGraw, Anthony, 186
McNamara, Robert, 31, 84, 166; position on ABM, 85
Mediterranean: denuclearization of, 56
Mexico, 44

Middle East, 86; denuclearization of, 56
Midgetman, 45, 147, 148, 152, 154, 155
Military balance, 121, 152, 174
Military decapitation, 9
Military disengagement proposals, 10
Military planning, 8
Miller, George H., 47
Miller, Judith, 189
Missiles: accuracy, 2; dual capability, 123; flight time, 2; heavy missiles, 122; mobile missiles, 102, 148, 154; throw-weight, 16. See also names and types of missiles
Mitterand, Francois, 134
MK 12A warheads, 45
Mohr, Charles, 191
Molotov, V. M., 55
Mondale, Walter, 160
Multilateral Force (MLF), 58
Multiple aim point, 102
Multiple independently targetable reentry vehicle (MIRV), 88, 90, 95, 103, 150, 173, 176; first U.S. and USSR tests, 90; test restrictions 95; verification 103
MX missile, 7–9, 138, 147, 148, 175; basing problems, 7, 9, 102, 147; Dense Pack basing plan, 138; first-strike potential, 8
Myrdal, Alva, 184

Nagasaki, 117
Nassau meeting, 30
National Academy of Sciences, 158
National command authorities (NCA), 88
National Security Council and the build-down proposal, 149
National technical means of inspection (NTM), 99, 104, 130, 140, 143, 166, 176
NATO Council, 119
Natural Resources Defense Council, 33, 48
Negotiating behavior: bargaining chips, 7, 105; effect of domestic divisions, 178; third party role, 29–31
Nehru, Jawaharlal, 15
Netherlands, 132
Neutron bomb. See enhanced radiation warhead
Nevada test site, 45
New Look strategy, 16
New Zealand, 57
Newhouse, John, 105, 188

Nike-Zeus, 16, 85
Nimitz-class carrier, 169
Nitze, Paul, 123, 124, 126, 127, 129, 133, 135, 189, 190; cites Soviet retractions, 133; evaluation of Soviet concessions on INF, 135; "walk in the woods" proposal, 126
Nixon, Richard M., 28, 36, 39; and bargaining chips, 107; linkage policy, 86; position on nonproliferation, 69; signing of SALT I agreements, 87
Nixon Doctrine, 66
Nonaggression pact, 20, 131
Nonaligned states: concern about security guarantees, 64; role in test ban negotiations, 30
Nontransfer agreements, 55
North Atlantic Treaty Organization (NATO), 20, 56, 58, 155, 175, 177; 1979 decision to deploy INF, 118, 119, 129; conventional capability, 129; opposition to efforts to reinterpret ABM Treaty, 162; reaction to efforts to dismantle SALT, 141
Nova Scotia, 141
Nuclear blackmail, 65
Nuclear deterrence, 3, 4, 9, 49, 53, 154, 177; stability, 3, 148, 154; U.S. effectiveness, 4
Nuclear energy: peaceful uses, 56, 67–69
Nuclear explosions: distinguished from earthquakes, 24
Nuclear fallout, 15, 50
Nuclear free zones, 56, 57
Nuclear freeze movement, 12, 118
Nuclear fuel cycle, 63, 70
Nuclear Nonproliferation Act (NNPA), 71, 76
Nuclear Nonproliferation Treaty (NPT), 34, 36, 43, 49, 52, 54, 58, 60, 70, 71, 75; Article 6, 36; reservations, 61; Review Conferences, 36, 43, 60; security assurances, 63–69; and the nuclear threshold states, 60; verification, 60, 61
Nuclear production ban, 55
Nuclear proliferation, 5; effect on security, 53
Nuclear Regulatory Commission, 62
Nuclear reprocessing plants, 63
Nuclear sharing, 59
Nuclear terrorism, 5

Nuclear test ban, 173; comprehensive or partial, 21; effect on nuclear proliferation, 18; inspection, 17, 19, 21–27, 32, 151, 176; linkage to other disarmament measures, 20; UN resolution supporting, 43. *See also* Limited Test Ban Treaty; Threshold Test Ban Treaty; Peaceful Nuclear Explosions Treaty; comprehensive test ban
Nuclear testing: decoupling of tests, 23; distinguished from earthquakes, 44; importance for developing SDI, 47; moratorium, 151; number conducted through 1986, 33; Soviet 1985 unilateral ban, 151; underground tests, 23
Nuclear threshold states, 31, 60
Nuclear throw-weight, 149, 156
Nuclear war: accidental, 4, 5; by miscalculation, 5, 54; false alarms, 4
Nuclear weapons: destructive power, 1, 2; production cut-off, 15, 20; reliability testing, 46; tactical, 16; unauthorized use, 6; utility of, 53; verification problems, 79
Nuclear winter, 2, 118
Nye, Joseph S., 185

O'Connor, Rory, 184
O'Toole, Thomas, 184, 186
Oberdorfer, Don, 185, 190, 191
Omang, Joanne, 270
Open skies proposals, 22, 171
Oppenheimer, Robert J., 152
Organization of African Unity, 130
Osnos, Peter, 191
Outer Space Treaty, 82, 97, 166; and the Strategic Defense Initiative, 162

Pakistan, 60, 64, 74; nuclear proliferation, 70, 73
Panofsky, Wolfgang, 46
Partial disarmament: problem of expansion elsewhere, 125
Pauling, Linus, 17
Peace movement, 12
Peaceful nuclear energy, 67; verification, 151
Peaceful nuclear explosives (PNEs), 16, 37, 38, 49, 68
Peaceful Nuclear Explosions Treaty, 37–39; on-site inspection, 38
Percy, Charles, 42

Perle, Richard, 41, 124, 128, 142, 185, 189
Perry, William J., 100
Pershing IA missiles, 135
Pershing II missiles, 11, 135
Persian Gulf, 73
Petersen, Nikolaj, 189
Phased-array radars, 162
Philippines, 135
Pincus, Walter, 183, 185, 189–91
Plowshare program, 37, 68
Plutonium, 58, 61, 62, 67, 68, 70, 72, 75, 77, 84
Poland, 56
Polaris, 46
Pope Pius XII, 17
Poseidon, 46, 122, 138, 139, 143
Potter, William C., 187
Preemptive strike, 5, 149
Presidium of the Supreme Soviet, 160
Preventive strike, 8

Quester, George H., 187

Radioactive debris, 16, 24, 26, 37
Rapacki, Adam, 12, 56
Reagan, Ronald, 48, 133, 174; attitudes on arms control, 117; and cruise missiles, 127; effort to improve peace image, 132; Eureka College speech, 145, 153; Geneva summit, 154; on limited nuclear war, 66; offer to meet Andropov at summit, 128; position on a comprehensive test ban, 20; and Reykjavik Summit, 155; Soviets as the focus of evil, 129; Star Wars speech, 156; and test ban issue, 41; willing to accept interim INF, 121
Reagan administration, 12, 45, 46, 144, 179; accelerated testing and deployment of ABM, 165; allegations of Soviet violations, 176; argues SDI tests will not violate ABM Treaty, 160; arms build-up, 118; bureaucratic in-fighting, 119; decision not to undercut SALT, 137; nuclear assistance pact with China, 74; nuclear nonproliferation policy, 71; and Pakistani proliferation, 73; and SALT II Treaty, 137; and South Pacific Nuclear Free Zone Treaty, 57; START deep-reduction proposals, 145; and the Strategic Defense Initiative, 175; and the issue of verification, 99, 156
Reciprocity of concessions, 179

Reconnaissance satellites, 166
Reprocessing plants, 70, 72
Reston, James, 170, 191
Richter, Roger, 186
Richter scale, 25
Robinson, Clarence A., 188
Robles, Garcia, 185
Rockefeller, Nelson, 27
Roosevelt, Franklin D., 29
Rosenfeld, Stephen S., 190
Ross, Anthony C., 185
Rumania, 12
Russell, Christine, 185
Russett, Bruce M., 47, 185

Sagan, Carl, 2, 183
SALT (Strategic Arms Limitation Talks), 11, 78–116, 130, 176; verification, 98–104
SALT I: compliance with, 137–44; missile freeze, 92; who gained, 113, 114; why lower numbers do not disadvantage the United States, 92. *See also* Anti-Ballistic Missile (ABM) Treaty; Interim Offensive Arms Agreement
SALT II Treaty: compliance with, 137–44; forward-based systems, 91; MIRV restrictions, 100; missile restrictions, 100, 113; protocol, 113; reaction against efforts to dismantle, 141; Reagan decision that U.S. will no longer be bound, 139; Reagan's position on, 100; restrictions on qualitative improvements, 96; verification, 9, 137; who gained, 109–13
Sartori, Leo, 189
Satellite verification, 9, 12
Satellite Inspection Technique (SAINT), 165
Scandinavia: denuclearization of, 56
Scheer, Robert, 186, 189
Scheinman, Lawrence, 186
Schell, Jonathan, 2, 183
Schlesinger, James, 40
Schmidt, Helmut, 120
Schneider, Stephen H., 183
Schriever, Bernard, 166
Schweitzer, Albert, 15
Scoville, Herbert, 190
Seaborg, Glenn T., 46, 184, 185
Secretary of Energy, 40
Seignious, George M., 106

Seismic detection stations, 23, 25, 40, 41, 44, 48
Senate Committee on Foreign Relations, 42, 61, 104, 137
Shah of Iran, 66
Shaw, Lisa D., 183
Sherr, Alan B., 199
Shevardnadze, Eduard, 134
Schultz, George, 135, 153
Simpson, John, 186
Singer, J. David, 187
Sino-Soviet split, 12
Sivard, Ruth, 183
Smith, George C., 185
Smith, Gerard, 107, 170, 185, 186, 188, 190, 191
Smith, R. Jeffrey, 186, 190, 191
South Africa, 60, 74; alleged nuclear explosion, 26; nuclear proliferation, 70
South Korea, 135; nuclear proliferation, 70
South Pacific Nuclear Free Zone Treaty, 57
South Vietnam, 66
Space satellites, 16, 166
Space weapons: Soviet proposed test ban, 162
Spain, 60
Sputnik, 165
SS-4, 131; SS-16, 173; SS-18; 142, 145, 147, 149; SS-19, 147, 173; SS-20, 120, 123, 125, 126, 128–33; SS-21, 125, 130; SS-22, 125, 130, 132; SS-23, 125, 130, 152; SS-24, 140, 151, 152, 154; SS-25, 139, 140, 152, 154
Stalin, Joseph, 3
Standing Consultative Commission (SCC), 103, 132, 142, 144
Stein, Eric, 184
Steinberg, Gerald, 191
Steinbrunner, John, 5, 183
Stevenson, Adlai, 84
Strategic Arms Limitation Talks. *See* SALT
Strategic Arms Reduction Talks (START), 71, 131, 132, 136–38, 144, 146–49, 156; reasons why U.S. START proposals were unacceptable to the Soviets, 145; verification, 147
Strategic balance, 4, 91, 121, 152, 174; and the issue of equivalence, 91; the problem of asymmetry, 176

Strategic Defense Initiative (SDI), 157; cost estimates, 158; description of system, 157; destablizing qualities, 159; position of U.S. allies, 158; relation to existing arms agreements, 160; ways of countering, 157
Strauss, Lewis F., 17
Strontium, 90, 31
Submarine-launched ballistic missiles (SLBMs), 2, 83, 89, 130, 145, 148; MIRVing of, 130; U.S. advantages, 92
Summit Conferences: Geneva (1985), 133, 154, 155; Moscow (1974), 35; Moscow (1979), 40; Reykjavik, 135, 155, 156, 164; Vienna (1961), 28; Vladivostok, 92
Surprise Attack Conference, 80; open skies proposals, 12, 98
Sweden, 44, 131
Sweet, William, 185, 187
Sykes, Lynn R., 44, 185

Tactical nuclear weapons, 18; U.S. stock in Europe, 125
Taiwan: nuclear proliferation, 70
Talbott, Strobe, 124, 189, 190
Tanzania, 44
TASS, 131
Technical Group I, 26
Technological change: as an impediment to arms negotiation, 177
Teller, Edward, 16
Thatcher, Margaret, 32, 141
"The Day After," 128
Thermonuclear weapons: prospects for a radiation free bomb, 16
Third World countries, 55
Thompson, Starley L., 183
Three Mile Island, 67
Threshold Test Ban Treaty, 14, 34–36, 38, 41, 42, 45, 48, 49; on-site inspection, 42
Titan missile, 104
Treaty of Tlatelolco, 57
Trident, 45, 138, 139, 143, 152, 173
Troop movements: verification, 176
Truman, Harry S.: position on arms control, 52
Tsarapkin, Semyon K., 20, 38
Two-key system, 6
U.S.S. *Alexander Hamilton*, 143
U-235, 58, 84

Underground nuclear explosions: detection, 26

Unilateral approaches to arms control, 9, 180

Union of Soviet Socialist Republics (USSR): alleged arms control violations, 103, 109, 117; ASAT development, 165; balance sheet on SALT, 110; and bargaining chips, 108; domestic divisions on arms control, 178; first strike capability, 117; general and complete disarmament proposals, 82; heavy missile capability, 8; military balance, 121, 152, 174; nuclear nonproliferation proposals, 70; peaceful nuclear explosives, 38, 68; political settlement and arms control, 7; position on French and British nuclear forces in INF, 130, 134; position on multilateral force, 59; preoccupation with defense, 88; propaganda efforts to stop INF deployment, 118, 152; resumption of nuclear testing, 20, 144, 156; return to disarmament talks, 133; risk-taking behavior, 3; and START, 145; test ban moratorium, 17; and verification, 156, 176; walks out of START and INF negotiations, 132

United Arab Republic, 64

United Kingdom, 29, 31, 52, 62, 65, 69, 84, 162; comprehensive test ban, 40, 41; nuclear capabilities, 91, 121, 123; and nuclear test bans, 16, 18, 27; role as mediator in test ban talks, 30; security guarantees, 65

United Nations, 159; Atomic Energy Commission, 78; General Assembly, 43, 79; police force, 7; Security Council, 41; Special Session on Disarmament, 68

United Nations Charter: Article 51, 65

United States: alleged arms control violations, 109; alleged missile gap, 84; balance sheet on SALT, 113; general and complete disarmament proposals, 82; missile vulnerability, 8; multilateral force proposal, 59; and the nuclear test moratorium, 18; peaceful nuclear explosions, 68; security guarantees and NPT, 65. *See also* Congress; individual executive agencies such as Department of State, Arms Control and Disarmament Agency.

United States Geological Survey, 48

Uranium, 58, 62, 63, 67, 69, 70, 72

Uranium enrichment plants, 63, 70

V-2 rockets, 81

VELA system, 26, 27

Verification, 22–27, 32, 44–45, 61–63, 98–104, 167, 176; control posts, 24; Gorbachev's concessions, 151; on-site inspection, 90; national technical means, 99, 113; Nazi Germany's evasion of the Versailles restrictions, 98

Vietnam, 69, 86

Viotti, Paul R., 183, 185, 191

Volga River: diverting water to, 68

Voss, Earl H., 183

"Walk in the woods" proposal, 126

Waltz, Kenneth N., 53, 186

Warnke, Paul C., 106, 138, 161

Warsaw Pact, 20, 65

Watergate, 36

Weapons Systems: negotiability of, 172–76

Weapons testing, 8, 173; ease of verification, 14; importance for weapons development, 14

Weinberger, Caspar, 159; efforts to end U.S. SALT compliance, 139; efforts to push broad interpretation of ABM Treaty, 164; view of Midgetman, 154

Western Europe: concern about decoupling of U.S. deterrent, 53; concern about SS-20, 125; nuclear freeze movement, 118

Weston, Burns H., 187

Whelan, Joseph G., 184

Wicker, Tom, 183

Wilmhurst, M. J., 187

Wilson, George C., 183

Window of vulnerability, 117

Wolfe, Thomas W., 188

Woodward, Bob, 187

World War II, 81

Wright, Sir Michael, 27, 184

X-ray laser, 43, 45, 162

York, Herbert F., 184

Zero-option proposal, 120–121, 124, 127, 129

Zuckert, Eugene, 166